Mastering Amiga
Beginners

Mastering Amiga Beginners

Revised Edition

Bruce Smith and Mark Webb

Mastering Amiga Beginners

© Bruce Smith and Mark Webb 1993
ISBN: 1-873308-17-5 Revised Edition: April 1993
(Previously published under ISBN: 1-873308-03-5)

Additional material by John Ransley.
Editor: Peter Fitzpatrick
Typesetting: Bruce Smith Books Limited
Cover artwork concept: Ross Alderson

Workbench, Amiga and AmigaDOS are trademarks of Commodore-Amiga, Inc. UNIX is a trademark of AT&T. MS-DOS is a trademark of Microsoft Corporation.

Disclaimer: While every effort has been made to ensure that the information in this publication (and any programs and software) is correct and accurate, the Publisher can accept no liability for any consequential loss or damage, however caused, arising as a result of using the information printed in this book.

Bruce Smith Books is an imprint of Bruce Smith Books Limited.

Published by Bruce Smith Books Limited,
PO Box 382, St Albans, Herts, AL2 3JD
Telephone: (0923) 894355 – Fax: (0923) 894366.

Registered in England No. 2695164.
Registered Office: 51 Quarry Street, Guildford, Surrey, GU1 3UA

Printed and bound in the UK by Ashford Colour Press, Gosport.

The Mastering Amiga series provides top quality guidance for Amiga users.

The Authors

MARK WEBB bought one of the first Amiga 1000s to appear in the UK and was inspired to launch, as Group Editor, the monthly magazine *Your Amiga*. Since then, whatever computer he has been obliged to use at work, he has returned to an Amiga at home.

A computer magazine pioneer, he also launched the first UK magazine with a disk on the front (Disk User). Mark has turned to books so that he can do some editing at home where he has to keep an eye on two unruly sons, Anthony and Karsten, and where wife Anne can keep an eye on him.

BRUCE SMITH is an award winning journalist with over 40 book titles to his credit. His style is renowned for being easy going and highly readable and led one reviewer to write "This is the first computer book I have read in bed for pleasure rather than to cure insomnia!"

In addition to the computer scene he is well known as a football journalist and his dulcet tones can generally be heard on BBC Radio Bedfordshire on Saturday afternoons.

He is the founder of Bruce Smith Books – a publishing house dedicated to the support of the Amiga and lives in rural Hertfordshire.

Contents

1: In the Beginning **17**

What Amiga? 18

Amiga A500 Plus..20

Amiga A600/A600HD 20

Amiga A1200 21

Workbench Versions 22

2: Switching On **23**

A500 Plus 23

A600 24

A1200 24

The Workbench 24

Mouse Matters 27

Keymap Confusion? 27

3: WIMPs **29**

Close Gadget 31

Title/Move Gadget 32

Front/Back Gadget 32

Scroll Gadgets 33

Zoom Gadget 33

Icons 34

More Menus 35

Screen Dragging 35

Workbench Hot Keys 36

4: Floppy Disks **37**

Formatting 38

System Requests 39

Hard Disks 41

Working Disks 41

Backing Up Masters 42

Renaming Disks 42

Corrupted Disks 43

How Much Space? 44

5:   Copying and Moving **45**
The Ram Disk...46
Deleting Ram Files 46
Copying Two Files 48
Trashcan 49

6:   About AmigaDOS **51**
Command Examples 52
The Shell 53
Directory Listings 54
Making Mistooks 55

7:   Utilities and Tools **57**
Clock Alarm 59
Setting the Date and Time 59
Extras Disk 61
The Calculator 61
Colors 63
KeyShow 64

8:   Some Preferences **65**
Workbench Patterns................................66
The Pointer 69
Saving Individual Pref Sets 71

9:   AmigaDOS & the Shell **73**
Shell Commands......................................75
Shell Special Effects 75

10: Drawers and Directories **79**
A Hierarchical Filing System.......................80
Trees, Roots and Branches 80
Directory Path.......................................82

11: AmigaDOS Format and Copy **83**
Formatting on an External Drive 85
Copying Disks with AmigaDOS....................85
AmigaDOS Backup 86
Making Drawers with AmigaDOS 88

Changing Directory 89
DIR Again 89

12: ED the Text Editor 91

Editing with ED 93
Extended ED...93
Block Actions 96
On the Menu 97
ED and AmigaDOS Scripts.......................................97
Script Creation 98
More Scripts...99

13: Icon Creation and Design 101

Icon Edit...103
The IconEdit Menus 105
Iconology 106

14: Choosing and Using a Printer 109

Types of Printer 110
PostScript Printing..111
Graphics Printing..112
Text Printing 113
Printing From Programs..113
Paper Chase 113
Background and Buffers 114
Inking Up 115

15: Printer Installation 117

Printer Driver...118
Printer Initialisation 122
PrintFiles...123

16: Printer Graphics 125

Colour Correction..126
Dithering...127
Scaling 127
Limits...128
Image Aspects..130
Shade 131

Threshold 131
Density 132
Graphic Dump 132

17: Fonts 133
Amiga Fonts 135
Fonts 2.1 136
Fonts Preferences 136

18: Graphics Galore 139
Bits and Pieces..140
Graphics Processing 140
Pictures as Objects 142
Computer Aided Design 142
3D Sculpture..144
Toon Town...144
Desktop Video 145
Ray Tracing..146
Fractals and Mandelbrots 147
Getting to Know Deluxe Paint...............................148
Flipping Great 149

19: Video Link Up 151
Linking Amiga with Home Video 151
Video on the Desktop 152
Soundtracks...153
Locking On...154
Frame by Frame 154
Compact Video 154
Professional Pixels...155

20: Communications 157
What You Need 158
Terminal Type 158
Feature Phoning..160
Getting the Best from a BBS 160
Forms of File...162
Where to Dial..163
General Interest 163

Multi-User Games 163

Crossing the Divide 163

Pay Phones..164

CompuServe...164

Silicon Village 165

Numbers Game 166

Hosting the Party 167

Comms Turn-on...167

And Last, Safety First..................................167

Commercial Subscription Services 168

21: Music and Sound.................................**171**

Sound Production 172

Sound Sampling..172

Using Samples 173

Hints and Tips 173

Trackers And Sequencers 174

Real Music...174

MIDI 175

22: The Offices: Home and Business...............**177**

The Big Three 177

Wordprocessing..178

What's in a Word? 178

Selecting a Wordprocessor 179

Editing and Checking 179

Presentation..181

Choosing and Using a Database 182

What do You Need?....................................183

Searching and Reporting 183

Transferability..184

Relationships...184

Collecting Data 185

Hypermedia 185

Spreadsheet Selection and Use 186

Manipulating Numbers 186

Text Labels and Reports 187

Integrating Software 187

Presentation Graphics 187

Desktop Publishing.. 188

More Figure Work 189

23: Programming Languages 191

AmigaDOS... 192

ARexx 192

BASIC and AMOS 193

Assembly Language 194

Development Languages... 194

24: Art of Programming 197

Taking the Lid Off.. 197

Mind Your Language 197

String Serenade... 200

Going Slightly Loopy 201

Proper Procedures 201

25: Access to AMOS 203

Ahead of the Game 203

Paging M Lionet 204

Not so Basic 204

Getting a Move On 204

Back to the Drawing Board 205

Now You See It.. 205

Definitely a First... 206

Heavyweight Professional 206

Bells and Whistles... 208

TOME of Your Own 208

Sprites and Types 208

Joining the Club.. 208

Library Steps.. 209

Contacts... 209

26: Virus Menace 212

Strains of Virus... 213

Signs of Infection.. 214

Nuisance Effects 214

Nasty Effects 214

Protecting Against Them 215

Killing Viruses 215

Virus Killers 215

27: Upgrading 217

The Importance of RAM 218

Adding On 218

Adding an Extra Floppy 219

Adding a Hard Drive 219

Different Technologies 221

Hard Drive Speeds 221

Hard Drive Backup 222

File Management 223

Matching up with a Monitor 223

Input Devices 224

Digitisers 225

Scanners 226

MIDI 227

Control 227

Networking 227

Genlocks 227

Fax Modems 228

Accelerator Cards 229

CD 229

Serial Communications 229

Card Sharp 230

Emulation 230

PC Software 231

Compatibility 231

28: Software Choice 233

That's Entertainment 233

Tweaking the A1200 235

Creative Classes 236

Learning Fast 237

Is it for Me? 238

29: Cheap Software 241

Definitions 242

How to Get PD Software 243

Using PD 245

Magazine Disks and Disks on Magazines 247

Fish Disks 248

Shareware 248

30: Multimedia 251

What Is It? 251

Authoring Programs 252

Dynamic Total Vision 253

Movies and PhotoCD...................................255

31: PCs and Amigas 257

CrossDOS...258

DOS Access 259

File Compatibility 260

32: Startup Commodities 261

AutoPoint..261

ClickToFront 262

Blanker..262

Exchange 263

FKey 264

NoCapsLock 265

33: Bits and Bobs 267

WBStartup 267

MultiView 268

SetMap 269

A: Glossary 271

B: Contacts 289

C: Mastering Amiga Guides 297

Index 313

Contents

1:
In the
Beginning

Beginning to learn any new subject matter is always a little daunting. Beginning to learn about a computer – the Amiga – and how to use it is perhaps particularly so. Or so it would appear. In fact it's not really the case; it just seems that way because there is a certain mystic quality that has developed about computers in the past ten years. Because they are mass market consumables they are affordable in the same way that VCRs are. Ah, but I can't even program my VCR you say. Who can? is the reply!

Long gone are the days when using a computer was only about typing in strings of incomprehensible words and numbers. The Amiga is easy to use; be assured. However, you must be prepared to experiment and make your own mistakes – in that way you will learn. And making mistakes is all part of the fun – take it from those who have been there many times before!

OK, first and foremost let's set out a few ground rules. This book is definitely not going to turn you into an expert in all things Amiga. This book won't make you an expert in any one area of the Amiga. What this book will do is to give you a general grounding in what the Amiga is, the sort of things it is capable of and how you can go about doing the things you want to do with it. This book will also set about showing you how to do some of the basic tasks that you will need to use your Amiga. It will introduce you to the jargon (and that is half the battle) and also give you an insight into the different types of programs (both fun and serious) available for your Amiga. In short what *Mastering Amiga Beginners* aims to do is to get you through those first few months of Amiga ownership and provide you with enough of an insight to allow you to determine your own areas of interest and show you how to pursue them further.

As a general guide to layout you will find that *Mastering Amiga Beginners* is roughly divided into two. The first part of the book gets you using your Amiga and the disks that come with it while the second half looks at what else is available for it and how to get more more from it at very little additional cost!

What Amiga?

One of the biggest problems with the Amiga is that it is such a superb computer! Not just that – it gets better and better on a regular basis because its manufacturers, Commodore, are continually improving it and releasing new hardware and new software.

Hardware refers to the physical being, so releasing new hardware means releasing a new model of Amiga. In much the same way that you have different models of the same car (A BMW comes in various flavours – a Three Series, a Five Series etc) you also get different models of Amiga, for example the A500 Plus, the A600, the A600HD, the A1200, the A3000, the A4000 and so I could go on.

Software refers to the information on disk – if you like the *program* – which is used to drive the Amiga. Before you can use your Amiga you have to insert a disk into its integral disk drive so that it can read the instructions it needs to run. This software – which is generally called *Workbench* – is also undergoing continual revision and in order to distinguish one version from another each one is given a version number.

The earlier versions of Workbench were called Workbench 1.1 and Workbench 1.2. When the Amiga experienced its first big boom in sales Workbench 1.3 was the order of the day. During the early 1990s Workbench 2.0 was released and this has been followed by Workbench 2.1 and, at the time of writing, Workbench 3.0.

Confused? Yes, who wouldn't be? Bear with us.

Thankfully, things are made a bit simpler because most versions of Workbench can be tied to specific types of Amiga as the following table shows for the more popular home versions.

Amiga	Workbench
A500	1.3
A500 Plus	2.0
A600	2.1
A1200	3.0

Table 1.1. Versions of Amiga hardware and Workbench software.

This book concentrates mainly on versions 2.0, 2.1 and 3 of Workbench. Thankfully, although there are major differences between each of them, the underlying look and feel of each and the basic philosophy of their operation is the same. More importantly, because we won't be going to those sorts of depths, any differences can largely be ignored. Where they cannot we will point out very clearly and very loudly! But what of Workbench 1.3? Well, although this formed the basis of the development of Workbench 2 and beyond it does look and feel very different. The predecessor to this book written by Phil South and published by Bruce Smith Books covers version 1.3 in detail and copies of this may still be available. See the relevant appendix for more details.

The final act in this chapter is to look at each of the main home Amigas in a little more detail, because what you get with each does vary. Locate your machine and read the details specific to you.

Before you do that though, a word about disks. All Amigas are fitted with an internal 3.5" floppy disk drive, located on the righthand edge of the machine. We'll come onto the technicalities of what a floppy disk is capable of storing in due course, but suffice to say it is the mechanism by which you can transfer software and save and load your own software and the information that it might be able to create. The 3.5" refers to the size of the disk – and in this case a 3.5" floppy disk measures 3.5" square! The term floppy disk is also a little bit misleading because there is actually nothing floppy about the plastic case of the disk. However, the magnetic tape which is held inside the case is indeed floppy and, rather like cassette tape, easy to damage. More on that later.

An alternative to a floppy disk is a hard disk. A hard disk is usually fitted permanently to the side of the Amiga or even inside it such that it is always available. Whereas you can insert and remove floppy disks in and out of a floppy disk drive, you cannot readily do so with a hard drive. However, the advantage of a hard disk is that it is capable of holding a great deal more information than a floppy disk drive. For example, the smallest hard disk drives can hold as much information as you could store on around 25 floppy disks, whereas the biggest can hold many more times this. We'll devote a chapter to hard disks later in the book, but will come back to them from time to time when relevant to you as a hard disk user.

Amiga A500 Plus

The A500 Plus is supplied as a basic system. The A500 Plus uses Workbench 2. To be more correct it uses Workbench 2.04 and you will probably have just three disks with it, these will be:

> Workbench 2.0
>
> Tools 2.0
>
> Fonts 2.0

Now I say "probably" advisedly because the A500 Plus was sold in a variety of different theme packs, some of which contained games, some of which contained more serious software. The above named disks, though, will be common to all and sundry.

Amiga A600 / A600HD

If you have read the adverts and reviews or have had some good sales advice in the shop you will already be aware that the A600 comes in two flavours – plain vanilla (that's the A600 itself) and raspberry ripple (that's the more expensive and slightly more tasty A600HD). Fundamentally the A600 and the A600HD are one and the very same – they run the same software – but HD stands for Hard Disk and that's what you get for your extra cash: a hard disk fitted internally.

Although both the A600 and A600HD run the same software, the inclusion of a hard disk does drastically increase the functionality of the computer because it means you have virtually instant access to all your software.

I have flipped between descriptions of the A600 and A600HD with regularity so far. Don't be put off by this because it won't happen that much more. The reason being is that the software on both machines is the same.

Having said that the A600 comes in two flavours, it also comes into a couple of different wrappings in terms of the software supplied with the machine. If you bought your machine after the Autumn of 1992 it is likely that you will be supplied with version 2.1 of Workbench. Prior to this it may well be Workbench 2.04 or 2.05. The simplest way to find out is to look at the label on the Workbench disk. If it says Workbench 2.1 then you have Workbench 2.1. If on the other hand it says Workbench 2.0 then you will be using version 2.04 (A600) or version 2.05 (A600HD).

The differences are not great. Basically version 2.1 provides some extras in terms of utilities. It has also been upgraded a little in the way that information is presented on screen. Additionally the positioning of the software across a couple of the disks has been rearranged. All that said, in terms of you actually using the software very little has changed.

No matter whether you have an A600 or an A600HD you will find that your Amiga pack has a set of floppy disks, the master disks. These are very important so treat them with respect. If you are an A600 user then these will form the focal point of your attention for the rest of this book. If you have a hard disk system then you can put them away somewhere safe as the programs and information they contain are already in position on the hard disk – but more on that later.

The disks are labelled:

> Workbench
>
> Extras
>
> Fonts

Under Workbench 2.1 there is an extra disk called:

> Locale

and, if you have an A600HD there is one extra disk:

> A600HD Install Disk

Amiga A1200

The A1200 is primarily a floppy disk based system and the initial rush of machine were sold in this configuration. However, there are now a number of hard disk systems becoming available and some of these may be fitted inside the machine or connected externally. Fundamentally these versions of the A1200 are one and the very same – they run the same software.

Although all A1200s run the same software, the inclusion of a hard disk does drastically increase the functionality of the computer because it means you have virtually instant access to all your software. At times we may refer to the A1200HD, meaning an A1200 fitted with any hard disk. All A1200s are ready to accept a hard disk and that's why you'll find a light with the legend H.DISK beside it above the floppy disk power light.

The A1200 is supplied with Workbench 3. This version first appeared on the Amiga 4000 but popped up surprisingly quickly afterwards in the A1200. If you are using the A1200 after earlier experience of another Amiga model then you will immediately notice some differences in the way that the Workbench appears and in where some files are located on the suite of disks which comes with the computer. Interestingly, from a superficial point of view, there is not a great deal of difference in the look and feel of Workbench 3 and Workbench 2.1.

No matter whether you have a standard A1200 or a hard drive system, you will find that your Amiga pack has a set of floppy disks, the master disks. These are very important so treat them with respect. If you don't have a hard drive then these will form the focal point of your attention for the rest of this book. If you have a hard disk system then you can put the floppies away somewhere safe as the programs and information they contain are already in position on the hard disk – but more on that later.

The disks are labelled:

Workbench

Extras

Fonts

Locale

Storage

Workbench Versions

If you are a bit confused by all these Workbench version numbers, don't be. Essentially, they are just numbers which allow you to distinguish between upgraded and rewritten software and the number tells you how significant the changes were from a previous version.

For example, a major change will generally have taken place when the whole number is changed. Thus Workbench 3 is a major change from Workbench 2 which was itself a major change from Workbench 1. Most version releases also have sub-version numbers and releases. For example, the first three releases of Workbench were called:

Workbench 1.1

Workbench 1.2

Workbench 1.3

These were all essentially the same but show that minor revisions were made. Thus Workbench 2.04 had minor improvements over version 2.0, while Workbench 3 was another major revision.

2: Switching On

You should have no trouble connecting your Amiga's leads and cables. There are only a few to do and they cannot be accidently plugged into the wrong socket – or port as it is more correctly called on the Amiga. Each Amiga does come with a small booklet which graphically illustrates what you need to do.

Once it is all connected you are ready to turn on. Once you do this the process you follow at this point will depend on what Amiga you have so we'll once again look at each of the models we are covering in turn.

A500 Plus

When you switch the power on and flip the rocker switch on the power supply you will be presented with an animated cartoon of a disk flying up and inserting itself into a disk drive. The Amiga is prompting you to insert the Workbench 2 disk into the disk drive.

Locate the disk called Workbench and pop it into the drive (Workbench title facing upwards and metal slider innermost). The A500 Plus will now read all sorts of information from the Workbench disk and within about 30 seconds will display the Workbench screen.

A600

When you apply power the actual startup process will vary depending on whether you have a A600 floppy disk system of an A600HD hard disk system.

A600: When you turn this on your screen will show an animated cartoon of a disk flying up and inserting itself in a disk drive. This is the A600's way of asking you to insert the Workbench disk into the internal floppy disk drive. Locate the disk called Workbench and pop it into the drive (Workbench title facing upwards and metal slider innermost). If you are running Workbench 2.1 then within a handful of seconds the Workbench screen will appear. If however you are using Workbench 2.04 or 2.05 a screen called KeyMap Selection will appear. If this happens press the Return key on the keyboard (that's the one with the big right-handed arrow on it located to the right of the main keyboard across rows 2 and 3). Within a few seconds the Workbench screen will appear.

A600HD: When you switch on the A600 will go through its starting up procedure, the technical term for this being *booting,* or *kickstarting* (basically the terms relate to being booted into life or kickstarted into action). If you are running Workbench 2.1 then within a handful of seconds the Workbench screen will appear. If however you are using Workbench 2.04 or 2.05 a screen called KeyMap Selection will appear. It this happens locate the 8 key on the keyboard and press it once. Then press the Return key (that's the one with the big right-handed arrow on it located to the right of the main keyboard across rows 2 and 3). Within a few seconds the Workbench screen will appear.

A1200

On a floppy system when you turn the power on your screen will show an animated cartoon of a disk flying up and inserting itself in a disk drive. This is the A1200's way of asking you to insert the Workbench disk into the internal floppy disk drive. Locate the disk called Workbench and pop it into the drive (Workbench title facing upwards and metal slider innermost). Within a handful of seconds the Workbench screen will appear.

On a hard disk based A1200 system once you flip the switch there will be a short delay and shortly thereafter the Workbench screen will be displayed.

The Workbench

OK, through the various outlines of the start-up processes above I come to an end point which is a single common denominator – the Workbench screen. The Workbench provides you with an environment where you can do all your day-to-day tasks such as running games and application programs and copying disks to name but three. The Workbench is itself a program that runs in the Amiga with the sole aim in life of providing you with a user-friendly (ie simple to use) interface with it – no matter which model you are using.

The term Workbench is a good one because that is exactly how you should treat it – a screen version of a work area where you do all of your computing. For this reason Workbench is sometimes referred to as the Desktop

The Workbench displays several features which characterise it, many of which you will learn about during the course of this book, however the most major characteristic of the Workbench is that it is a WIMP system. The term WIMP is an acronym which stands for: Windows, Icons, Menus and Pointers.

The Workbench is itself a window and it exhibits all of the qualities of the many other windows you will be encountering in the coming chapters – all of which will be fully described. A computer window works very much like a normal house window – you look through it (or into it) and see what it reveals on the other side. The larger the window the more you can see, the smaller the window the less you can see. A window only allows you to see part of the world, it doesn't show you everything (though it could if you made it big enough) as there may be items outside the area of view covered by the window. All these facts are true of household windows, they are also true of the Amiga Workbench windows.

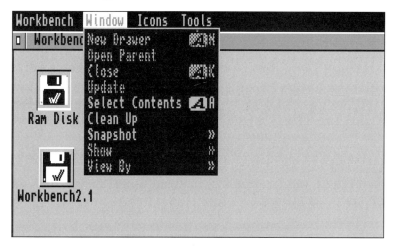

Figure 2.1. A typical Workbench display showing a selection of icons and a pull-down menu. The Workbench 3 display is very similar but the menu colours have changed! But as this is a black and white book...

While Window puts the W into WIMP, Menus supplies the M. All Amiga menus are accessed via a menu bar that invariably sits across the top of the screen. When you are working at the Workbench then you will easily see the Workbench menu bar strung across the top of the Workbench screen.

In addition to displaying the version of Workbench you are using it also displays a number which represents the amount of memory that is available to you and your programs. This number will vary depending on whether you have had a memory upgrade fitted to your Amiga or not.

The P in WIMP is for Pointer and the pointer is the arrow that you can move around the Workbench by moving the mouse across the table surface. The pointer will move in the direction you move the mouse.

If you move the Pointer so that its tip sits over the word Workbench and then press (and keep pressing) the right mouse button the Workbench changes and reveals some new legend – these are the names of the Workbench menus and they are Workbench, Window, Icons and Tools. If you move the pointer across each of these in turn you will find that a list of menu options pops down under each one.

Note that these pop-down menus only remain visible while you keep the mouse button depressed, when you release the button the pull-down menu disappears until recalled in similar fashion.

Selecting a Workbench menu option is relatively straightforward and really just requires some coordination between mouse and eye. For instance if you move the mouse to the menu bar, press down the right mouse button and move over the Workbench menu option you'll see that the first option on the menu is Backdrop. Move the pointer so that its point sits over the word Backdrop – you should notice that the option becomes highlighted – now release the mouse button. All being well you should have now selected the Backdrop option and the effect of this should be to turn or convert the Workbench from a window into a non-window environment called a Backdrop. If this hasn't happened then try the process again. You can return the Workbench to a Window by repeating the process, ie select Backdrop again. It's worth practicing this a few times as menu selection is an important part of using your Amiga.

If you hadn't already guessed from above the I in WIMP stands for Icons. These are the small picture images that will appear on your Workbench and in windows that you open. You will be able to see a couple of icons on your desktop already – the Ram Disk is one and also the Workbench disk – if you are a hard drive user the latter will be replaced by System and Work icons. More on icons later.

Mouse Matters

If you don't already own one, then you will find a mouse mat a worthwhile investment. Table and desk tops tend to be slippery and offer the roller ball fitted in the base of the mouse no real surface to grip on and roll. A mouse mat is specially designed for use with a mouse and it also ensures that you keep a bit of the desk free for its use. Mouse mats vary in cost and dearest isn't always best. Always try any mouse mat out before you buy it.

Get into the habit of mouse-lift and move. You don't need an entire desktop to move the mouse around on – a small mouse mat is ample room. Simply push the mouse to its edge, lift and replace it on the opposite side of the mat, before continuing movement. It soon becomes a natural process.

To use the mouse effectively place it to the right of the Amiga with its tail (the wire) running away from you. Lay the palm of your hand over it with your index finger on the left button and your middle finger on the righthand button. This assumes you are right-handed like me! Obviously if you are left handed you will need to reverse these arrangements.

The left mouse button is the one which is used most so when you need to use the mouse button, press the left one unless you are told otherwise. Because the lefthand mouse button is used to select items it is often referred to as the Select button. The righthand mouse button is often called the Menu button as it is used to make the menus pop-down.

Keymap Confusion?

If you are using version 2.04 of Workbench then you will be aware that when you first turn on your Amiga it does not go straight to the Workbench screen but to a simple screen which is entitled KeyMap Selection. An explanation may be in order for one and all at this point.

The Amiga is an international computer. That is great but in itself it also creates an awful lot of problems – not least those encountered by the language barrier. For example, although English and German may be reasonably closely related, the German language has many characters not included in the English alphabet.

It is reasonable to expect that an English Amiga would have an English keyboard and a German Amiga a German one. To enable this to happen the Amiga is supplied with a map of each of the major keyboard configurations, English, German, French, Swedish and several more. This keymap is not a map in the traditional sense but a set of numbers that reflect the keyboard characters.

KeyMap select allows you to set the correct keymap for your use and under Workbench 2.04/2.05 this is done when you first startup. This has been further rationalised under later versions of Workbench and details of this can be found in Chapter 33.

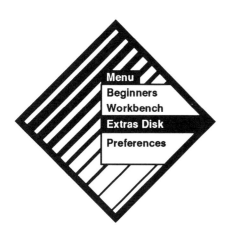

3:

WIMPs

All windows on the Amiga exhibit similar characteristics, a fact which makes them very easy to use because, once you have learnt how to use one, you have also learnt how to use every other one!

The Workbench is by default a window but does differ in one respect from other windows in that you wouldn't really want to close it, otherwise you'll be left with nothing to work on or with! So to that end it's best to experiment with another window and the best one for that purpose is the Workbench disk window.

If you are using a hard disk system then for the following you could insert the Workbench disk itself or pretend that the System icon on the Workbench is the disk icon in question.

At the moment the Workbench disk is represented by a disk icon (ie a cartoon of a disk with some legend underneath it). You can reveal its components by moving the pointer over it and then pressing the left mouse button twice in quick succession. This process is called *double-clicking*.

At this point the disk drive should spring into life and soon the Pointer will metamorphose into a small clock indicating to you that your keyboard has gone to sleep while the disk is being read – in other words while information or data is being located on it. If this does not happen then you have probably not double-clicked the mouse button quickly enough, or you haven't positioned the Pointer correctly over the disk icon. Try again. When you are successful the Workbench disk window will appear on the screen and then various icons will be displayed inside it.

Figure 3.1. When you insert your Workbench disk you will find it displays a disk icon on the Workbench desktop. A disk icon for Workbench 3.0 is shown above – you can see an example of the Workbench 2 disk icon as it appears on the desktop in Chapter Two as part of Figure 2.1.

Once the window has opened you will see that it becomes filled with a number of different icons each representing the various files that are held on the disk and which go towards the total working environment of the Workbench. Figure 3.2 shows a typical Workbench disk window for Workbench 2.1.

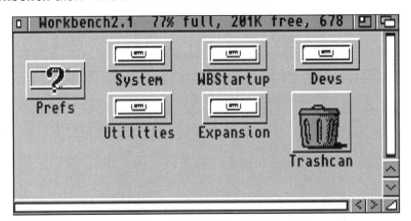

Figure 3.2. A typical Workbench disk window.

If you study the physical structure of the window you should see that it is composed of a number of elements, all of which are also reflected in the Workbench window. These elements are often called *gadgets* in Amiga parlance. From the top righthand corner, these are:

- Close gadget
- Title/Move Bar
- Zoom gadget
- Front/Back gadget

- Scroll gadgets

- Sizing gadget

Each of these is described individually below and shown graphically in Figure 3.3.

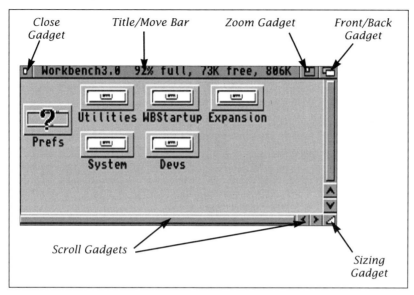

Figure 3.3. A typical Workbench disk window. Each window is accompanied by a number of gadgets which you can use to control what it shows.

Close Gadget

The small square gadget with a white dot inside it situated in the very top lefthand corner of the window is the Close Window gadget. As its name suggests, this is used to close the current window, effectively removing it from the Workbench screen. To use this gadget, position the tip of the Pointer so that it lies over the white dot and click on the mouse. The window will disappear from the screen. You can reopen the window again at any time simply by double-clicking again on the relevant icon. Try this a few times to get used to the process as it is a fundamental operation in the running of your Amiga Workbench.

The most readily distinguishable of the windows features runs almost right across the top of the window and is sandwiched in between the Close gadget and the Zoom gadget. This is the Title/Move bar which contains details about the disk and also allows you to move the window around the desktop.

When a window is opened it will always display its name in the Title/Move Bar. This will generally be the same as the name assigned to the icon you used to open the window in the first place.

The window name provides a useful point of reference which becomes important when you have several windows open on the Workbench at once.

The bar also contains information relating to the physical contents of the disk, namely the number of files on the disk and the amount of free space it contains. This free space size is important as it gives you an indication as to the amount of information that can be stored on it.

You can also use the bar to move the window around the desktop. This is done by positioning the Pointer anywhere within the bar and depressing the left mouse button. While keeping the mouse button depressed, when you move the mouse the window will be dragged around the Workbench in the same direction! Releasing the mouse button fixes the new window position until you reposition it once again. Try this with the Workbench disk window and notice that you are only dragging the outline of the window about, the window itself doesn't move until you release the mouse button.

Title/Move Gadget

This gadget, which is immediately to the right of the Title/Move bar allows you to change the size of the window. The action of the gadget is to switch between two sizes. Generally, if a window is small when you open it, clicking on the double gadget will make it large. Clicking on the gadget again will restore the original window size.

Front/Back Gadget

In the far top righthand corner of the window is the Front/Back gadget. This has a dual action. If you have several windows open on screen at once then the Workbench can become a very cluttered place. Windows will generally overlap one another, partially obscuring the contents of the others around them. When you have several windows open they are said to be stacked. The topmost window, which is called the *current window* is by definition in the foreground. All other windows are in the background. By clicking the Pointer on the Front/Back gadget the window is either sent to the back or brought to the front.

If the window you click on is the current window it will go to the very bottom of the stack of windows. Any other window which is not the current window will be brought to the top of the stack and made the current window. If you click on this gadget with just the Workbench disk window displayed you will find that the window disappears! In fact it has simply gone behind the Workbench window – to bring it back click in the Workbench window's own Front/Back gadget!

Scroll Gadgets

Because it is possible to make a window smaller, there may be occasions when it is simply too small to show you all the icons it contains. Equally, you may have so many icons in a window that there isn't enough room to make the window big enough to show all the icons! This is where the scroll bars come into play. The scroll bars are located across the bottom and down the righthand edge of the window – they are therefore normally referred to as the horizontal scroll bar and the vertical scroll bar.

The Scroll Bars are held within the Scroll Boxes. By dragging the Scroll Bars inside their Scroll Boxes you can make other areas of the window come into view. The best way to see this is to make the window about half its present size and then practice the technique. The window can be made smaller using the Sizer gadget detailed next.

An alternative method is to click the Pointer over the arrow gadgets which will force the window to scroll the icons and shift their positions in the direction indicated by the arrow head.

Zoom Gadget

When you open a window it is displayed in a predetermined size. However, you will invariably wish to alter the size, making it either larger of smaller. The Window Sizer gadget allows you to do this.

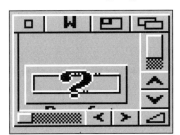

Figure 3.4. A typical zoomed window.

You use this gadget in much the same way as you would do the Move Window gadget. Place the Pointer over the gadget, keep the left mouse button depressed and then drag the Pointer. You can perform the drag in any direction. For example to make the window wider, drag right. To make it narrower, drag left. Similarly, to make the window taller, drag down and drag up to make it shorter. If you wish to make the window taller and wider then drag diagonally down to the right. Dragging up to the left will make the window shorter and narrower.

Note that adjusting the size of a window may well alter the state of the scroll bars. For example, by making a window larger more icons can fit into the field of view. If all icons can be shown the scroll bar gadgets become ghosted as they are not needed any more. The converse is also true.

Icons

Icons are pictorial representations of various aspects of your Amiga. We have already seen one in the Workbench disk icon. The other icon on the standard Workbench is the Ram Disk – as you should be able to see this icon is similar to the Workbench disk icon. It is a sort of pseudo disk that uses some of the Amiga memory to store information – we will be looking at it in due course. If you double-click on the Ram Disk icon you will see that it displays its own window.

The disk icon is just one of several icon types that are used by the Amiga. There are several other types and you can get a good idea of what each of these types looks like by opening the Workbench disk window.

If you do this you will see it is rather dominated by a series of icons that look like drawers – these have names such as Utilities, System, Monitors, Expansion and so forth. Not surprisingly these types of icon are called drawer icons and they too can display their own windows. If you double-click on the drawer icon (more simply drawer) called System it will open a window displaying yet another set of icons.

The icons in the System drawer are all examples of program icons (don't try double-clicking on any of these yet). Programs are often also called Tools in Amiga parlance and they often have their own distinctive icon. For example, a wordprocessor called Wordy might have an icon which incorporates its name utilising a big W. The wordprocessor files (called projects) it creates will also often use a clone of this icon to tie it into the Wordy family. Notice this use of terminology on the Amiga: you use Tools to create Projects or if you prefer, Projects are created on the Amiga by using Tools.

Under Workbench 2.1 and earlier the Workbench disk also contains a special type of icon labelled Trashcan. This is in fact a drawer icon but a special type of drawer. You can use this to dispose of projects and tools that you no longer require. We'll look at this again in due course – don't try experimenting now because anything you throw away you cannot get back. You have been warned! The Trashcan was discontinued with the release of Workbench 3.

There are other icon types that you will come across during your Amiga travels especially if you start designing your very own icons using the IconEdit project which is covered in a later chapter. The bottom line is that you needn't be phased if you encounter an icon type that you haven't seen before.

More Menus

The Workbench menus provide you with the tools that you will need to carry out general run of the mill operations. Now that you hopefully have a better insight into the Amiga Workbench, have a look at the menus again and you will see that they are arranged quite logically. The headings are:

> Workbench
>
> Windows
>
> Icons
>
> Tools

The options listed in the Workbench menu are those that relate to operations to be undertaken at a Workbench (overall) level. Those that are grouped under the Windows heading are options that relate to and act on the current window. Finally, those listed under the Icon heading are particular to icons. The last menu is Tools and at present this contains just one option ResetWB which effectively resets the Workbench.

We will be looking at several of the options in these menus in greater depth as we progress.

Screen Dragging

While windows play a big role in the organisation of your Amiga Workbench so do screens. The best way to illustrate what a screen is, is to show you one. Go to the Workbench menu and select the Backdrop option. The Workbench window disappears and the various icons it held now appear on a screen. Note that the Workbench menus are still available to you.

As you become more familiar with Amiga software you will find that some of it runs in windows and some of it runs on screens. Just as it is possible to have multiple windows stacked, it is also possible to have screens stacked.

You can reveal screens by dragging the uppermost ones down. For instance, if you have converted the Workbench window into a screen via the Backdrop option, move the Pointer to the menu bar, press and keep depressed the left mouse button and then drag the Pointer down. The Workbench screen comes down with you to reveal a blank background (if another screen was active it would be revealed at this point). You can move a screen up and down in this way, but not side to side.

If you now release the mouse button you will find the Workbench remains in place and that you cannot move the mouse Pointer off the top beyond the Menu Bar. To move the Workbench back to its normal position, simply repeat the process. It is not generally necessary to drag the Workbench in this way, but you will wish to drag other windows in a similar fashion.

Workbench Hot Keys

You may well have already noticed that numerous items on the Workbench menus – though certainly not all – have an Amiga A symbol and letter on the extreme right of the menu. This is known as a *hot-key assignment*. Basically each one allows you to get to that particular command using a keypress combination rather than having to go to the menu to select it, thus saving time and effort. The down side is that you need to know what the key press is in the first place. However, as the key used is normally the first letter of the option you want, it isn't that difficult and once you have used hot-keys a few times, they become automatic.

To use a hot-key you need a little bit of manual dexterity. First press and hold down both Amiga keys. They are the keys with slanted As juxtaposed either side of the spacebar. Then press the hot-key you require, at which point the desired operation should be implemented and you can let go of all three keys.

For example, you can select the Backdrop option using the two Amiga keys and the B key. To do this hold down the two Amiga keys and then press the B (for Backdrop) key. Under Workbench 3 you need only hold down the righthand Amiga key.

4: Floppy Disks

No matter which type of Amiga you have – and no matter whether you have a hard disk installed or not – the floppy disk will be your most effective way of exchanging information with the outside world. Almost without fail any programs or games you might buy will be supplied on one or more disks.

Many Amiga magazines nowadays come with at least one disk taped to the front. And as you become more confident in your use of the vast array of features of the Amiga you will want to save your own information for later use or to give to someone else – be it a high score table from your favourite game or the text of a book created using one of the Amiga's text editing programs.

Put bluntly, if you want to get anywhere with your Amiga you must be able to do the following tasks:

- handle disks without damaging them

- prepare disks ready for use

- make copies of your most important disks

- load data from thrm and save data to them.

Thankfully these tasks are not difficult and, once mastered, are like learning to ride a bike, you never forget them. What is more, these techniques are used on computers the world over so you really are learning for the future. To work through the following examples you will need a couple of new (blank) disks handy.

Formatting

The problem with standards is that they lead to incompatibility! Whilst most computers in the world are standardising on 3.5" sized disks, the way they store information on them differs! That said the way in which the Amiga stores information on its disks is the same across all machines and versions of Workbench. For the former reason, disks are normally supplied in a blank format. So before you can use them you must perform a process called *formatting.* The formatting process lays down a sort of electronic map that the Amiga can use to enable it to save and retrieve your information quickly and efficiently. Because this process is so vital it is made relatively easy to perform, and whenever you purchase a box of disks it is always worth spending some time formatting them in one go. This way you'll always be able to place your hands on a disk ready to use whenever you need it. Because you must format a blank disk before you can use it, new blank disks are normally called *unformatted* disks.

To format a new disk remove the Workbench disk from the internal drive and insert a new blank disk. The Amiga will try to read the contents of the disk – it needs to do this so it knows what icon to display and what name to place under the disk icon. As the disk is unformatted it won't be able to obtain this information, so after a few moments it will display the disk icon on the Workbench with the name:

DF0:????

DF0: refers to the disk drive number. The Amiga calls its internal disk drive number 0, therefore DF0 is Disk Floppy drive 0 (or floppy disk drive 0) and ???? signifies that the Amiga cannot use the disk as it is unformatted. Note that on some early versions of Workbench 2 the ???? is sometimes replaced with the word BAD, ie:

DF0:BAD

Before you can format the disk you must select it. You do this by moving the Pointer over the disk icon and clicking the left mouse button once. Because we are dealing with an icon the Format option is conveniently located in the Icon menu. Display the Icon menu and you will see the Format Disk... pretty well down the list. Move the Pointer down over Format Disk... and a selection bar will appear over the option. Let go of the mouse button to select it.

System Requests

During your hopefully long usage of the Amiga, it will often wish to inform you of certain matters. Things might not be turning out as it expected or it can't find something and wants your help. To do this the Amiga uses something called a System Request box. This is rather like a miniature window which is used to display a message and there will normally be a couple of button gadgets for you to click on. Typically OK if you want to proceed or Cancel if you want to stop what it was you were going to do! Normally these messages are pretty succinct and shouldn't give you too many problems.

When you select Format Disk... a system request box will appear on the screen requesting you to insert the Workbench disk back into the disk drive. (If you have a hard disk fitted this actually won't happen because the formatting program is located on the hard disk which the Amiga has instant access to.) The Workbench needs to read the formatting program off the Workbench disk into memory before it can proceed. So, remove the unformatted disk and insert the Workbench disk. Within a couple of moments the System Request box will appear again, this time requesting that you insert the disk to be formatted back into drive DF0:. Do this.

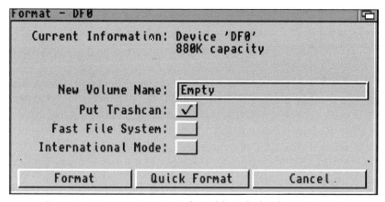

Figure 4.1. Later versions of Workbench display a Format options window when Format is used.

Under Workbench versions 2.1 and later, another window will appear and this will list the various format options available to you. For instance, as you will see later it is also possible to format PC disks, equally you can format special smart card devices that plug into the slot in the lefthand edge of the casing. For the moment though simply click on the disk device you wish to format on, namely DF0:.

Under 2.1 and later, a second Format window is displayed on screen and you can select a number of options via this, such as the disk's name and whether you want the Trashcan to be be placed on the disk. Clicking on the Format button starts the formatting proper.

Another requester box will then appear on the screen, this time labelled Format, asking if it is OK to format the *volume*. The volume is simply another word for disk. This may seem silly because you have physically set about to do this! In fact this type of prompt is called a safety net because it ensures that you cannot accidentally format a disk without really wanting to – the formatting process destroys any information on the disk. To continue, move the Pointer over the Format or Continue button and click the lefthand mouse button once. Of course, if you wish to stop the process select the Cancel button.

Under Workbench 2.1 and later there is a Quick Format button which allows you to reformat previously formatted Amiga disks. This should not be used when a disk is being formatted for the first time or if you are reformatting after a disk has become corrupted.

If you click on the OK gadget the Amiga will set about formatting the disk. The disk icon title:

DF0:????

will be replaced by:

DF0:BUSY

and the requester box will keep you informed of the formatting process by displaying Formatting and Verifying messages. Under Workbench 2.1 a sliding bar illustrating the amount of disk formatted in percentage terms is shown. In releases of Workbench prior to version 2.1 the display will be in a small requester type box and will typically look like this:

Formatting cyl 0, 79 to go

cyl stands for cylinder – perhaps more commonly referred to as a track. Cylinders are numbered from 0 to 79, giving 80 tracks per disk.

The System Request box or requester mentioned above is a common occurrence on the Workbench screen, so get used to seeing it. It is issued by the Amiga whenever it needs something from the user or needs to inform the user that something is not quite right. The message inside the requester details exactly what the problem is.

Hard Disks

If you already have a hard disk then the Workbench disk contents will have been transferred onto your hard disk. This means that you will not have to reference the floppy disk version of the Workbench disk itself. To format a floppy disk on a hard disk system you insert the new disk into the floppy disk drive, highlight the ???? disk icon and select Format Disk... from the Icon menu.

Working Disks

Disks are wonderful devices but they are also fallible devices. Consider this for a moment. What would happen if you spilt some coffee over your Workbench disk? Well for a start your disk would almost certainly be corrupted and totally unusable. Then, unless you were using a hard disk system, you wouldn't be able to boot your Amiga – it would be unusable until you went out and found yourself another copy of the Workbench disk. You could get the new Workbench disk from a friendly dealer but this takes time and would probably cost you a few bob. Why have all that hassle when you are quite at liberty to make a copy of the Workbench disk? You can then use this working copy for everyday use and lock the original master copy away – just in case.

Now, I make the point above about being at liberty to make a backup copy. Commodore allows you to do this, but while most companies who produce software allow you to make a working copy, it is against the law to give people pirate copies of your software.

Making a backup copy is straightforward. You will need:

- The original Workbench disk
- A blank floppy disk
- A disk label

The original master Workbench is the disk from which information will be copied and thus it is known as the *source* disk. The blank floppy (it does not have to be preformatted as the backup process does this) is the disk onto which files will be copied, therefore it is the *destination* disk. The label can be written and then stuck to the destination disk. "Workbench disk – working copy" is a good enough title for the label.

Next you should write protect your master source disk. To do this turn the disk so that the rear is facing you and with the tip of a nail or ball point pen, slide the small plastic tag in the lefthand corner of the disk up so that it reveals a square hole. Whatever happens now you cannot write information to this disk – ie you cannot accidentally format it or overwrite it. This is not essential for backing-up but it is a good habit to get into as it ensures that you should not be able to backup your blank disk onto your master disk by mistake!

Backing Up Masters

Backing-up a disk is straightforward but can be a tedious chore, especially if you are using a single drive only. This is how to back up your Workbench disk.

First place the Workbench disk in the drive, select it by clicking on it once and then select the Copy option from the Icons menu. This will display a System Request box titled DiskCopy. This is the name of the program that does the backing-up. For Workbench versions 2.1 and later this will tell you the number of disks swaps (assuming you are using a single disk drive) needed to perform the backup.

The requester will be asking you to insert the SOURCE (FROM) disk into drive DF0. In fact this should already be there so click on Continue. Information will now be read from the source disk into the Amiga's memory. When it has read as much as it can, it will ask you to replace the source (FROM) disk – the Workbench disk – with the TO (destination) disk. At this point insert the new disk into the disk drive and click on Continue. The information read from the FROM disk is now written to the TO disk. This process will repeat several times until the backup copying process is completed.

When the DiskCopy window disappears the backed-up disk icon will appear – the copy has been made and is about ready for use. Now that you have a working copy of your Workbench disk I would strongly recommend that you back-up and make working copies of the other disks that were supplied with your Amiga – the Extras disk for example. Place the original master disks in a safe place and keep the working copies handy for everyday use.

Renaming Disks

When the backed-up copy of the Workbench disk has been completed the DF0:BUSY icon is replaced by a disk icon with the name copy of xxxx where xxxx is the name of the disk copied, in this case Workbench 2. In other words it should read something along the lines of Copy of Workbench2.1 or of Copy of Workbench3.0.

This is a little long winded and it is somewhat neater and more convenient (as you will come to realise as you read further on) to rename this to plain old Workbench2.1 or Workbench3.0. This is easy to do.

To rename a disk, first highlight the disk to be renamed (ie click on it once) and then select the Rename option from the Icons menu. A small simple window will appear on screen with the current disk name inside it. The small box over the initial letter is the *cursor* and this can be moved around to edit the name. To remove "Copy_of_" just press the Del key eight times until the cursor rests over the W of Workbench. Press the Return key (the large cornered arrow to the right of the main keyboard) to complete the renaming process.

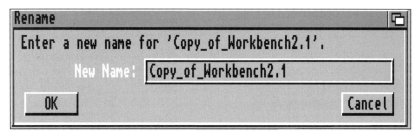

Figure 4.2. Renaming a disk is very easy using the Rename option.

Corrupted Disks

If you keep regular backups of all your disks then you should never be caught out if a disk becomes corrupted and unusable. If you back-up your important files at regular intervals then at worst you will simply need to do a bit of catching up. Of course you only need to back-up your projects as and when they have been extended, added to or contain some new but important information. And quite often it is easiest to do this simply by copying the file onto a backup disk rather than making a complete backup. Copying files is the subject of the next chapter.

However, there are a number of general rules that, if adhered to, should help prevent your disks becoming damaged or corrupted, rendering them useless:

1. Use good quality disks. The price of disks has fallen drastically in recent years and if you shop around you can purchase them at a very reasonable rate. However, cheapest isn't always the best and, as the saying goes, you get what you pay for. If you have friends with computers, ask them where they get their disks and if they are happy. Once you have found a reliable brand stick with them!

2. Always keep your disks in a disk box. If you get into the habit of locking your disks away in a disk box made for the purpose they are less likely to become contaminated or fall foul of coffee, dirt, dust and sticky fingers.

3.   Never, ever, touch the surface of the disk. The magnetic media where your Projects and Tools are stored is protected by a plastic shell. The disk drive has access to this via a metal slider. If you slide this back you can see the surface. It is via this that disks can become corrupted. Fingers are covered in oils that will damage the magnetic surface of the disk.

4.   Smoking is bad for your health. The smoke particles blown onto the disk surface will act as a contaminant. Give up!

How Much Space?

You may be wondering how much information can be stored on a single floppy disk. Well, when a Workbench floppy disk is newly formatted it contains 880K of space free for use. The term k, or K, is shorthand for kilobytes and it is a measurement of storage. One kilobyte (1k or 1K) equates to 1024 bytes. A byte is a standard computer unit, and it may be easier to think of a byte as being equal to a single character. Thus the alphabet can be stored in 26 bytes. Therefore an 880K disk can store:

880*1024 characters = 901,120 characters

For very large storage measurements the Megabyte is used. One Megabyte (1Mb) is equal to 1,048,576 bytes or 1024K.

However, not all this space is available to you as the Amiga needs some to store its own information in. A newly formatted Workbench disk will generally have about 834K available for you to use.

If you try to copy some information that is too big to fit onto a disk, either because the item is very large or because there isn't enough room on the disk because it is full with other files, a System Request will inform you of the fact.

Menu
Beginners
Workbench
Extras Disk
Preferences

5: Copying and Moving

Copying and moving files (Projects and Tools) from one disk to another is – despite what you may hear to the contrary – a very straight-forward process. What I'll outline here is the process for a standard floppy disk system. Hard disk users have life a smidgen easier in that files are normally copied to and from a hard disk which is on site permanently. But more on that later – for all Amiga users the ability to copy files to and from floppy disks is an important task to master.

Generally there are two types of copying you will want to do: copying a file from one position to another on the same disk and copying a file from one disk to another disk. The former is better termed a moving process because you don't actually make a copy of the file. When you transfer a file from one disk to another you make a copy of it as the original source file remains intact. We'll come back to this in due course.

The first thing to bear in mind is that there is only a single floppy drive on the basic Amiga system – therefore it should be obvious that to copy one file from a floppy disk to another will involve some disk swapping. This can become quite tedious if you are trying to copy a large file – perhaps a program – therefore it is best to use an intermediate copying stage and this is where the Ram Disk comes into play.

The Ram Disk

The Ram Disk is one of the most useful features of the Amiga and provides an added dimension of power for those of you who have a single drive Amiga because it effectively gives you a second drive, which can make the process of copying so much easier.

RAM is an acronym for Random Access Memory. This is the memory (internal section of the computer) into which your programs and applications are loaded from disk. By partitioning off an area of this memory, you can use it to save and load programs and data. The partitioned area is known as the Ram Disk and Workbench has immediate access to it as signified by the display of its icon on the Desktop.

From the outset the Ram Disk is displayed as an icon on your Workbench, and like any disk icon it can be opened by double-clicking on it to display its disk window. If you open the Ram Disk window you'll see that it's much like any other disk window.

You'll notice from the title bar that it signifies that the Ram Disk is 100% full, with 0K free and some amount of K in use. This seems weird as there are no files present – but remember that the Ram Disk is self adjusting and grows and shrinks to accommodate files deposited into it. The amount of K in use displayed under Workbench is simply a working overhead.

The Ram Disk offers a number of advantages over a standard floppy disk – the biggest being speed. The Ram Disk is an electronic device and has no moving parts. Accessing a file in it is virtually instantaneous. Also, in case you were wondering, you don't have to format it like a floppy disk – it is already formatted for you.

But there is a drawback: the Ram Disk is *volatile.* Being a software simulation of a hardware device it is only active while the computer is switched on. The moment you remove the power or reboot, the contents are lost forever. If you wish to preserve them you must save the Ram Disk contents onto a floppy disk first. However this is generally a small price to pay for the benefits it has to offer.

The process of copying a file from one place to another is straightforward and involves three simple steps:

1.   Opening the appropriate windows to display the file you wish to copy – the source or *from* file.

2.   Open the appropriate windows to display the destination you wish to copy *to.*

3.   Drag the file from 1 to 2.

Let's copy a file from the Workbench disk into the Ram Disk. We'll copy the Clock tool.

1. Open the Workbench disk window (if it is not already open) and locate the Utilities drawer. Open this by double-clicking on it.

2. Open the Ram Disk window by double-clicking on it.

At this point you may wish to reposition the windows so that the source window and destination window are juxtaposed. Note that, if you like, you can close the Workbench disk window at this point – it will not affect the Utilities drawer window which will remain displayed.

3. Locate the Clock tool. Move the Pointer over it and depress the left mouse button. Keep the mouse button depressed and move the Pointer so that it is over the Ram Disk window. Notice that as you move the Pointer a copy of the Clock icon comes with it. With the Pointer (and Clock icon) over the Ram Disk window, release the mouse button.

Within a few seconds the Clock icon will show in the Ram Disk window. You have successfully copied your first file!

To copy a file from the Ram Disk to a new floppy disk you just repeat steps one, two and three. Thus to copy the Clock to a new floppy disk (assuming you have already formatted the new floppy disk) proceed as follows:

1. Open the Ram Disk window (if it is not already open).

2. Open the window for the disk to which the Clock is to be copied.

3. Locate the Clock icon. Move the Pointer over it and depress the left mouse button. Keep the mouse button depressed and move the Pointer so that it is over the window of the destination disk and release the mouse button.

The above principle can be applied to copy any file – it is as easy as that. It is possible to copy files without the Ram Disk, but we'll look at that process later.

Deleting Ram Files

Deleting files from the Ram Disk is again a simple process – in fact there are two ways in which it can be performed. The first method is simply to turn your Amiga off and then restart it. Remember that the Ram Disk is volatile and by removing the power its contents are lost. This is not very practical though. (Note: If you turn your Amiga off, wait about ten seconds before turning it back on.)

The second method is to use the Delete option found in the Icons menu. Select the file you wish to delete (click on it once) and then choose the Delete option from near the bottom of the Icon menu. This will throw up a system requester to ensure that you wish to proceed, click on the OK gadget to go ahead or Cancel to abort the deletion.

Copying Two Files

You can copy more than one file at a time. In fact there is no real limit to the number of files you can copy in any one go other than that the destination disk (the disk where the files are being copied to) has to have enough room on it to accept the files. If it doesn't then the copy will proceed until the destination disk is full – any files remaining at this point will not be copied. Logical enough.

To copy two or more files you simply select them each in turn before dragging across into the destination window. You do this by keeping the Shift key depressed as you select each file in turn. For instance, suppose you wished to copy a couple of files from the Utilities drawer. Under Workbench 2.0 and 2.1 there are several files in the Utilities drawer – including Clock and More – these will be copied. Under Workbench 3 these have been replaced by just two files – Clock and MultiView – so if you are using Workbench 3 copy these. To copy your two files from the Utilities drawer onto the Ram Disk, you would proceed as follows, after first exposing both the relevant windows:

1.   Hold down a Shift (above Alt) key, either will do.

2.   Click once on the Clock icon to select it.

3.   Click once on the More or MultiView icon to select it.

4.   Move the Pointer (and copy icons) over the Ram Disk window.

5.   Release the Shift key and mouse button.

The copying process will then take place. Note that once you have selected the icons you wish to copy you can release the Shift key. So in the above numbered example, you could have let go of the Shift key at point 4.

If you have a lot of files to copy you can select them by using a technique called *marqueeing.* This involves creating a marquee box (which is a box made of dashed lines down each edge) by dragging it out with the Pointer around the icons you wish to select. For example to select the Clock and More/MultiView icons in this way you would:

1.   Position the tip of the arrow of the Pointer in the top lefthand corner of the Utilities window, just above the Clock icon.

2.   Press and keep pressed down the left mouse button.

3.   Move the Pointer down and to the right across the Utilities window to the lower righthand corner of the More/MultiView icon. As you do this a rotating dotted line will appear – this is the marquee.

4.   Drag the marquee until it engulfs all the icons you wish to select (Clock and More/MultiView in this case), at which point you can release the left mouse button.

5.   Depress the Shift key and keep it depressed.

6.   Move the Pointer over one of the selected icons and press the left mouse button and keep it depressed.

7.   Release the Shift key but keep the left mouse button depressed.

8.   Drag the copy icons over the destination window and release the mouse button.

And that's it. It sounds complicated but it isn't – it's one of those things that, once you have done it once or twice, becomes second nature.

Trashcan

Whenever you format a floppy disk from the Workbench you have the option of including a Trashcan on it (under Workbench 2.04/05 and earlier this is created automatically). The Trashcan is where you put Projects and Tools that you wish to delete – note that simply putting them in the Trashcan does not delete them.

To see how this works take a formatted disk and copy some files onto it as outlined above. Then select one or more of the files and drop them into the Trashcan. To do this drag the file or files over the Trashcan icon and let go. The trashed icon(s) will disappear from the main window – they are in fact now in the Trashcan!

The Trashcan itself is in reality a Workbench drawer but one that has a special purpose. If you double-click on the Trashcan icon now its window will appear and you should be able to see the trashed icon(s) inside. To delete the contents of the Trashcan, first ensure it is selected and then select the Empty Trash option from the Icons menu. Note that this deletes everything inside the Trashcan and there is no safety net, ie no system requester will appear.

Because the Trashcan is a Workbench window you can see what files, if any, it contains by double-clicking on the Trashcan icon. This also means that you can recover a file from the Trashcan simply by dragging it back into the drawer from which it came (or any drawer window for that matter). However, once you have selected Empty Trash the file is gone for good and will no longer be present in the Trashcan drawer.

6:
About
AmigaDOS

Jargon is often the most confusing aspect of learning an alien subject matter. One term which you have probably come across is *AmigaDOS*. This becomes all the more confusing because the terms Workbench and AmigaDOS seem to be used as one and the same. Really they are not so, first of all, what is AmigaDOS?

AmigaDOS stands for Amiga Device Operating System and, like Workbench, it has version numbers which relate to the release of Workbench. Thus Workbench 3 and AmigaDOS 3 were launched at the same time.

Theoretically, if you could break down the Amiga into little bundles of component parts you would find yourself with bits of hardware and software, each of which has a particular responsibility – these are called *devices.*

The Amiga's device operating system allows you to control many of these devices via a series of commands. A command is a word typed in at the keyboard. This is a simplistic overview but hopefully you now have the idea of what is going on.

So what is the relationship between Workbench and AmigaDOS? Workbench is a front-end to AmigaDOS. It provides you, the user, with a friendly viz *user friendly* way to access the various aspects of the Amiga. For example, when you drag a file into the Ram Disk from a disk, you are graphically issuing an AmigaDOS command. In this case the command would be the COPY command.

This may all sound complex, and I suppose to a large extent it is, but let me assure you that there is a great deal of satisfaction at the end of the road once you have mastered it. Thankfully many of the AmigaDOS commands you will want to use are straightforward and their title relates directly to what you want to do. For example, if I asked you what command do you think you would use to find out what version of software you are using, what would be your guess? To find the version you use the command VERSION. To rename a file you use the RENAME command, to format a disk use the FORMAT command. Simple really.

However problems do occur because in many respects AmigaDOS – like any other programming language – is an exact science. You have to be absolutely accurate in what you type at the keyboard – even the ommision of a space can render what you have typed totally useless!

This chapter is by way just a short introduction into AmigaDOS – it is itself a vast topic and if it tickles your fancy there are a couple of books in the *Mastering Amiga* range to help you along the way – see the appendix on Bruce Smith Books titles.

Command Examples

In the above examples of AmigaDOS commands (namely COPY and RENAME), I have used the command names in capital letters. This is not normally necessary but it helps distinguish AmigaDOS command names from the body text so it's a convention I'll continue to use.

So how do you enter and execute an AmigaDOS command? For the odd one-off command you can use the Execute Command option in the Workbench menu. When selected, a requester window is displayed on the screen under the heading Execute a File. To the right of the heading Command you will see a text gadget and you can now use the keyboard to enter the command you wish to be executed. If you make a mistake you can use the Del key to delete it should you so wish.

Try this example. Select the Execute Command option and then type:

VERSION

and press the Return key or select the OK gadget. The requester will disappear and will be replaced by a window entitled Output Window. Inside here will be printed the current version numbers of

Kickstart and Workbench. Click on the close gadget to remove the output window. If you decide against executing the command you can abort the whole operation by clicking on the Cancel button.

To show you how this VERSION command relates to the Workbench, go to the Workbench menu and select the About... option. This produces a window that lists the same information, albeit in a slightly different format.

You can close the Output window generated by Execute Command in the normal fashion.

The Shell

The Execute Command option is fine for the odd command, but if you are going to use AmigaDOS reasonably frequently (and you will as you become more experienced) then the AmigaShell or Shell for short is a much better option. Under Workbench 2.1 and later you will find the Shell icon in the System drawer – prior to this it was located in the Workbench disk window along with the other drawers. If it makes it more palatable for you then think of the Shell as being a sort of continual Execute Command window!

Running or opening the Shell is performed in the normal fashion. Simply double-click on the Shell icon. The Shell window appears and displays an area into which you can type commands. On startup it displays a prompt in the form of:

Workbench2.1:>

or:

Workbench3.0>

To enter a command at the AmigaShell simply ensure that it is the currently selected window (by clicking the Pointer in it) and type a command at the keyboard. Try this now, type:

VERSION

and then press Return.

When we did this before, a system requester was displayed containing the version details. Because the Shell is a direct link with AmigaDOS any information to be displayed (or returned) by a command is displayed in the AmigaShell window itself.

While interesting, VERSION isn't an AmigaDOS command that you will be using regularly. The more interesting commands to the Workbench user are detailed in later chapters but we'll take a look at a few now to give you a flavour.

Directory Listings

When you open a window you see what it contains in the form of pictures – icons. Because the Shell, and indeed AmigaDOS, is a text based interface you are not provided with icons of the files available to you when you open a Shell. However you can obtain a list of the file names by cataloguing the disk – the listing provided is called a *directory* of the files or directory for short. This is done with the DIR command. Because DIR is a shortened version of DIRectory, you are producing a directory of the files on the disk! So with the Workbench disk in the internal disk drive type at the prompt:

DIR

remembering to press the Return key at the end. (The Return key should be pressed at the end of each command entry to terminate it and execute it. Take this as read from now on.) The Workbench disk will spin into life and very shortly a list will appear on the screen.

The directory produced lists two main groups of files. Those with (dir) after them are in fact drawers and you may recognise many of them. Some you will not have seen before! The files without (dir) after them are just that – files. Note how they are displayed grouped and in alphabetical order for you!

A point of possible confusion: the terms drawer and directory are interchangeable – they mean the same thing. It is tradition to use drawer when working from the Workbench and directory when working from the Shell.

The list produced by DIR is too long to fit within the AmigaShell window. However, remember that the AmigaShell can be treated like any other Workbench window. You can move it and, by using the enlarge gadget at the bottom righthand corner, enlarge it. If you enlarge it to the full screen you will be able to see all the items listed by DIR.

If you wanted to see the files located in the Utilities drawer at the Workbench you would open its window, ie double-click on the Utilities drawer icon. To catalogue the contents of a particular drawer (directory) you simply specify its name after the DIR command ie:

DIR UTILITIES

Note that there is a single space between DIR and UTILITIES. Shortly a list of files will appear on the screen and many of these relate to the files you will have already seen as icons on the Desktop. You might like to try cataloguing other Workbench disk directories in a similar fashion. For instance try each of these in turn:

DIR PREFS

        `DIR SYSTEM`

You can even catalogue the Ram Disk by using:

        `DIR RAM:`

Making Mistooks

If you type in an AmigaDOS command incorrectly and you notice the error of your ways before you press the Return key you can simply use the Del key to erase what you have typed up to the point of the error and then start again from that point.

If you have pressed the Return key then – unless you are using a fairly dangerous command such as one that deletes files – nothing major will happen. For example if you went to type VERSION but instead entered VRESION then you would simply get the following message:

        `VRESION: Unknown command`

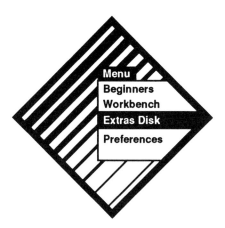

7:
Utilities
and
Tools

OK, by now you should have a pretty good idea how to operate the various basic Amiga mechanisms, namely the mouse and pointer, windows and menus. In this chapter we'll look at some of the more interesting and practical stuff possible with your Amiga, including a look at how we can use the various Utilities and Tools it is supplied with. Like all aspects of the Amiga, once you have mastered one you will have gone a very long way towards mastering all the others!

Essentially there are two drawers containing useful files on the Amiga that you will use more than most. These are the Utilities drawer and the Tools drawer. The latter is on the Extras disk, the former on the Workbench disk and that's the one which holds the Clock and More tools (Workbench 2.1) or Clock and MultiView (Workbench 3.0). On releases prior to Workbench 2.1 there were other tools available in the drawer but in this chapter we'll concentrate just on the Clock tool from the Utilities drawer and come back to More/MultiView in due course.

The Clock

If you open the Workbench disk window (the System drawer on hard disks) and then the Utilities drawer, you will see the Clock icon staring at you. If you double-click on this icon, within a matter of seconds, an analogue clock will appear in front of you – and all being well it should even be telling you the right time. Chances are it won't – so don't worry we'll see how to set the correct time, and date for that matter, in due course.

Notice how the Clock is running in a window that features all of the aspects of all the other windows that we have dealt with bar one. If you can't tell, it's the scroll bars. They are not needed as there is nothing to scroll onto. You can make the window bigger by using the window sizer gadget. If you do this you will see that the clock adjusts to fit the size of the window. Neat!

Ensure the Clock window is the currently selected window (the Clock title/move bar will be blue if it is – if you are not sure just click the Pointer inside the Clock window at some point) and move up to the Workbench screen title bar. If you now press the right mouse button you will see that the standard Workbench menu has been replaced with a new one. Under Workbench 2.1 and later there are two headings and under Workbench 2.0 there are five headings which all belong to the Clock and what you are now looking at is the Clock menu bar.

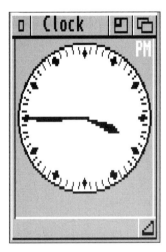

*Figure 7.1. The Clock is displayed in its own window which
exhibits many of the normal window characteristics.*

Not all tools have their own menu bars, some do, some don't. Just bear in mind that to get to a particular menu you must ensure that the menu of the Tool you wish to display is in the current window.

Some of the menu items can be turned on and off, in this case the currently selected mode of operation is highlighted by a tick. To see what I mean go to the Clock menu and display Project (Workbench 2.1 and above) or Type (Workbench 2.0 and below). As the Clock is currently being displayed in analogue mode this is ticked. Select the Digital option and watch the analogue Clock disappear, to be replaced by a digital Clock.

Figure 7.2. The Clock also has menus associated with
it which allow you to use its many functions.

Notice also how the window has now changed to suit the display of the analogue Clock. I normally have the Clock running in this way but position it so it is located on top of the Workbench menu in the Workbench menu bar so it is easily visible at all times.

With the Clock in analogue mode you might like to experiment with some of the other options on the menu.

Clock Alarm

The Clock has an alarm built into it. Setting the alarm is straightforward. First select Set from the Alarm menu and a small window will appear called Alarm Set. To set the hour, click the Pointer in the hour gadget box, ie over the hour counter. Use the up and down arrow gadgets to set the hour.

Repeat the procedure with the minutes gadget. Under Workbench 2.0< there is a separate AM/PM gadget to set the alarm for the appropriate half of the day. Select Use to set the Alarm. Selecting Cancel aborts the setting. Finally select Alarm On from the Alarm menu to enable the alarm. When the appropriate time arrives the screen will flash once and a high pitched noise will be produced by the speaker.

Setting the Date and Time

The Amiga can be pretty much customised to suit your own particular needs as we shall see in a forthcoming chapter. These customisation choices are called Preferences and are controlled by a series of Tools that are located in a drawer on the Extras disk called Prefs. Note that under Workbench 2.0 and earlier these Prefs files are in fact on the Workbench disk. Prefs is a drawer icon even though it looks somewhat different from other drawer icons – but we warned you about that didn't we?

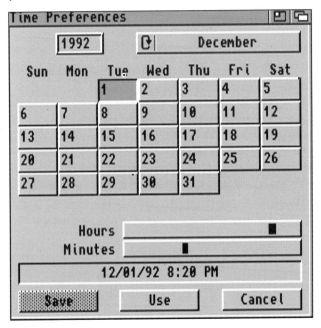

Figure 7.3. You can set the date and time of the Clock using the
Time Preferences editor. This has to be done every time you use
your Amiga unless you have a battery powered clock installed.

If you double-click on the Prefs icon a window will open displaying the various Preference icons – again each of these is dominated by a question mark. Each of these icons provides access to Preferences Editors when run. These are simply windows which provide a variety of gadgets which allow you to define and change settings.

At this point we are interested in just one particular Preference editor, the one that controls the time and date setting and this is the Time Preferences editor. When you double-click on this it opens a window.

To set the current date first enter the year in the year string gadget. Click in the gadget to display the cursor, use the backspace key to delete what is there and enter the new date. The month is set using a cycle gadget – keep clicking on the cycle gadget until the correct month is displayed and then click on the date in the calendar to set the day.

The time is set using a 24-hour clock and simply by dragging the hour and minute slider bars up and down until the correct time is displayed at their top. When you are happy that your settings are correct click on the Save button or on Cancel if you want to abort the process.

Extras Disk

The Extras disk is nearly as important to you as your Workbench disk. It contains a lot of important files which you will need to use from time to time. As already mentioned, from Workbench2.1 it contains the Preferences editors which allow you to define exactly how your Amiga works. For now though, we will be concentrating on the drawer called Tools. If you are using a hard disk system then you will find that the Tools drawer is located in the System drawer displayed on the Workbench.

If you are using a single drive system then – to prevent disk-swappingitis occurring – you will probably find it easier to copy the projects you might want during the course of an Amiga-using session onto the Ram Disk.

The Calculator

Traditionally everyone thinks of a computer as a great calculating device. Although in reality that is exactly what the Amiga is, the manner in which those numbers are calculated and the results are displayed determines what task your Amiga carries out. However, not to disappoint you the Tools drawer contains a Calculator icon which, when double-clicked, displays a non-sizeable window and provides some useful basic mathematical tools. It functions just like any other desktop or pocket calculator and you can use it by clicking on the number button gadgets with the mouse Pointer.

Thus to perform 5+2= from the on-screen keypad you use the Pointer to click on the following button gadgets on the face of the calculator:

5

+

2

=

The CE key is a Clear Entry gadget and this allows you to delete/remove the last entry only. So, if you meant to calculate 5*6 and actually entered 5*7 and noticed your error at this point, you could select CE to remove the 7 and then carry on.

One key that is not on most calculators is the << and this allows individual characters to be removed from the currently typed number. Thus entering 1234567 and then selecting << would remove the 7 from the number sequence. Selecting it again would remove the 6 and so on. The +/- key *toggles* the sign of the number, ie changes it from a positive to negative value and vice versa.

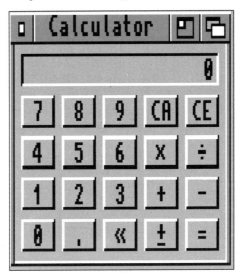

Figure 7.4. The Calculator window.

From Workbench 2.1 there is an additional window available to users of the Calculator called Calculator Tape. With the Calculator window selected move to the menu bar and open the Settings menu. Select Show Calculator Tape. Now any actions you perform on the Calculator will be listed blackboard style in the Calculator Tape window.

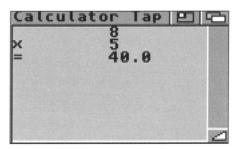

Figure 7.5. The Calculator Tape window.

Colors

Colors allows you to alter the individual colours of Amiga screens opened from the Workbench. When you double-click on the Colors icon a window is displayed on screen. Across the top of the Colors window are four default colour blocks which are the basic four building blocks of standard Workbench colours. By default these are normally Grey, Black, White, and Blue. You can select any of these by clicking on them, at which point the colour gadget will be highlighted by a box. Select the colour you wish to alter and then move the colour slider gadgets to edit the colour. The process is fully interactive and, as you move the sliders, the appropriate colours on the screen will change. For example, select the rightmost colour (blue) and then drag the R(ed) slider across to the right. Blue represents the colour used under many releases of Workbench for the window name bars. The blue in the Colors window name bar will become pink. If you click in any other window you will notice that its name bar is pink.

You can restore the default colours at any time simply by selecting the Reset button. The Cancel button ignores any changes you have made while Use implements the changes you have made, closing the Colors window.

The number displayed to the right of the G(reen) slider gadget is a hexadecimal representation of the colour weight. The three digits refer (from left to right) to the weight of the R, G and B components. The number 0 means no element of that colour, while F means 100% of the colour. These numbers cannot be edited directly so they are really only a numeric reference point for you.

As mentioned, Colors can be used to edit the colours used by any screen displayed by a program launched from the Workbench. To change a particular screen's colours proceed as follows:

1   Open the Tools window on the Workbench to display the Colors icon. It might be convenient to copy this into the Ram Disk.

2   Launch the application if this is not already up and running.

3   Drag the window down the screen until the Colors icon is revealed.

4   Double-click on the Colors icon. This will be displayed on the program screen (not on the Workbench screen).

5   Edit the colours accordingly and close the Colors window.

The colours and number of them displayed by the Colors window will depend on the number actually used by the application running.

KeyShow

Because alphanumeric needs differ from country to country so do keyboards. For instance in England there is the need for a £ character unlike in the USA, Germany or Sweden where it is likely to be substituted by a different, more appropriate, character. When you run the KeyShow program it displays a graphical representation of the keyboard in a window marked with the character each key will produce when depressed. A600 users will notice that the graphic displayed shows a separate numeric keypad which the A600 doesn't have – just ignore that bit.

Several of the keys are shaded – these are the qualifier keys, namely Ctrl, Shift and Alt. When you hold down one of these keys the result of a keypress will normally differ from what would have been produced had it not been held down. You can simulate what you will get by clicking on one of the greyed keys. For example, click on one of the grey Shift keys. The Shift keys become blue in colour to show they are in effect and the keyboard characters change accordingly. Thus a becomes A etc. To remove the Shift qualifier simply click on it again. Press (with your fingers) on Alt and Ctrl to see what these do.

The KeyShow window sometimes uses a few extra characters to represent a particular action. When Ctrl is the qualifier many keyboard alpha keys are prefixed with a caret symbol (^) or a tilde (~) which indicate control characters.

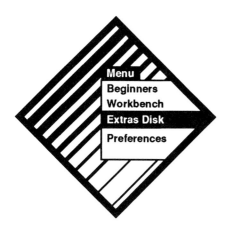

8: Some Preferences

One of the useful things about the Amiga from your point of view is that you can define the way it operates and how it looks and feels to use. In other words you can really personalise your own Amiga pretty much to suit your own needs and also to make it look and operate very differently from any other Amiga. The implementation of some of this is quite advanced and beyond the bounds of the aim of this book. However, some of this is quite straightforward and can have an immediate effect on the look of the Workbench for instance.

Many of these user-definable aspects are defined by what are called the Preference editors. The Preference editors were introduced, albeit briefly, in an earlier chapter. To recap, they are a series of windows each of which relates to a particular aspect of the Amiga's operation. Each contains a number of gadgets which allow you to change the way in which the particular aspect of the Amiga operates.

The settings in the various Preference editors are defined by Commodore and they are ideal for most uses. However, individuality is a great thing and you may feel you either wish to make your set-up look different or fine tune a particular operation or function to suit your own special needs. And there's nothing wrong with that!

Once you have mastered how one or two operate you should have no problems coping with the rest of them. In this chapter I'm going to concentrate on those that are particularly useful, either from a particular point of view, or because they allow you to personalise the look and feel of the desktop.

One thing to point out at this stage is that invariably the look of the Preference editors is undergoing continual enhancement and you may well find that some of the more specific items differ from what you have displayed on the screen. For example, between Workbench 2.1 and Workbench 3.0 the arrangement of colours for the Workbench palette has been turned around through 90 degrees. Don't let this throw you – the functionality remains the same. Honest!

The Prefs drawer itself is something of a rover. You will find one on the Workbench disk but it may not contain the Preference editors in earlier versions of Workbench, ie 1.3 and 2.0. For Workbench 2.1 and 3 (and probably subsequent releases as they appear) you will find them in the Prefs drawer on the Extras disk.

Workbench Patterns

The WBPattern editor allows you to change the background colour or pattern on both the Workbench backdrop itself and all windows. The backdrop can be changed independently of all windows and vice versa.

When you double-click on the WBPattern icon the WBPattern Preferences window is displayed. This is a window that has had some of those subtle changes made to it that I was warning you about earlier.

Under some versions (typically Workbench 2.1 and below) you will find that there are two radio buttons positioned in the top lefthand corner of the window labelled Workbench and Windows. By default the Workbench button is coloured blue and this indicates that any changes you are about to make will be to the Workbench backdrop. If you wished to change the window's pattern then you just click on the Windows button gadget. Both buttons are mutually exclusive so effectively you simply toggle from one to the other.

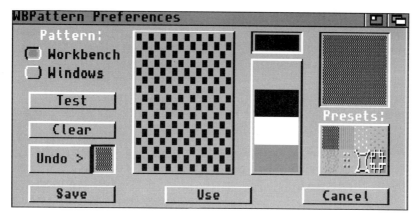

Figure 8.1. WBPattern Preferences editor a la A600.

Under later versions (Workbench 3.0 and later) there are two cycle gadgets at the top slightly left of centre called Placement and Type. By default Workbench and Pattern are displayed and this indicates that any changes you are about to make will be to the Workbench backdrop and will done using a selected pattern. The Placement gadget can be cycled through two other settings, namely Windows and Screen.

The Type cycle gadget allows you to choose between Pattern and Picture. If you choose Picture then the Select Picture... item will become active. Clicking on an active Select Picture gadget brings up a file requester for you to locate an IFF picture to act as a backdrop to your Workbench screen. There are no IFF pictures on the distribution disks so we'll leave this advanced stuff to our sister title *Mastering Amiga Workbench 3*. The rest of the window is about editing a pattern.

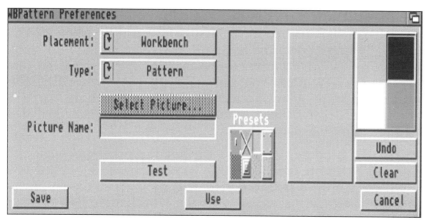

Figure 8.2. WBPattern Preferences editor a la A1200.

There is a large rectangle to the right of these buttons which dominates the main area of the window and this is the magnified viewing box and this shows you a magnified view of the pattern you are using. To one side of this is a slightly smaller rectangle which holds within it the four Workbench colours – this is the colour palette. You can select any one of these colours just by clicking on it – the current colour is then displayed in the smaller box above this. This is the selected colour.

Another area is the Presets area which shows predefined patterns. You can select from any of the patterns therein simply by clicking on one of them. Try clicking on the one in the top right containing the grey looking dots. When you do this the pattern appears in another box and in a larger form in the magnified view box.

With this selected, click on the Test button and the selected pattern will be applied to the Workbench backdrop so that you can see what it looks like. To remove this, click on the Undo button and then select Test again. At this point you might like to play around with the various other patterns to see how they look. Remember you can also apply them to windows by selecting the Windows button.

If you get confused at any point remember that you can abort the whole lot at anytime by selecting the Cancel button. This will close the WBPattern Preferences window but you can then reopen it.

Workbench patterns are built up from a series of square dots – these are the picture elements and are more commonly called pixels. The purpose of the magnified view box is that it allows you to edit patterns at this pixel level. You do this by positioning the Pointer tip at the desired point and pressing the lefthand mouse button. This will set a small block in the colour of the currently selected colour. To set a blue block click on the blue rectangle so that blue is displayed at the top of the colour palette and then move the Pointer accordingly. You can apply a sweep of colour simply by holding down the lefthand mouse button and moving the Pointer. Note that as you make the changes they appear en bloc in the Preset preview area. You can make up your own colours from scratch simply by selecting a base colour – say blue – and then selecting the Clear button. You can then draw your own design using the magnified view area.

WBPattern is good fun to play with but for practical reasons you will probably find it easier to stick with the base colours. One area it would be useful in is in the colouring of individual windows. For instance setting the background of the Workbench disk window to black would make it instantly recognisable amongst a desktop of many. Unfortunately though, changing the appearance of individual windows in this manner is not possible via WBPattern.

You will probably have noticed by now that the WBPattern Preferences editor has three buttons strung across the base of the window. These are titled Save, Use and Cancel and are found on all the Preferences editor windows. If, after playing around with the WBPattern editor, you decide that you don't like your creation – click on Cancel and everything you have done will be forgotten and the window will close, at which point you can start again if you so wish.

On the other hand, if you like what you have done, you can select either Save or Use. Save will record your new design on the Workbench disk and whenever you reboot your Amiga it will be used until you change it again using Save. If you only wish to use your new design for a limited period select the Use button and the changes you have implemented will be forgotten when you reboot your Amiga.

The Pointer

By now the Pointer will be a familiar object to you and because of its importance some people like to give it a bit more of a personality by changing its appearance or completely replacing it. The Pointer Preferences editor allows you to do just that. When you double click on the Pointer Preferences editor it displays its own window which houses all the gadgets you will need to customise the thing!

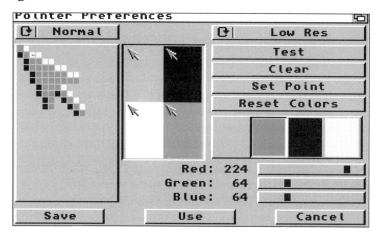

Figure 8.3. The Pointer editor window.

The window is divided into four distinct regions. The main area to the right is the editing gadget and it is here where you make your additions and deletions in a magnified view box. To the upper right of this are four representations of the Pointer against each of the Workbench colours so you can see how the finished article will look against any Workbench background. To the right of this again there are four operational button gadgets and below this the colour palette and sliders.

Using the editor is very intuitive and a couple of minutes practice will make you an expert without too much trouble! You select a colour by clicking on one of the four in the palette so that it is displayed in the selected colour box to the right. Alternatively you can construct a new colour using the palette slider bars (note that you cannot change the Workbench background colour composition though). Then you move across into the magnified view box and position the tip of the Pointer at the position you wish to set a point, and then click. You build images up in this way:

1.   Select colour

2.   Position Pointer

3.   Click

To erase a pixel from the Pointer design you simply set the colour to the background colour. Position the Pointer over the pixel to be erased and click.

The four button gadgets provide a number of useful facilities and are detailed below:

Test   Select this and the current Pointer takes on the image of that shown in the magnified view box. This way you can see what the Pointer looks like on screen.

Clear   This erases the entire contents of the magnified view box.

Set Point   The pointer has a hot-spot. This is the single pixel point on the Pointer which is used to define what you are selecting. Normally the hot-spot is at the very tip of the Pointer and is signified by a small yellow pixel with a hole in the middle. When you select Set Point the next time you click the Pointer in the magnified view box will set the hot-spot at that point.

Reset Colour Restores the last set of saved colours to the palette.

Editing the Pointer can be fun but if you get yourself in a pickle remember that you can always select the Cancel gadget to forget what you have done prior to starting again.

For now you might like trying to add your initials for a totally personalised Amiga Pointer!

Saving Individual Pref Sets

Some of the Preferences editors allow you to save named settings which can be recalled as you want to use them. For instance using the WBPattern Preferences editor you could sit down and create a whole library of Workbench and window patterns and recall any particular one for use at whim.

If, with the WBPattern Preferences window open and selected, you move to the Workbench menu bar you will find that the menu bar has at least three menus which can be used in conjunction with it, they are Project, Edit and Options. Note that some editors also add their own additional menus.

These menus are there to make it easier for you to work with Presets and the best way to see these in operation is to look at a practical example using the WBPattern editor explained at the start of this chapter. For this we'll make two Workbench patterns which we'll call Dots and Arcs.

First open the WBPattern editor and select the black dots backdrop from the Presets box (the top lefthand one). Now move to the menu bar and select the Save As option from the Project menu. A Save Backdrop Pattern window will appear on the screen.

You will see from the Drawer setting in this that the default storage for these is in the Presets drawer. By default, the name for the file is set at WBPattern.pre. The .pre signifies that the file is a preset and it's worth keeping this. You should edit the rest of the filename though to signify what it is. The name:

WBPdots.pre

is good for that purpose. When you have done that select OK. Then exit the WBPattern editor. If you now open the Presets drawer you should see the WBPdots.pre file present. The icon has already been assigned to this because by default the Save Icons? setting in the Options menu is selected (signified by a tick). This option toggles on and off each time you select it. If it is disabled then the file will be saved in the Presets drawer but with no icon so you will not be able to see it.

Now create the second Workbench pattern in a similar way, this time selecting the Arcs pattern from the Presets box in the WBPattern Preferences editor – this is located on the lower line, third from the left. Save this using the Save As option, calling it:

WBParcs.pre

You will notice that when you display the Save Backdrop Pattern window the previously saved definition is listed in the scrolling file window. In fact there are two listed: the plain settings file plus a .info file which is the icon. Finally you may wish to save a copy of the standard default setting and call this:

WBPstandard.pre

At the conclusion of this you should have a Presets drawer with three icons in it similar to that illustrated in Figure 8.4.

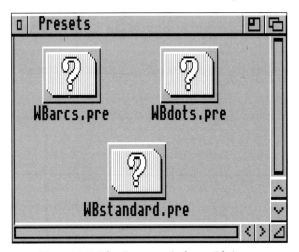

Figure 8.4. The Presets window with icons.

To set the Workbench pattern to any you have defined, simply double-click on the appropriate icon – what could be simpler? The beauty of having a standard setting there is that you can reset the desktop back to its original detail at any point simply by double-clicking on it. You can save window patterns in a similar way and there is no limit to the number you can define other than the physical limit imposed by available space on your Workbench disk.

If you want to load a previously defined definition to edit some more then you can by using the Open option from the Project menu. This displays the Load Backdrop Pattern window, the contents of which will be familiar to you. Simply double-click on the named definition (ignore the ones with .info appended to them) and its details will be loaded into the WBPattern Preferences editor.

Menu
Beginners
Workbench
Extras Disk
Preferences

9: AmigaDOS & the Shell

The Shell – or AmigaShell as it is often known – was introduced in Chapter Six. As you become more familiar with and more experienced in using your Amiga you will soon come to realise that you will get the best performance out of your Amiga using a combination of the dynamic duo Workbench and AmigaDOS. Therefore, as the Shell is a prime route to using AmigaDOS, a good working knowledge of what the Shell has to offer is well worth having.

As a newcomer to the Shell you will make mistakes so it is worth knowing how to use the Shell's simple but effective editing facilities. The most important keys are the four arrow or cursor keys, the backspace key and the Del key. The arrow keys normally sit at the extreme bottom righthand corner of the keyboard and the backspace (left arrow) and Del keys are situated immediately to the left of the Help key in the top righthand corner of the keyboard. The latter two allow you to delete characters to the left or immediately under the cursor in the normal fashion.

If you have the AmigaShell open, close it and then reopen it. Now enter the following commands one after the other:

        DIR

        LIST

        DIR DIRS

pausing after each command to watch what happens. Each command will generate some output to the screen. When the prompt reappears, press the up arrow key. The DIR DIRS command appears at the prompt. Press up arrow again and the LIST command appears. Press the down arrow key and DIR DIRS appears. Press Return and the command DIR DIRS is executed.

Each time you enter a line of text and complete by pressing the Return key the Shell records the fact and archives the command. This in effect gives you a complete command *history* and you can scroll backwards and forwards through it as you wish using the up arrow and down arrow keys.

Unless you are a pretty proficient typist then you will invariably make mistakes. The Shell provides a number of key combinations to make editing these out of your commands as simple as possible. These are normally simple dual-key combinations which operate from the current position of the cursor. Some examples of these dual combination commands are listed in Table 9.1.

Command	Action
<Del>	Delete character under cursor
<Backspace>	Delete character to left of cursor
<Ctrl-A>	Move cursor to start of line
<Ctrl-K>	Delete from cursor to end of line
<Ctrl-U>	Delete from cursor to start of line
<Ctrl-Z>	Move cursor to end of line

Table 9.1. Some Shell key commands.

For instance, you can delete from the current cursor position to the end of the line by pressing <Ctrl-K>. The two chevrons, <>, signify that it is a single key press and the two keys involved are the Ctrl and K keys. In other words press Ctrl and K together and the text to the end of the line from the current cursor position will be deleted!

The best way to become familiar with these is simply to use them. A few minutes using each is all it takes and from that point on you will find a significant difference in your use of AmigaDOS. The only point to note is that the Del key deletes the character under the cursor. The cursor is normally placed at the end of the line, so if you wish to delete the character to its left you must first move it there using the left-arrow key.

The Shell also provides a useful search facility in that it allows you to seek out the last occurrence of a particular command, thus avoiding the need to scroll through a potentially long command history list. To use this simply type the start of the command name and then press Ctrl-R. For example:

DIR<Ctrl-R>

will locate the last time the DIR command was used. Typing:

<Ctrl-R>

again will seek out the next previous occurrence and so on.

Note that this facility is case sensitive and so it is important that you use the same case (upper or lower) when typing in.

Shell Commands

The Shell also has a few inbuilt commands which can be quite useful. You must bear in mind that Shell commands belong to the Shell and are not AmigaDOS commands. They would not work therefore if you typed them into the Execute Command window.

To use any of these commands simply type them at the Shell prompt and press the Return key. The most interesting of these I find is REVERSE. This reverses the colours in the AmigaShell window making it readily distinguishable from other windows and also easier on the eye. The NORMAL command restores the original colours. Note that these two particular Shell commands were removed with the release of Workbench 3 – but it is possible to re-introduce them as we shall see.

Another useful Shell command is CLEAR. Entering this will clear all previous activity from the current Shell window leaving just the prompt sitting at the top of the screen as though you had just opened the Shell itself.

Shell Special Effects

As we've seen, the Shell allows you some editing shortcuts using special key press combinations and some more interesting visual effects on-screen using the Ctrl and ESC keys respectively. Let's take a further look at the editing keys first which are implemented via the Ctrl key – the most popular ones are listed in Table 9.2.

Key	Action
<Ctrl-h>	Deletes last character
<Ctrl-w>	Delete last word
<Ctrl-x>	Delete current line

Table 9.2. Some popular Shell editing shortcuts.

The best way to understand these is to play with them. Of them all <Ctrl-X> is by far the most useful and can save having to press the Delete key to remove an erroneous command line.

The ESC key provides for some rather more interesting effects on-screen, such as coloured text and italicised text to name but two. To see just how this works from the Shell enter the following command (after making a Shell the active window):

<ESC>[3m

and press Return. The text inside the Shell, from this point, will be displayed in italics!

Note that when you press the ESC key in the Shell an inverted [is displayed (inverted means displayed as a character in the background colour inside a white box). You still need to press the [after ESC though. You will also find that you get an "Unknown command" error message on-screen. This should be ignored.

When you try entering these ESC commands from a Shell nothing is displayed on screen after pressing ESC until you have pressed the Return key. Have faith!

The above key combination would normally be written as:

<ESC>3[m

as it is not necessary to keep the ESC depressed while you press the subsequent keys. To set things back to normal type:

<ESC>[0m

Some of the various ESC key commands that you can use to create a wide range of effects are listed in Table 9.3 opposite.

As always, try experimenting with the above to see how you get on and what weird or wonderful effects you can come up with. If you get into problems press <ESC-c> (the Esc key and c together) to restore the status quo!

Keys	Action (Workbench 3 in brackets)
<ESC>[0m	Cancel all effects
<ESC>[1m	Bold text enabled
<ESC>[3m	Italic text enabled
<ESC>[4m	Underlined text enabled
<ESC>[7m	Inverted text enabled
<ESC>[30m	Set text colour to blue (grey)
<ESC>[31m	Set text colour to white (black)
<ESC>[32m	Set text colour to black (white)
<ESC>[33m	Set text colour to orange (blue)
<ESC>[40m	Set background colour to blue (grey)
<ESC>[41m	Set background colour to white (black)
<ESC>[42m	Set background colour to black (white)
<ESC>[43m	Set background colour to orange (blue)

Table 9.3. Some Shell special effect key sequences.

10:
Drawers
and
Directories

This chapter is mainly a theoretical one. That said, it is a very important one because it will help you understand how drawers (directories) and files are handled and used by the Amiga.

For the purposes of this chapter we intend to look into how the concept of directories works by using the Workbench as an example. The concepts involved are all widely applicable and the graphical nature of the Workbench will help get them across. As the saying goes: "Every picture..."

With your Amiga up and running and the Workbench disk in position double-click in the Workbench disk icon. After a few moments, in which AmigaDOS is reading the contents of the disk, you will be presented with a window in which some of the contents of the disk will be displayed in the form of small pictures or icons – OK, this we have encountered before.

If you look in the Workbench disk window you will notice that several of the icons displayed are shaped like drawers. Well that's exactly what they are, software drawers into which you can place your files and information and indeed other drawers if you so wish.

We have seen that drawers also have their own windows. If you double-click the left mouse button when the Pointer is positioned over the Utilities drawer icon, a window will open displaying the contents of the drawer! You might like to try this now and see what the end result is. In fact the drawer window is very much like the disk window in that it has all the same gadgets.

A Hierarchical Filing System

Why drawers? AmigaDOS supports what is called a hierarchical filing system which means that it can have multiple levels. At this point it's probably worth drawing an analogy.

Imagine your desk at home, office or school and that you have no access to files, or drawers or cupboards. You would have to keep every single book or sheet of paper on top of the desk. This would produce a cluttered area which would be difficult to work in and would raise your blood pressure when you tried to locate a particular item. In an organised working environment you would arrange your books and papers into folders or drawers which would themselves be held in a desk or filing cabinet.

Workbench drawers – and therefore AmigaDOS drawers – are designed to emulate this same process. Every AmigaDOS disk has enough space on it to hold tens of thousands of pieces of information. Most files don't come anywhere near this in size and so it is possible to store many files on a disk. For instance, a disk might contain 30 files. If these were all stored in the main disk window it would make locating a particular file troublesome and involve a fair amount of scrolling around the window. Equally you would have to have 30 very different names so each one was clearly distinguishable from any other.

Drawers can be used to organise your files. You can create a drawer, give it a name and then place the relevant files inside the drawer. For instance, you may wish to use your Amiga as a wordprocessor and as a means to hold bank statement details. You could create two drawers on a disk and label them Wordprocessing and Statements. You could then save each file you created in the relevant drawer. You might call the disk Current Work.

But, you can also go a step further. Drawers may themselves contain drawers. Let's take the Wordprocessing drawer a step further. You might find that you are producing several types of documents. For example, Home, Business and Club. You could create suitably named drawers inside the Wordprocessing drawer and then place the relevant files in the appropriate drawers. And we could take it a step further again. You might create two types of wordprocessor file for your Club – namely Letters and Memos. Once again these drawers could be created and used in similar fashion. In fact there is no limit to the number of drawers that can be nested inside drawers, subject to there being enough space on your disk to do so.

The term drawers is sometimes interchanged with the term directories, and it is quite common to refer to directories stored inside other directories as *subdirectories.* As a rule of thumb, drawers belong to Workbench, directories to AmigaDOS. Even though they mean the same thing, this allows you to illustrate clearly which one you are talking about.

The thing that should become immediately apparent from arranging your files in this way is that it makes it very easy to locate files when you next want them. If you want a Club memo file you'll know exactly where to look!

Trees, Roots and Branches

Because of its arrangement it is sometimes called a tree or tree directory. You can imagine the various subdirectories being the roots of a tree, or if you turn the lot upside down, the branches of a tree. The very top of the tree structure, ie the top directory (this is the one that is displayed when you open a disk icon) is normally referred to as the root directory for this reason.

If you look down the root structure of the Wordprocessing directory as illustrated in Figure 10.1 you will notice that several directories are on the same level but they are not connected directly.

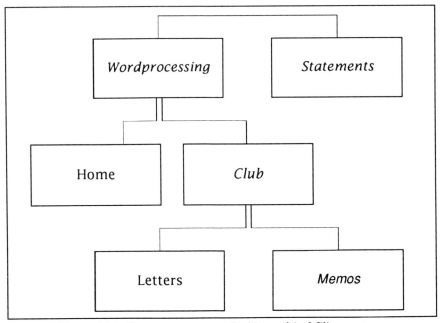

Figure 10.1. The root structure of a hierarchical filing system.

For instance, the directories Home, Business and Club are all sub-directories of Wordprocessing but there is no direct connection between them other than via the Wordprocessing directory. This is a very important concept and one that you should fully understand.

Imagine you are working on a file stored in the Letters directory. This is called the current directory. To go to the Memos directory you must first go up to Club (ie up the directory tree) and then down to Memos (ie down the directory tree).

Quite often a subdirectory of a directory or drawer is referred to as being the *child* directory of a *parent* directory in which it is located.

Directory Path

When you need to reference a particular file you can do so by giving what is called its *path name*. The path name consists of the file name preceded by any directories and subdirectories which must be accessed to reach it. Each directory name is separated by a slash character. So to write the path name of a file called Report in the Memo directory we would use:

Current-Work:Wordprocessing/Club/Memos/Report

The last name is generally a file and not a drawer. Also it isn't always necessary for you to give the disk (volume) name in the root if the disk to be used is implied, in which case the path name becomes:

:Wordprocessing/Club/Memos/Report

Note the use of colon (:) which implies the root directory of the current disk. If you have more than one disk drive attached to your Amiga then you might wish to state the disk drive number and we shall cover this in due course.

The directory from which all other files and directories are accessed is often referred to as the root directory. All the directories that radiate from it are known as branches of the root directory.

Another analogy that is often used is that of parent and child directories. The starting directory is called the parent directory and any directories created here are child directories. Obviously directories created within the child directory will become its child directories whilst it, in turn, becomes their parent directory! If you are struggling to understand this terminology then simply apply your family tree to it. Your father is your parent and you are the child. Your father is the child of your grandfather while also being your grandfather's child!

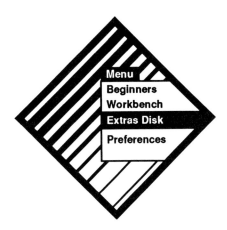

11: AmigaDOS Format and Copy

In an earlier chapter we saw how to use the various Workbench options to format a floppy disk – a very important task. When you use the Format Disk option from the Workbench menu it simply invokes an AmigaDOS command called FORMAT.

Let's examine how to use the FORMAT command itself directly from the Shell. Again, this is one of those items that has been developed during each subsequent release of AmigaDOS and Workbench, so although the way in which you enter the command on the Amiga hasn't changed, there has been a development in how the Amiga responds. If you get something that isn't *exactly* the same as what follows, don't panic. Just use a bit of common sense and – if you need to – experiment!

When a disk is formatted from the Workbench using the Format option you are required to supply two items of information, even if you don't know it. Firstly you must indicate the disk to be formatted by selecting it and then you must supply a name for the disk. The latter is actually done for you, and a name of Empty is assumed by default. You do have the option of changing this of course.

When disks are formatted from the Shell the same two items of information are needed. The disk is identified courtesy of the device name of the drive it is placed into. The disk name can then be specified. You can use Empty if you wish or alternatively supply any legal disk name.

The layout of the disk formatting command is shown below. In computer terms this is normally referred to as its *syntax.*

FORMAT DRIVE <drive name> NAME <disk name>

The commands that must be typed are shown in capital letters, the text inside the angled brackets indicates that you must supply some information here. In this case it is the drive name, ie the one where the formatting is to take place, and then the disk name, ie the name to be assigned to the disk when formatting has completed.

The rules are exactly the same for formatting from the Shell as they are from the Workbench. Formatting destroys anything that may be on the disk.

To format a disk in the internal drive (drive DF0:) and call it MyDisk, use the following command:

FORMAT DRIVE DFO: NAME "MyDisk"

Note that the name to be assigned to the disk must be enclosed within double quotes (not under AmigaDOS 3). As with all AmigaDOS commands the case of the letters for the command is irrelevant although the combination used inside the double quotes to name the disk will be used exactly. Note that AmigaDOS 3 ignores the quotes in commands but quotemarks used in naming a disk are included as part of the name.

You will then be asked for the Workbench disk and within a few seconds a message will appear inside the Shell window along these lines:

Insert disk to be formatted in device DFO

Press RETURN to begin formatting or CTRL-C to abort

Do this and the procedure is then much the same as described earlier. The DF0:BUSY icon appears on the Workbench and then formatted and verified. Unless you are working from a hard disk based system you will almost certainly need to do a little bit of disk juggling in repost to the various messages that will be echoed into the Shell window. On completion the formatted floppy disk will take its place on the Workbench as an icon.

```
┌─┬────────────────────────────────────────────────┬──┬──┐
│ □ │ AmigaShell                                     │ ▣ │ ▱ │
├─┴────────────────────────────────────────────────┴──┴──┤
│4.Workbench3.0:> FORMAT DRIVE DF0: NAME "MyDisk"         │
│                                                         │
│                                                         │
│                                                         │
│                                                         │
│                                                         │
│                                                      ◹ │
└─────────────────────────────────────────────────────────┘
```

Figure 11.1. Using the FORMAT command from the AmigaShell.

```
┌─┬────────────────────────────────────────────────┬──┬──┐
│ □ │ AmigaShell                                     │ ▣ │ ▱ │
├─┴────────────────────────────────────────────────┴──┴──┤
│4.Workbench3.0:> FORMAT DRIVE DF0: NAME "MyDisk"         │
│Insert disk to be formatted in device DF0               │
│Press RETURN to begin formatting or CTRL-C to abort: ▮   │
│                                                         │
│                                                         │
│                                                      ◹ │
└─────────────────────────────────────────────────────────┘
```

Figure 11.2. Follow the prompts carefully.

Formatting on an External Drive

If you have access to an external floppy disk drive then you can use this to format disks should you so wish. The syntax of the command to do this is pretty much the same – in fact the only item of information to change is the drive details. Normally this would be DF1:, therefore the command becomes:

FORMAT DRIVE DF1: NAME "Empty"

Formatting will then continue as for a single drive system. If you are using a floppy disk system keep your Workbench disk in the internal disk drive so it can automatically access the programs it needs.

Copying Disks with AmigaDOS

AmigaDOS provides the command DISKCOPY to totally copy the contents of one disk to another. The net effect is the same as that described using the Workbench. The syntax of the command is:

DISKCOPY FROM <source> TO <dest> NAME <new name>

As you can see, AmigaDOS can take three different parameters and provides you with the opportunity to rename the destination disk. This last part of the command is optional and if you don't wish to rename the disk then you can use a shortened version of the command as follows:

DISKCOPY FROM <source> TO <destination>

In this case the disk is given the exact name of the one it was backed up from, ie it does not have "copy of" prefixed to it. In both forms the relevant drive device names are substituted for <source> and <destination>.

The utility works by reading each of the tracks from the source disk and writing them to the destination disk and includes the information laid down on the source disk when it was originally formatted. This means that when using DISKCOPY to backup a disk you don't have to format it first, this is effectively done as the backup takes place. An obvious time and effort saver.

AmigaDOS Backup

You can backup a disk using a single disk drive. To make a backup disk with a single drive system, calling it BACKUP use the following syntax:

```
DISKCOPY FROM DFO: TO DFO: NAME "BACKUP"
```

You will be invited to insert the source disk in drive DF0: and to press Return. The process of reading information, swapping disks and writing information will take place as with a Workbench based backup.

If you have two floppy disk drives you will find it even easier to backup disks. The command form is almost identical to the above process but does not require the swapping of disks. Ideally you should place the source disk in DF0: and the destination disk in DF1: and issue the correct form of the command. From the example given above this would be:

```
DISKCOPY FROM DFO: TO DF1: NAME "BACKUP"
```

Copying Files

DISKCOPY is all encompassing and makes clone copies of disks. This is ideal for that purpose but a more sedate version of a copy command, called COPY, allows individual files and directories to be copied. The syntax of the command is:

```
COPY FROM <source> TO <destination>
```

in which <source> can be a directory, file or the full path of a filename to be copied. <destination> is the information as to where the file is to be copied. Because of ambiguities arising, it is very difficult to copy a file or files from one disk to another directly, using a single disk drive. If a single drive system is in use then files can be copied onto another disk via the Ram Disk.

If you are using Workbench 2.1 then to copy the Clock from the Utilities drawer of the Workbench disk into the Ram Disk you would use the following two command lines:

```
COPY FROM Workbench2.1:Utilities/Clock TO RAM:
```

```
COPY FROM Workbench2.1:Utilities/Clock.info TO RAM:
```

Alternatively, if you are using Workbench 3.0 you would use:

```
COPY FROM Workbench3.0:Utilities/Clock TO RAM:
```

```
COPY FROM Workbench3.0:Utilities/Clock.info TO RAM:
```

(If you are having trouble understanding exactly what is happening here – it might be worth rereading Chapter 10 again where the directory structure of the Amiga is explained.)

Note that when you copy an icon file across, you must also copy the .info (pronounced dot-info) file across as well. If you open the Ram Disk window you should now see the Clock in position and ready to use.

If you wish to copy a file between two floppy disks using only the internal disk drive then you must include the disk name. For example to copy the Clock from the Workbench disk onto a disk called TIME use:

```
COPY FROM Workbench2.1:Utilities/Clock TO TIME:
```

```
COPY FROM Workbench2.1:Utilities/Clock.info TO TIME:
```

Alternatively, if you are using Workbench 3.0 you would use:

```
COPY FROM Workbench3.0:Utilities/Clock TO TIME:
```

```
COPY FROM Workbench3.0:Utilities/Clock.info TO TIME:
```

For dual drive systems things are easier as you can simply use the disk drive device names – DF0: as the source and DF1: as the destination. The command to do this is:

```
COPY "DFO:Utilities/Clock" TO "DF1:clock"
```

The disk drives will come into action and the Clock file will be copied across.

Copy files from a hard disk to a floppy disk is just as simple, providing you remember that the hard disk device name is DH0:. Thus to copy the Clock from the Utilities directory of the hard disk into the Ram Disk you would use:

```
COPY FROM DHO:Utilities/Clock TO RAM:
```

```
COPY FROM DHO:Utilities/Clock.info TO RAM:
```

Finally as you get more confident you can drop the FROM and TO out of the command line thus:

```
COPY Workbench2.1:Utilities/Clock RAM:
```

```
COPY Workbench2.1:Utilities/Clock.info RAM:
```

or:

```
COPY Workbench3.0:Utilities/Clock RAM:
```

```
COPY Workbench3.0:Utilities/Clock.info RAM:
```

AmigaDOS is clever enough to know what you mean!

Making Drawers with AmigaDOS

Under Workbench a new drawer is created using the New Drawer option. Under AmigaDOS a new directory is created with the command MAKEDIR (ie MAKE DIRectory). The full syntax of the command is:

```
MAKEDIR <name>
```

where <name> is the name you wish to call the directory including the disk name or, on a multi-drive system, the drive name as well. In this instance double quotes are not required. For example, to create a directory called Wordprocessing on the Ram Disk you would use the following command:

```
MAKEDIR RAM:Wordprocessing
```

Again you can use the MAKEDIR command to create a directory on any disk simply by using the disk drive name or the name of the disk. For example, to create the same directory on a disk in the internal floppy drive you would use:

```
MAKEDIR DF0:Wordprocessing
```

Note that the MAKEDIR command always places the new directories in the current directory. To change directory the command CD is used (CD=Change Directory). To move into the newly created Wordprocessing directory in the Ram Disk you would use the command:

```
CD RAM:Wordprocessing
```

You will now be in the Wordprocessing directory – as should be reflected by the prompt – and MAKEDIR commands issued now will create further directories inside the Wordprocessing directory and place them here.

Important: If you are working with a single disk drive Amiga always specify the disk name at the start of any filename to ensure the task you are performing works on the correct disk. If you do not then it is likely that the command will be performed on the Workbench disk.

Changing Directory

So much for moving down the directory tree, but how do we go up it towards the top or root directory? The CD command is used once again but rather than specifying a name as the parameter we use a back slash character. For example to move up out of the current directory (assuming it isn't already the top root directory) use:

> `CD /`

If you wish to move up two directory levels use two back slashes:

> `CD //`

CD can also be used to Change Disk, in other words to change from the disk in one drive to the disk in another assuming you are using a dual drive system. For instance if you are using DF0: and wish to use RAM: type:

> `CD RAM:`

Alternatively you can change the drive or directory simply by typing its name, ie you don't have to include the CD portion. Thus to change to the Ram Disk and then back to drive DF0: use:

> `RAM:`

> `DF0:`

DIR Again

The back slash can be tagged onto the end of the DIR command as well, thus allowing you to catalogue the directories above you. For instance, if you were in the Utilities directory on the Workbench disk and typed:

> `DIR /`

you would see a list of the files in the root directory above it.

In addition it is also possible to use full file path names in association with the DIR command should you so wish. For instance, on a dual drive system you may wish to catalogue the disk in drive DF1: which can be done using:

> `DIR DF1:`

Commands such as:

> `DIR Workbench2.1:Prefs/Presets`

or:

> `DIR Workbench3.0:Prefs/Presets`

and:

> `DIR DF0:Utilities`

are also legitimate.

You may also use DIR in a more selective manner by the use of several options tagged onto the end of the command.

For example, suppose you only want a list of all the directories held in a particular directory, you could use the DIRS option. For example to catalogue the Workbench disk so that only the directories are listed you would enter:

DIR Workbench2.1: DIRS

Likewise you can use the FILES option to list only the files in a directory:

DIR Workbench2.1: FILES

12: ED the Text Editor

The Amiga contains a number of text editors – the most easy to use of which is called ED. Text Editor? Well, a text editor is most readily described as a wordprocessor without the thrills. In fact it's probably better to call it a wordprocessor minus just about everything! That said, it does make it very easy to use!

ED helps you to create files of text. It contains a number of editing facilities which allow you to edit the text. Thus it is possible to write letters, articles, reports and even books using ED. Although I wouldn't recommend the latter.

Unlike many of the tools you have available to you on the Amiga, ED does not have an icon for you to double-click on to start it. Instead you must start it using either the Execute Command option or the Amiga Shell. The syntax of the command is:

ED <filename>

where <filename> is the name you are giving to the project file. I would suggest you use the AmigaShell to run ED until you get the hang of it. While you practice it is a good idea to save your files in the Ram Disk so make this the current directory by typing:

CD RAM:

The prompt in the Shell should change to something like:

1.Ram Disk:>

Then enter the following from the AmigaShell:

RUN ED TestED

ED will load and open a large window on screen. In the bottom lefthand corner of the screen the following message will appear:

Creating new file

This will create a file called TestED.

The window for ED is much the same as those allocated to Shell windows, however the Pointer is of little use for entering text but it does allow access to the three menus used by ED, titled Project, Movement and Edit. However, for the most part, ED is keyboard controlled and without the frills of the WIMP.

As your first ED lesson let us enter a simple two line text file. Ensure the ED window is selected and then type the following at the keyboard:

This text is typed into ED the Amiga text editor.

With ED I can create simple text files.

ED uses Ctrl and Esc key combinations to invoke the various commands at your disposal. To save this small file to the Ram Disk and then quit ED use:

<ESC>X

When you do this the following should appear in the bottom lefthand corner:

*x

This is the command display area and *x represents <Esc>X. While you're using ED, it's best to think of Esc as being the command key. To execute the command you now need to press Return.

If you catalogue the Ram Disk by typing:

DIR

into the AmigaShell you will see that the file has indeed been created.

Once you have created a file you can load it up and carry on adding more to it as your needs are. To reload the TestED file simply ensure that you have set the current directory to the one containing the file and type:

ED TestED

If you were in another directory you could still load the TestED file simply by specifying the directory path, ie:

ED RAM:TestED

Editing with ED

Like the Shell, ED provides a number of editing facilities and these are listed with brief descriptions in the box opposite. Most of these command actions are fairly straightforward and easy to understand, however a few are worth a few words of expansion and this is given below. In all cases experiment with a simple ED file such as TestED.

TAB ED does not contain any Tab stop positions that can be adjusted to suit your own needs. Instead it assumes a standard Tab setting of three character spaces and each time Tab is pressed it moves the cursor three positions to the right. The effect is exactly the same as having pressed the right arrow key three times in succession.

<Ctrl-F> This swaps the case of the character under the cursor and moves it right one position. Thus if the letter under the cursor is an e and <Ctrl-F> is pressed it will become an E.

<Ctrl-G> ED supports a number of extended commands accessed with the Esc key (see below). This repeats the last extended command.

<Ctrl-O> This command deletes the characters from and to the right of the cursor position up until the first space character. If the character under the cursor is a space it deletes all spaces to the right until the first non-space character.

Extended ED

ED supports a wealth of extended commands. These are commands which generally require more than one letter used in combination with the Esc key, or require information to be supplied with the command. In some versions you can press the Esc key and then the letter keys in sequence afterwards.

For example the command:

    <ESC-SH>

can be used to display the file information that ED keeps on each file it creates (this is saved with the file). The above command can be entered as <Esc-S> and <Esc-H> or as <Esc-S><H> or as <Esc>SH. As with all ED commands, extended commands are displayed in the bottom lefthand corner of the screen and are not executed until the Return key is pressed. Some of the more important extended commands used by ED are given in the following descriptions.

As with the standard Ctrl commands, many of these command actions are fairly straightforward and easy to understand, however many are worth a few words of expansion and these are given below. In all cases experiment with a simple ED file such as TestED.

Note: All ED's extended commands use the slash (/) symbol to delimit characters from either the command or from each other. Slash means the same to ED as the space does to AmigaDOS so it's important you fix the distinction in your mind.

<Esc-A>   Insert Text: This command can be used to insert text at the current cursor position. Its effect is really just like typing directly at the keyboard. For example:

           <Esc-A>/ECHO "This is an example of ESC-A"

<ESC-BE>   Mark Block End at Cursor: Blocks of text can be marked for various reasons. These are outlined below under the section headed ED Blocks.

<ESC-BF>   Find String Backwards Search: Specific strings of text can be located using ED's find facility. Searches can be carried in either direction from the cursor position. This command searches backwards, ie from the cursor towards the start of the file. To search for the string Echo use:

           <ESC-BF>/Echo

           Note that by default the search is case dependent, ie the case of letters must match exactly. For instance, searching for Echo will not recognise echo or ECHO. The command locates the very first occurrence. Repeat command with <Ctrl-G>.

<ESC-BS>   Mark Block Start at Cursor: Blocks of text can be marked for various reasons. These are outlined below under the section headed ED Blocks.

<ESC-DB>   Delete Block: This command deletes the marked block of text. If no block is marked the error message No block marked is returned. See the section headed ED Blocks.

<ESC-E>   Exchange Characters: This command finds the first occurrence of the specified character and replaces it with the second specified character. For example, a common mistake is to use an O in place of a zero. This can be rectified by moving the cursor to the top of the file and then proceeding as follows:

           <ESC- E>/O/0/

           <Ctrl-G>

When there are no more occurrences, or if an occurrence is not found, the error message Search failed is displayed.

<ESC-EQ>   Exchange Characters With Query: The above example of using <Esc-E> is fine but it will mean that each occurrence will be replaced. Of course you might have Os in your text which are vital. This command allows you to account for this. To search for occurrences of O and possibly substitute them for zeros use:

<ESC-E>/O/0/

On finding the first occurrence the following message will be displayed in the bottom lefthand corner of the ED window:

Exchange?

Pressing Y (or y) will effect the change. Pressing N (or n) will move the cursor on ready for the next instance. Pressing any other key will abort the command without any change. Pressing <Ctrl-G> will execute the command once again.

<ESC-F>   Find Text String: This command searches forward to find the first occurrence of the string, which may consist of a word or phrase. For example:

<ESC-F>/Hello there mate/

By default the search is case dependent.

<ESC-I>   Insert Text Before Cursor: This command works like <Esc-A>, however the text is placed directly before the cursor as opposed to after it. For example:

<ESC-I>/This is before the cursor/

<ESC-IB>   Insert Copy of Marked Block: This command locates the marked block of text and inserts a copy of it at the position of the cursor. See the section headed ED Blocks below for a full explanation.

<ESC-IF>   Insert Named File: This command locates the ED file named and reads it into the body of the current text at the position of the cursor. The file being read remains unaltered. For example to load a file called Tester into the body of a current ED text file you could use:

<ESC-IF>/Tester/

<ESC-LC>   Distinguish Character Case: This is the default state of ED and is used to countermand the action of <Esc-UC>. After being executed, searches will be carried out and will be case dependent. Therefore the three words:

ECHO

echo

Echo

will be seen as three different words.

<ESC-M> Move To Line Number: This command becomes very useful when dealing with long ED files as it allows you to move to specific lines. For example to move the cursor to line number 10 use:

<ESC-M> 10

and press Return. The line numbering starts from the top and the first line is always line number one.

<ESC-SA> Save Text To File: This command saves the current file but without quitting ED. A filename can be included to save the text under a new filename. For example:

<ESC-SA>/NewFile/

<ESC-SB> Show Block On Screen: When a block has been marked, issuing this command will move the start of the marked block to the top of the screen. See the section headed ED Blocks immediately below.

<ESC-UC> Renders any search non case-dependent.

<ESC-WB> Write Block to File: This command writes the marked block of text to the named file. For example:

<ESC-WB>/Marked/

The current text is unaffected as is the current ED file.

Block Actions

ED allows sections of text to be identified by enclosing them within bounded areas. These areas are defined by the use of two markers inserted into the text using the commands <Esc-BS> and <Esc-BE>.

The text to be marked can vary from just a few characters up to a few hundred lines. The markers are not shown on screen but you can identify the start of a marked block using <Esc-SB>. Note that markers only remain until you start typing into ED, they are not affected by ED commands however.

ED markers have several uses: they allow you to move a section of text from one part of a file to another; to copy a repetitive section of text quickly and simply; to allow you to delete a section of text; and to allow you to save a marked section of text to a file. So get used to the markers, they play a very big role in effective use of ED.

Inserting a marker is easy. Move the cursor to the exact position at which you wish the marker to be placed and then press <Esc-BS> (Block Start). The marker does not occupy any space on screen and may, and generally will, occupy the same position as a character from your text. The second marker is placed in the same way but, as it is marking the Block End, use <Esc-BE>.

Blocks that are to be copied to a new position are always copied to the current position of the cursor, so always reposition this first before executing the <Esc-IB> command.

Note: Markers affect complete lines – you cannot mark sections of a line in ED as you could in larger editors. However, you don't have to move the cursor to the start of a specific line.

On the Menu

ED is complemented by a series of menus. These provide instant access to a variety of the extended commands discussed in the preceding pages. They are used in the normal fashion: select the menu option required and its function is carried out. If the option requires further user input then this is requested at the base of the window just as though you had issued the command from the keyboard. The menu options and a brief description of each is given in the box below. As always try each of these out to see how they work.

All of the menu options have direct hot-key equivalents and these are listed on the menu. More detailed explanations of many of the above can be found in the preceding four pages covering the extended command set.

ED and AmigaDOS Scripts

One of the more useful applications of ED – and really the reason why it is a text editor as opposed to a wordprocessor – is the creation of AmigaDOS scripts. In the past chapters we have been entering simple one or two line commands. This is fine for the occasional one-off task like formatting a disk or copying a file. However, suppose you had a task that you wanted to carry out that required 20 lines to be typed in. It could be done simply as we have seen in the past chapters. However, you leave yourself open to mistakes. If you inadvertently typed in something wrong then you might have to start all over again. No problems if it is in line one, but if the mistake is in line 19...

Equally, the lines of command that you are going to type in might form something that you are going to use over and over again. Typing them in every time would not only be prone to error but also boring and wasteful of your time.

AmigaDOS provides you with a way around this, called a script file. A script file is simply a file on disk that contains the lines of AmigaDOS that you wish to be executed – this is the script. To enter and save AmigaDOS scripts you need to use a sort of wordprocessor, in fact something called a text editor. Your Amiga is supplied with one of these and it is called ED. In case you are wondering, in terms of functionality there is little basic difference between a text editor and a wordprocessor. A text editor is effectively a very basic wordprocessor without the thrills of special effects and other goodies such as spell checking.

Script Creation

Creating a script file is just like creating an ED file. Start ED with a new file name. For example, select the Ram Disk as your current drive with:

```
CD RAM:
```

and call the file SCRIPT with:

```
ED SCRIPT
```

Ensure the ED window is selected and then type the following at the keyboard:

```
CD DF0:
DIR DIRS
```

Save and then quit this small ED file using:

```
<ESC-X>
```

The AmigaDOS command EXECUTE carries out the task of executing the contents of a script file. The format of the EXECUTE command is:

```
EXECUTE <filename>
```

Again <filename> is the name of the script file you wish to be executed. The command works very simply. It reads the first line from the file and acts on it just as if it had been typed in at the keyboard. When it has completed it, it goes back to the script file and reads the second line. This continues until there are no more lines to be read and the command then terminates.

Execute the SCRIPT file by typing:

```
EXECUTE SCRIPT
```

Both commands will be executed, providing you with a list of the directories stored on the disk in drive DF0:. It will also leave you set with DF0: as the currently selected drive!

AmigaDOS script files can be used to do some very clever things – in fact much of the Amiga's start-up process is carried out by such a script file!

We can now make a simple addition to the SCRIPT batch file to ensure it returns to the Ram Disk after it has completed executing. Make the Ram Disk the current directory and then re-enter the command that was initially used to create the file SCRIPT:

RUN ED SCRIPT

Whenever ED is asked to create a file it looks in the current directory (or the directory specified) to see if the named file exists. If it does it opens it and displays its contents. If no file exists it creates one and signifies the fact by displaying the Creating new file message. The cursor can be moved to the end of the file with the aid of the down-arrow key, at which point the CD RAM: command can be added. The batch file should now read:

CD DF0:

DIR DIRS

CD RAM:

This can be saved with <Esc-X> and then re-executed with:

EXECUTE TestED

When executed this will switch to DF0: and catalogue the directories in the root directory of the disk before returning to the Ram Disk.

More Scripts

When a batch file is executing, it is common practice for the file to display status messages to inform the user what is happening. This is what happens when you boot your Amiga when it displays various copyright and status messages as the start-up process is carried out. These can be inserted into batch files quite simply by using the ECHO command. The syntax of the command is:

ECHO "<text to be printed>"

Here are a couple of examples that can be inserted into the SCRIPT file after the first and second commands:

ECHO "Changed to DF0:"

ECHO "Returning to Ram Disk"

The new extended script should look like this:

CD DF0:

ECHO "Changed to DF0:"

DIR DIRS

    ECHO "Returning to Ram Disk"

    CD RAM:

By default the ECHO command prints a Return character after it has echoed the message within the double quotes to the screen. There will be occasions when you don't wish this to happen. The NOLINE option stops this Return being printed. For example, to display a message followed by the date and time:

    ECHO

This could be added to the end of the SCRIPT file to finish it off looking like this:

    CD DF0:

    ECHO "Changed to DF0:"

    DIR DIRS

    ECHO "Returning to RAM Disk"

    CD RAM:

    ECHO "Today's date and time is: " NOLINE

    DATE

Save this with <Esc-X> and re-execute with:

    EXECUTE SCRIPT

13:
Icon
Creation
and Design

One of the features that makes the Amiga unique, is its icons. They are distinctive and intuitive to use. They have a look which tries to approximate the type of *tool* or *project* they are associated with. There are five basic icon types – although you may not have seen all of these to date.

Amiga icons are not stored as part of the original program or file they create. They are stored as .info (pronounced dot-info) files. For instance the icon associated with the Shell is in fact called:

Shell.info

You can see these and other .info files simply by opening a Shell window and typing:

DIR

to list all the files, picking out the ones with the .info suffix. These hold the information which displays the picture on screen and also the information or pointer linking them to a particular file.

If you examine the listing in relation to the Workbench disk window itself you will see that there is a .info file for each of the icons that are displayed.

What might not be apparent at this point is that there are several basic icon types although the typical on-screen appearance of the icon may change. These basic icon types are:

Disk

Drawer

Tool

Project

Trashcan

and these are illustrated in Figure 13.1.

Figure 13.1. Amiga Icons. Top: Disk and Drawer.
Middle: Tool and Project. Bottom: Trashcan.

A Disk icon represents any disk that is available or accessible by the Workbench. The Ram Disk and Workbench disk icons are the standard format although, as you may have already noticed from third-party applications, icons can be vastly different and may even be very much larger! When you open a disk icon, a window will always appear on the screen displaying any icon files that are available in the disk's root directory.

A Drawer icon represents a subdivision of the disk's storage area. When a drawer icon is opened a window will appear displaying any icon files that are held within the drawer's directory. The System drawer is a typical drawer icon, however the Prefs icon is also a drawer icon!

A Tool icon represents a program. The appearance of these is normally unique. When you open a tool icon you start the program it is linked to. The Clock and Calculator icons are examples of Tool icons.

A Project icon represents a file that has been created by a tool, ie a program. Again it may be very specific in appearance but as a general rule it will look similar to the tool icon from which it was created. When you open a Project icon it will normally first load the tool which created it and then the file associated with the project.

The Trashcan icon represents an area on the disk where unwanted items are stored until you decide to discard them by emptying the trash!

IconEdit

Supplied on your Amiga master disks is the means to enable you to create, edit and even personalise your own icons, either starting from existing icons or from scratch for new projects you are yourself creating. With just a little imagination you could transform your Workbench to make it look like nobody else's.

The key to achieving this is IconEdit, which can normally be found in the Tools directory on the Extras disk.

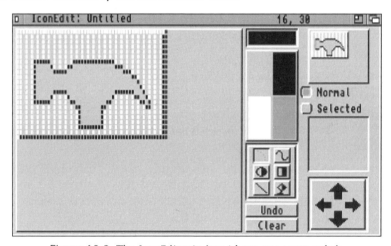

Figure 13.2. The IconEdit window (there are some subtle differences on different Workbench versions).

When you double-click on the IconEdit icon it reveals its own window along with a full set of menus. By default the IconEdit window contains a magnified version of an icon, a hammerhead, in the drawing area, a colour menu to its right and a toolbox of drawing tools. The extreme right of the window also contains an actual size image of the current icon – you may already have noticed this. As always do remember that the actual layout in the IconEdit window may change between releases of Workbench.

From this point you can create your own icon using the hammerhead as a base to work from or, alternatively edit an existing icon by loading it into IconEdit, or perhaps clear the field to start from scratch.

If you wish to create your own icon from scratch locate the Clear gadget at the bottom of the drawing tools and click to clear the drawing area to a grid pattern. This is useful for guiding your drawing tools especially since icons are usually pretty structured designs. However, it can be turned off via the Settings menu.

Each of the grid squares represents a pixel and these can be set in any of the four Workbench colours – the desired colour being selected from the colour menu. You can clear the background to a particular colour simply by selecting the colour required and then clicking on Clear. You can then select a desired colour and click the left mouse button within the drawing area to set points and thereby build up your design. The point to be set should be positioned centrally within the cross-hair cursor. To aid you further the coordinates of the cross-hair cursor are displayed in the window title bar and run from 1,1 in the top lefthand corner to 80,40 in the bottom right. Therefore the desired area is 80 pixels wide and 40 deep.

One important gadget to be aware of at the off is the Undo button. Pressing this will undo your last action – but only the last one.

The toolbox below the colour menu provides six simple but effective drawing tools which are easily learnt by a bit of experimentation. The tools are:

Freehand   This is a sort of perpetual draw tool and while you keep the mouse button down it will draw a continuous line of pixels in the currently selected colour as you move the mouse over the drawing area.

Continuous   This gadget is similar to the Freehand gadget described above except that it will always produce a continuous line. That said, to create the continuous line you must move more sedately than you might for the aforementioned Freehand gadget.

Circle   This gadget allows you to draw a circle in the selected colour. To draw a circle, click at the point in the drawing area where you wish the centre of the circle to be. Then drag the Pointer away from the point to create the circle size you wish. You can move the Pointer to and from the centre to alter the size of the circle. You can even extend the circle off screen. Once you release the mouse button the circle will be set.

Note that the icon of the gadget has a filled half. If you select this you will get a circle that is filled in the selected colour. If you select the unfilled segment you will get only the circle outline. In the case of the latter, if you draw the circle and then press the Ctrl key before releasing the mouse button the thickness of the circle outline will be doubled!

Box   The box gadget works in much the same way as Circle to create rectangles except that the initial mouse click sets the top left corner of the square and you then drag down and across to the desired bottom righthand corner. In addition to doubling the line thickness as indicated above you can also create a 3D box effect (similar to that shown around Workbench icons) by holding down the Alt key before releasing the mouse button.

Line   Not surprisingly this allows you to draw a line at any angle. Simply click at the start point and drag the Pointer to the desired end point. If you press Ctrl before releasing the mouse button the line thickness will be doubled.

Fill   The fill gadget allows you to fill an enclosed area with a selected colour. For example you could draw a rectangle in black on a white background and then in-fill it with blue. To do this simply select the fill colour, the fill gadget and move the Pointer inside the enclosed area before clicking the left mouse button.

The IconEdit Menus

IconEdit provides you with a total of seven menus which offer between them a host of useful features. The function of many of these should be reasonably clear to you as we have encountered options with similar actions before. Some of the more erudite functions are explained below.

The Project menu is a standard interface that allows you to open and save icon files for editing or creation. The Save As Default option allows you to design your own default tools and save them. For example, the default tool icon is the hammerhead icon – you could change this by using the Type menu to select the desired default tool and then edit it. The default disk icon – as used by the Ram Disk etc – has no colour but you could change the black tick into a blue one as follows:

1.   Select Disk from the Type menu.

2.   Select New from the Project menu.

3.   Select the blue colour from the colour gadget.

4.   Click on each black pixel comprising the tick to make it blue.

5.   Select the Save As Default Icon option from the Project menu. (The default information is saved to your Workbench disk.)

6.   Insert a new disk into a disk drive.

If you have proceeded correctly the icon representing the new disk – and all subsequent disk icons – should now have a blue tick!

The Edit Menu introduces the concept of the *clipboard.* In reality this is simply an area of Amiga memory into which images can be held temporarily. Like the Ram Disk it is volatile so its contents are lost when you close IconEdit or reboot. Note also that only one image can be held in the clipboard, so loading a second will cause the original or previous image to be overwritten.

The Highlights menu includes the Image option that can be used to create a second icon to be shown when the original is displayed (this is explained shortly). It also includes two other interesting options in Complement and Backfill. If you select Complement when designing an icon (with the Normal button checked) then when you select the icon it will be highlighted, including the background of the box. You can see the physical effect of this by clicking once on the Ram Disk icon for instance. The Backfill option works in much the same fashion except that the background box is not highlighted.

A word of warning. Those big black arrows in the corner of the IconEdit window can erase your work if you are not careful. While they are great for getting an icon in the right position on-screen, if any part of the icon goes off-screen it will be lost. Take care in using them and don't scroll too fast.

Iconology

Creating simple but effective icons is quite an art and it may take you a good deal of practice to produce designs you find really appealing. For the most part, if you should get into icon design then concentrate on editing existing icons so that your Workbench becomes a more personal affair.

Remember though to only edit those on the working copy of your Workbench disk, not on the master copy.

Remember also that icons should be recognisable for what they represent and you have been alerted to the real-size picture which is displayed in the top righthand corner of the IconEdit window. Keep glancing across at this to see if your magnified design is making visual sense at the reduced size.

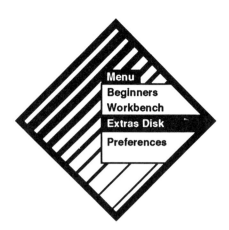

Menu
Beginners
Workbench
Extras Disk
Preferences

14:
Choosing
and Using a
Printer

The Amiga can produce such colourful pictures and such smoothly curving characters on screen that, in an ideal world, we would want to reproduce them faithfully on our printer so that the rest of the population could enjoy them too. But it's no straight-forward matter.

Graphics and typefaces are held as computer data in memory and displayed by different methods on different devices such as a TV screen, a computer monitor, a plotter and, the subject of this chapter, the ubiquitous printer.

The key to using a printer with the Amiga is the availability of a suitable *printer driver* – this being the software interface between your Amiga and your printer. You need a driver because no two printers are the same and even though Epson printers are regarded as a *de facto* standard, standards are never quite that!

Most of the time you'll find a suitable driver supplied by Commodore for use with the Printer Preferences editor but, for the more unusual printers and those brought out since you bought your computer, you may need to get an equivalent printer driver supplied by a third party, often a public domain library – more on which in a later chapter.

The main complication is that not all printers are the same. There are different ways of reproducing the pictures you can see on your screen, such as hitting the paper with wire pins through an inked ribbon (dot matrix) and spurting drops of ink onto paper (ink and bubblejet) and putting a charge on the surface of the paper only to remove it where the ink must settle (laser). We'll go through the types of printer and then mention how your Amiga goes about printing and what to look for in printer consumables. Actually getting your printer set up is dealt with in the next couple of chapters. First, let's look at the various types of printers.

Types of Printer

There is a wide and varied range of printer types which are classified by the way in which they perform the process of printing. The more popular methods are detailed briefly below.

Daisywheel

>   The grand old daisywheel is still around with its typewriter action which results in perfectly formed characters if all you need is A to Z and 0 to 9. Not much use for a graphics-based computer but you can still drive one from your wordprocessor if daisywheel quality is needed for business letters or form filling. The appropriate Prefs driver will send the correct ASCII codes without batting an eyelid. ASCII codes are the numbers which computers use internally to represent letters of the alphabet and any other printable characters on your keyboard.

Thermal

>   The thermal printer for home computing has had its day but, if you've got an old one, treat it like a dot matrix of a certain age.

Inkjet/Bubblejet

>   The inkjet printer was pioneered for micros in this country in the early 80s by Olivetti but lost out to the rise of the dot matrix.

>   The inkjet has been joined by a near relation, the bubblejet. The Canon Bubblejet and the Hewlett Packard Deskjet have proved very popular because they can offer laser-like quality at prices substantially below that of most laser printers. The Canon Bubblejet for example has 48 jets which give a resolution of 360 dots per inch (dpi), a more detailed printout than most laser printers can achieve.

>   Inkjet printing is also the key to the best colour printing on the Amiga. The Hewlett Packard DeskjetC and Paintjet are both supported by printer drivers and give reasonable results.

The software however is not up to perfectly matching all available screen colours through mixing the printers' inks. Some inkjets improve colour printing greatly by offering a separate black cartridge so that any blacks in the picture do not have to be created by mixing coloured inks which can drown the paper in ink and result in brown *black!*

Dot Matrix

Dot matrix printers are the most successful breed of printers, partly because they are cheap to purchase and cheap to run, partly because they reproduce both text and graphics to an acceptable quality. Dot matrix printers fall into the two main categories of 9-pin and 24-pin, the latter offering better quality and speed in most cases. There are some 18-pin and 48-pin printers.

Dot matrix printers come in different carriage (paper) widths, can accommodate sheet feeders (like a photocopier) for business stationery and can be fitted with a mechanism to print in colour via four different colour ribbons. The versatility of the dot matrix is its strong point. Nor have the possibilities been exhausted as new methods of describing graphical displays to the printer mechanism are invented and incorporated into computer software.

The latest dot matrix printers have colour printing mechanisms as standard. These print through a multicoloured ribbon under software control. The printer driver detects which colour is being sent and sends the appropriate code to move the ribbon into position. 24-pin dot matrix colour printouts are very impressive, though a little slow and noisy.

Laser

The classic *office* laser printer is based on the Hewlett Packard Laserjet standard. Amiga graphics benefit less from mono laser than business documents with text and line drawings. Lasers come with trays which hold single sheets and their print quality is usually 300 dots per inch or 600 dots per inch. A variety of page description languages (see PostScript below) are built into these printers, most not supported by Amiga software. Running costs vary greatly and may be too much for home use.

PostScript Printing

PostScript has never featured high on the Amiga's list of printing priorities but it is now supported in Prefs so is worth a mention. PostScript is a page description language. You will be more used to a program displaying text and graphics on your screen and your screen is a pattern of dots turned on and off by the program. Well PostScript is a program which creates the dot pattern inside a printer, which is then transferred to paper for us to view it. Normal printing operations don't use PostScript to anywhere near its full extent. It comes into its own when used by applications for desktop publishing and complex drawing.

It is useful to be able to send the PostScript output to a file on a disk as opposed to sending it directly to the printer. This file, which is a computer program, can be sent to the printer at any stage and can also be copied to other computers such as PCs or Apple Macintoshes which are more likely to have a PostScript printer attached.

If professional printing is required, typically for flyers, newsletters, brochures etc created in a Desktop Publishing program, then *imagesetting* is the intermediate stage. You send your file to an imagesetting bureau and they run it through their typesetter. The typesetter usually outputs either a positive image on photographic paper (bromide) or a negative image on transparent film. If colour is involved then the bureau will *separate* the colours and output four films. The bromide or film (depending on what your printer requires) is then used to create the plates which go on the printing machinery.

Graphics Printing

Even when printing text, for example in a desktop publishing program, the Amiga will be printing graphically, in other words it won't be making use of any of the character sets which are built-in to the printer. Instead the whole page will be created from mixing patterns of dots on the paper. The driver software will create an appropriate dot pattern (dithering) to represent each of the colours or different grey levels which make up a screen picture. Different patterns are needed for the different available resolutions.

Monochrome graphics printing turns off any attempts by the printer driver software to do any dithering so you literally get a black and white version. Depending on the picture, this can result in an attractive print and you can use it for the ultimate draft or *proof* graphics dump. Avoid this setting if you are printing from a desktop publishing (DTP) program because it will distort the printing of fonts as well as conventional graphics. Fonts in DTP programs are created with grey pixels around the edges to help them keep their curves! Fonts in the DTP context are sometimes called *outline* fonts and are also referred to as *type*. Commodore supply some outline fonts with the Amiga but you'll need an appropriate drawing program or DTP program to use them in this form.

The dot matrix machines normally print bidirectionally, for speed, but since in graphics mode slight skew can be seen – especially in text – unidirectional printing may be selected.

Text Printing

Text printing relates to printing ASCII characters in the font styles which are built into the printer. These range from draft text with bold and italics to Near Letter Quality (NLQ) or LQ (Letter Quality) fonts with portrait or landscape orientations.

The ability to fit font cartridges and to download fonts from the computer is only relevant to printing in character mode. Plug-in font cartridges or cards are available for most 24-pin printers, and for the Deskjets and Laserjets.

Printing from Programs

Most of your printing will be done from within a program which will present you with certain options, such as turning the print sideways so that it fits better along the paper. You'll have noticed that, although the computer screen is usually wider than it is deep, printer paper is usually deeper than it is wide! Most programs however will pass the printer job, and your selections, onto the Amiga's Printer Preferences program before it gets to the printer. This means that you don't have to set up every program for your printer. Printer Prefs does it all!

Paper Chase

Tractor paper handling is best for fanfold continuous paper (for listings), labels on carrier paper, and for multi-part forms. However, only an impact (ie dot matrix or daisywheel) printer can print all parts of multi-part forms.

Cut sheet feeders holding 50 or more sheets are available as optional extras for most dot matrix and inkjet printers. This is particularly appropriate for office use, where cut sheets do not require that tractor margins be removed and look better than fanfold. Some printers can print on Overhead Projector (OHP) film, though each type may require an appropriate (eg coated) grade of film for best results. There are merchants who specialise in appropriate coated paper for, especially, inkjet and laser printing when quality really matters.

For printing wide tables and spreadsheets with a dot matrix printer, you can print sideways in graphics mode on a standard (8") model, or choose a wide (13") model. With the other printer types, it is usual to print sideways (landscape) in character or graphics mode since – even if available – models which can handle A3 paper are much more expensive.

For dot matrix printers the so-called *true A4* size (ie 8.25" x 11.66") is the closest possible to 210 x 297mm, while having a whole number of print lines spaced at one-sixth of an inch. You'll find that 70 gsm (grams per square metre) is a good weight as a compromise for both draft and correspondence use. It may be obtained with tractor margins that are micro-perforated which leave a reasonably clean edge when they are removed.

As for labels, you get them on fanfold carrier paper for use with a variety of software, such as a database printing out from a name and address list. If you buy them Indian file, one after the other, it's easier to set up the software! If your database can print onto two, or more, labels across the sheet then you will find you can get through your printing more quickly.

For page printers copier paper is quite acceptable and 80 gsm a good weight. The same paper may also be used (preferably with a cut sheet feeder) with dot matrix and inkjet printers. On occasion I have noticed the extra ink applied when printing *outline fonts* (which are constructed graphically) can spread and slightly distort the curves so, if this happens, try a coated paper of some kind.

The ribbons for dot-matrix printers are relatively low in cost, whereas the cartridges for inkjet printers work out at more per page. In the case of the page (eg laser) printers, the consumables include the toner and the development unit, which can be expensive.

Background and Buffers

The Amiga treats printing as a separate task and can do it at the same time as running a program. Further speed gains can be made by sending the data quickly to a temporary storage area in the computer's memory (called a buffer). Getting back control of the keyboard and mouse doesn't mean that printing has stopped, only that it is going on in the background as data is sent from the temporary store to the printer unseen.

The memory buffer can also be in the printer but the bigger the memory capacity of the printer, the more expensive it will be. Some laser printers have enough memory to form up complete pages in their own memory and can therefore be asked to print multiple copies without troubling the computer again.

Inking Up

Ink cartridges are an important part of the inkjet printing process and there are some companies who specialise in supplying inks, both standard cartridges and sets of ink which can, for instance, turn an ordinary black and white printer into a colour printer by changing inks and overprinting. To do this you need a program which will control the process, separating the colours out from the screen picture and printing them one at a time.

For instance any colour/shade which contains blue (cyan ink) will be printed on the first pass with a cyan cartridge fitted, any colour containing yellow will be printed on the second pass, and so on. For the Deskjets, Paintjets and Bubblejets you can get full colour printing systems which provide ink refills for the multipass process together with the software.

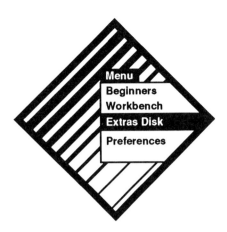

15: Printer Installation

We looked at the various types of printers available in the last chapter. It has to be said that of these the dot-matrix technology is certainly the most popular, not least because of its versatility but also because of its cost effectiveness. Certainly from the Amiga point of view it is the type that is connected most of the time and generally it is the printer type the Amiga is geared towards when it comes to use the Preferences editor PrinterGFX.

You connect your printer to your Amiga via a cable that is connected at the *printer port*. This can be either a *parallel port* or a *serial port*. Again, both are available but 99% of the time and, with a dot-matrix printer, 99.9% of the time, it will be through the parallel printer port.

The Amiga, and that includes Workbench and every other program or application you may run, knows how to talk to your printer because it follows a predefined set of rules for operation. This is more complex than it might seem at first sight because there are so many different models and types of printer and each differs from the other, not only in physical shape but also in the facilities they have to offer you as the user. Trying to write a single piece of software for the Amiga that can take into account these differences and also cater for all eventualities would be nigh on impossible. Therefore, it is common for separate printer driving programs to be supplied, each of which is custom written to do the right job for the right printer. This is called the *printer driver* and several are supplied with the Workbench, many more are available from a variety of sources – such as PD libraries – and you just install the correct one for your printer as part of Printer Preferences.

Now that we have got a few of the basics out of the way, and we'll assume that you have connected your printer to your Amiga at the relevant point, let's see how we get it up and running. Assuming you are using a dot-matrix printer, there are three essential steps to take:

1.   Choose and install the correct printer driver.

2.   Define the system defaults.

3.   Define graphics defaults.

We'll look at each of these in turn.

One point to bear in mind at the very off here is that while solving printer problems may be infuriating, do remember that one of the best ways of solving them is to experiment. By obtaining printed output at each stage you should be able to see what actions have what effect.

Printer Driver

As always you should be working with a backup copy of your Workbench disk. The main task is to select a printer driver or drivers from those that are supplied on the Storage disk and copy them to the relevant point on the Workbench disk. That relevant point is the Printers drawer which is itself located in the Devs drawer on the Workbench disk.

If you have bought a popular make of printer and have taken advice from a friend or dealer then you may already be pretty sure as to the identity of the printer driver you are going to use.

Chances are its name will stand out for you. If at the end of the day you're stuck, you probably need to experiment using the various printer drivers to hand. For instance, Star, Panasonic, Taxan, Citizen, Mannesman and many others are all highly Epson compatible so an Epson driver will do the job. The bottom line is to buy a printer which you have a printer driver available for – or a combination you know works. Common sense really. Table 15.1 shows a list of the more common printer drivers which are supplied under Workbench 2.1 and 3.

CalComp_ColorMaster	CalComp_ColorMaster2
CanonBJ10	CBM_MPS1000
Diablo_630	EpsonQ
EpsonX	EpsonXOld
Howtek_Pixelmaster	HP_DeskJet
HP_DeskJetOld	HP_LaserJet
HP_PaintJet	HP_ThinkJet
ImagewriterII	NEC_Pinwriter
Okidata_293	Okidata_92
Okimate_20	PostScript
Seiko_5300	Seiko_5300a
Sharp_JX-730	Tektronix_4693D
Tektronix_4696	Toshiba_P351C
Toshiba_P351SX	Xerox_4020

Table 15.1. Common printer drivers.

Once you have identified the printer driver you need (you can install more than one if you want) you should copy it, or them, from the Storage disk into the DEVS/PRINTERS drawer on the Workbench disk.

Copying should be straightforward. Simply open the windows so that the Printers window on the Storage disk and the Printers window in the Devs drawer of the Workbench disk are displayed. Locate the files you want on the Storage disk and then drag them into the Printers window on the Workbench disk. Incidentally, this window will already have a printer driver called Generic in place.

If you get a message displayed in a system requester box that your Workbench disk is full then you will need to make some room for the new file or files by deleting something that you do not use that often. For example, the Clock or MultiView. Remember that you should only delete such objects from your working copy of the Workbench disk – not the original. If you then need them you can copy them from the original into the Ram Disk or onto another backup copy of the Workbench disk itself.

The Printer Preferences editor is easy to use. It is located in the Prefs drawer on the Extras disk. When double-clicked, a Preferences editor window is displayed. There are slight variations between issues of Workbench.

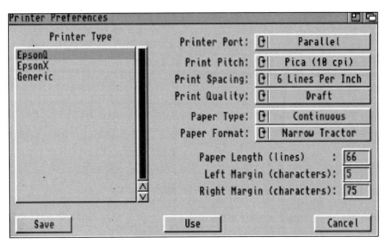

Figure 15.1. The Printer Preferences editor.

The editor window will display the printer drivers available for you to use. By default there is a single printer driver called Generic. If you have copied across a printer driver from the Extras or Storage disk(s) as outlined above, this should also be listed. The Generic printer driver is a general all-purpose interface. In most cases it will allow you to do standard text printing but without too many special effects. Generally you won't use it. You can have numerous printer drivers available to you simply by copying them into the DEVS/PRINTERS directory on your Workbench disk. However, do bear in mind that there is not a lot of spare space on your Workbench disk and every additional printer driver you copy eats into this. As a rule of thumb just limit yourself to the driver you are actually going to use.

The printer driver window is a scrollable window and you can locate the one you need by using the scroll gadgets should the list extend beyond the bands of the window itself. Click on the driver name of your choice once and its name will be displayed in the small window underneath the printer driver list window. This is now the selected driver. Incidentally, you can use this small text string to enter the full path name of a different driver which can be used at that point – it doesn't have to be located in the DEVS/PRINTERS directory.

The Printer Preferences editor window is then divided into three regions, each of which has three further options to make a selection. These mostly use simple cycle gadgets onto which you click to cycle through the available options.

Printer Port allows you to select where the Amiga sends the information to the printer – as outlined at the start of this chapter this will be set to Parallel nine times out of ten, but it can also be set to Serial.

Paper Type can be either Single of Fan-fold. The former is single sheets of paper whereas the latter is more commonly called continuous computer stationary. The Paper Format option is rather misleading, because it actually refers to the maximum length of the line you will be allowed to print. The default is suitable for most printers which offer an 80-column width. You may need to change this to wide tractor if you are using a wide carriage printer – 132 column for instance. As with many of the settings available here there is nothing to be lost, and indeed a great deal of experience to be gained, simply by trying each option out for yourself and seeing what the result is. The worst you can do is waste a few sheets of paper and if you use the same sheet each time...

At the righthand side of the window are three more settings. These are numeric values which you click on to highlight the text gadget and then enter a new value or edit an existing one. The first of these is Paper Length (Lines) which has a default value of 66. For a standard sheet of paper, single sheet or continuous, 66 lines is generally ideal but this is provided you don't change other options – as I said a lot of experimentation to suit your own needs! Left Margin (Chars) is the number of characters in from the left where the printer will start printing. Similarly Right Margin (Chars) is the position of the righthand margin of the text, calculated as the number of characters that will be sent to that particular line. Thus for any one line the actual number of characters printed is the Right Margin minus the Left Margin.

Again these figures are always slightly arbitrary, because in the first place it depends where you feed the paper through the printer. You can for instance vary the lefthand margin simply by feeding the paper through the printer further to the left or right. As I keep saying it's all down to you really. Fix a point in your mind's eye where you will feed the paper through – make a mark or set one of the paper guides that some printers have and use this as a reference point. Then if you prefer a wide lefthand margin increase this value to suit.

A finer point to bear in mind with regards to margin settings is that in Printer Preferences the left and right margin positions are specified in absolute character numbers starting from character position number one, however character positions in printers always start from zero. This should not be a problem but if you want to be totally accurate you should remember to add one to whatever value the printer manual indicates if you need to transfer printer command settings into Preferences. In other words in an 80 column printer character positions go from 0 to 79, but in Printer Preferences they go from 1 to 80.

Print Pitch has three possible settings, 10, 12 and 15 (15-17 on Workbench 3.0), though only 24-pin printers are likely to offer the latter. Old 9-pin dot matrix printers won't be able to handle it. The values refer to the number of characters printed in one inch of horizontal space. Thus in 10 pitch, there are 10 characters printed per inch across the page. Print Spacing refers to the number of lines printed per vertical inch of space – the default is 6lpi – that's 6 lines per inch. The higher the number here the less space there is between each line of text. Setting this to say 3 produces well spaced out lines.

Finally, there is Print Quality and there are two options here: Draft and Letter. Draft is a lower quality print output but is very much faster to produce and creates less wear and tear on your printer ribbon. Letter is a higher quality more dense output which takes longer to produce and has a wearing effect on the printer ribbon. For general purpose output use Draft and switch to Letter as and when you need it.

Backtracking a bit to the subject of spacing. When we talk of spaces we refer to the width of printed spaces, but the actual size of the space depends on the character size currently being used. A space is bigger in 10 pitch than it is in 12 pitch. If you set your printer's margins in Printer Preferences they're actually the real printer margins, but their physical positions will always depend on the typesize you have set in Printer Preferences.

Printer Initialisation

The offshoot of this is that if you later change the printer's character size and reinitialise the printer to force the changes into effect, unless you have adjusted the left and right margin values accordingly too, the printer's physical margins will move!

Once you have set the Printer Preferences to meet your requirements that is not the end of the story. All that has happened at this point is that the settings you chose have been saved on the Workbench disk as part of your preferences setup. The printer hasn't got the foggiest idea about what you have done – yet! To send this setting to the printer requires the use of InitPrinter, which is located in the Tools drawer. Its use is ultra simple. Firstly turn on your printer and ensure that it is on-line. This is usually signified by a small light being illuminated on the front panel of the printer and basically means that the printer is listening out for information from the computer it is connected to. Secondly double-click on the InitPrinter icon. And that's it. All being well your printer is now set up as you defined in your Printer Preferences.

A couple of points to bear in mind here. If you change any of the settings in Printer Preferences you have to send them to your printer. The best way to do this is to rest the printer – turn it off for a few seconds and then switch it back on before running InitPrinter again. Also, many modern printers have a control panel now which allows you to make specific changes at the printer itself – these will override any previous values sent by InitPrinter.

PrintFiles

In the Tools drawer you will find a tool called PrintFiles. This provides a most convenient way of sending a series of files to the printer for printing.

If you have a printer attached to your Amiga then you might want to try sending a file to it. For a test run I would suggest that you use a simple text file created using ED and with an icon attached to it using IconX as previously described.

To send a file first depress and keep depressed the Shift key. Next click on the icon you wish to print, and keeping the Shift key depressed double-click on the PrintFiles icon. The file will now be sent to the printer. Note that Workbench does not inform you of the fact – it just gets on and does it! If there is a problem, Workbench will inform you by displaying a System requester.

Note that you can print a whole succession of files at one time should you so wish. To do this locate the files to be printed and copy them to a common location along with the PrintFiles utility. Then select all the files to be printed as outlined above, simply press and keep depressed the Shift key and then select each file in turn. When all files are selected, and with the Shift key still depressed, double-click on the PrintFiles icon.

Menu
Beginners
Workbench
Extras Disk
Preferences

16:
Printer
Graphics

In the last chapter we examined the use of the Printer Preferences editor to control how the Amiga interfaces to a connected printer. Many of the settings in the Printer Preferences are fundamental to successful printer operation and in that respect are essential. There is a further Printer Preferences editor, PrinterGfx, and this is used to control the way in which a suitable printer – such as a standard dot-matrix printer – produces graphic dumps. A graphic dump is a printout of part of or all of a screen image. If you thought that producing a carbon copy of a screen from your Amiga was a simple matter, think again. The Amiga Workbench can make it a simple matter but there is an awful lot going on in the background!

The PrinterGfx Preferences editor is located in the Prefs drawer which will be either on the Workbench disk or the Extras disk depending on which version of Workbench you are using. When double-clicked it displays a relatively straightforward screen – illustrated in Figure 16.1 – but for a first time user the range and, in particular, the naming of some of the options can be more than a little off-putting.

However, the same basic principle that was laid down in the last chapter – and indeed the basic philosophy of using your Amiga in general – still remains. Don't be afraid to experiment with different settings and see what the results are. Experimentation is the key to getting the very best from your Amiga.

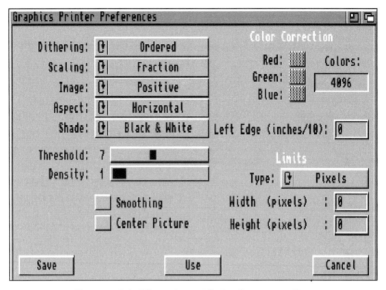

Figure 16.1. The PrinterGfx Preferences editor.

Colour Correction

Being American in origin this is actually labelled Color Correction in the Graphics Printer Preferences window. This option is only of relevance if you have a colour printer and are looking to produce a colour screen dump. What this tries to do is to produce a better match of the screen colours to those on the final printed output. You should bear in mind however that the end results are not going to be perfect. Colour perception is a personal thing and can be affected by monitor brightness, contrast and so forth.

There are three check boxes, R, G and B which stand for the Red, Green and Blue colours. To turn on colour correction you simply check the box of the colour you wish to try and correct. So if you decide that the red in the printed copy doesn't look right, you can check this box. You can check one, two or all three of the boxes but for each box you check there is a reduction in the number of colours the Amiga can actually try and print on your printer. Of course, the result of this might be that the colour is even more off the mark than before, but that's for you to decide! By default and with no corrections, the Amiga should be capable of producing thousands of different colours – the actual figure is displayed below the three Color Correction check boxes. For each colour you enable for correction there is a reduction of 308 in the total number of colours available to you – such is the price of perfection! Of course, this entire option is only available for colour printers!

Dithering

Dithering is one of a handful of cycle gadgets available as a block in the PrinterGfx preferences editor. The option can have one of three settings – Ordered, Halftone and Floyd-Steinberg.

Dithering is a technique which only applies to colour printing, and it plays an important role in the correct representation of colours. In Ordered dithering the coloured dots that compose the picture are printed in simple straight rows and columns. Using this method there is a very noticeable regularity to the printing of colour shades. Printing using this setting is the quickest of the three, the penalty for this speed is that the final results can look a bit false.

Halftone dithering is a method of varying both the density and the precise position of the individual coloured dots when mixed colour shades are required. Halftone images therefore appear a little softer and are easier on the eye.

Floyd-Steinberg or F-S dithering, employs a quite complex algorithm to manipulate the physical pixel data from the screen, so that in effect screen colours are slightly smeared before being translated into printer dots. This method of dithering takes time and hence should be limited to final printouts of images.

Sometimes when printing diagonal lines their edges can look jagged. One way to work around this is to check the Smoothing gadget in the PrinterGfx Preferences editor. With this enabled the printing software attempts to reduce the effect by algorithmically manipulating the data before it is translated into printer graphics. This takes some time and therefore with the Smoothing option enabled print speed is greatly decreased.

Scaling

The final size of your printed image can be affected by the setting of Scaling. There are two options, Fraction and Integer. The final size of the printed image depends on this setting and the printer's line length. This means that you are not just restricted to prints which are in a one-to-one ratio with the screen image.

Fraction, as its name suggests, allows the height and width of the image to be fractionally adjusted so as to maintain the correct overall proportions. This means that, depending on the values set by Limits (see later), individual screen pixels in either plane might be expanded or omitted altogether, so as to preserve the required image proportions.

Integer is the converse of Fraction. In other words every pixel on the screen is guaranteed to be reproduced in the printed output by an even number of dots, and the number will be in the same proportion as the adjustments made to all the other pixels in the printed area.

Limits

This gadget allows you to control the overall size and shape of your printed image. Used in conjunction with Scaling described above, you can create special effects, range the print size and even distort the final output. There are also two text string gadgets which allow you to define the Width and Height of the image to be printed. Click in either of these and delete, edit and enter new numeric values. The units of measurement are tenths of an inch and therefore a setting of:

> Width 60

and:

> Height 40

would give an image of six inches wide by four inches high, subject to the cycle gadget selections under which there are five options available – Bounded, Absolute, Pixels, Multiply and Ignore.

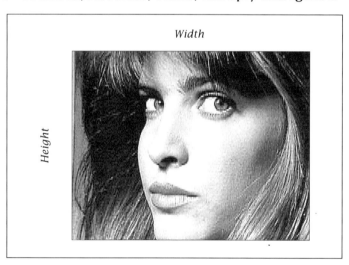

Figure 16.2.The aspect ratio of a graphic is expressed in terms of Width and Height. This picture has a 1 to 1 aspect ratio. A wider picture might have a 2 to 1 aspect ratio, a longer picture a 1 to 2 aspect ratio, and so on.

Bounded means that the size of the printed image will not be greater than the Height and Width values defined in the Limits settings (see below). Images may be smaller but not any larger when Bounded is selected.

Absolute can be used in any one of three different ways. If both Height and Width values are supplied the final printed image will be precisely the size specified, regardless of the screen image's true aspect ratio. If only one of the limits is set, either Height or Width, entering zero for the other, the printed image will have the correct aspect ratio while at the same time precisely matching the dimension specified.

Thus if 60 is specified as the Width then the width will be six inches and the height will be the correct Height to match the width. The final Absolute option is when both Height and Width are set to zero. In this circumstance the width will be the maximum possible – based on your Printer Preferences – and the height will be in proportion to this.

Pixels works in exactly the same way as Absolute except that the Height and Width values are taken as numbers of pixels rather than tenths of an inch.

Multiply is misleading in that it doesn't allow you to magnify the size of an image in the way you might think. Multiply allows the height and width of the printed image to be adjusted, in proportion to each other if required but based on a ratio. The units used in this case are simple number values, but represent pixels. For instance, if the Width is specified as two and the Height four, then the printed image will be twice the screen's image in width (in pixels) and the printed height will be based on four times the number of pixels on the screen.

With Ignore selected the Width and Height limits are totally ignored and the printed image's size is the size determined by the application that should now be responsible for printing the image.

Image Aspects

Image can be set to Positive or Negative and you can think of the difference between the two like being the difference between a photographic positive and negative. Positive produces a (normal) printer dump while negative swaps the blacks and whites over. It only applies to monochrome images though.

Figure 16.3. A negative image is useful for printing out screens with dark backgrounds – to save on ink – but it can also look good!

The Aspect setting effectively defines the orientation of the image on the paper. When set to Horizontal the image is printed across the paper as it appears on the screen of the monitor. When set to Vertical the image is printed sideways with what appears at the top of the screen running down the righthand side of the paper. This can be useful when you want to print images that are quite wide so that you can use the full length of the paper.

Figure 16.4.When printing, a Horizontal aspect results in a normal print across the printer paper, a Vertical setting turns the picture on its side. Many pictures are wider than tall so this is a very useful feature.

The Left Offset gadget allows you to define the number of inches to shift (or offset) the image. This is much the same as the Left Margin option in Printer Preferences really. The offset can be defined in steps of tenths of inches, thus a value of 1.5 would be one and one half inches. The Centre Picture gadget allows you to ensure that the printed image is produced centrally on the page. With this gadget checked the Left Offset gadget is inoperative and any values entered will be ignored until Centre Picture is disabled.

Shade

The last of the cycle gadgets, this one has four options which allow you to define what colours to print, or perhaps more correctly, how colours are printed. This option, like many others, is rather dependent on your printer being able to support it. The four options available are Black & White, Grey Scale 1, Grey Scale 2, and Color.

The first option Black & White, when selected, means literally what it says – the image printed will be limited to black and white with no colours being used (this does assume that you are using a ribbon that has a black component in it). This is a useful option to select if you simply want to print out a trial image to check on the picture itself, plus its other components such as size and position.

In contrast to Black & White prints, Grey Scale 1 allows each of the colours on the screen to be printed in a particular shade of grey which best represents the colours on screen. This is achieved by varying the dot-patterns printed. Grey Scale 2 offers a more restricted form of grey scaling, such that only a maximum of four dot-patterns are used for any image in any printer graphics mode. This option is in fact designed to match the standard monitor display.

Color is only applicable if you have a colour printer. If selected, instead of varying the dot-patterns to reproduce a screen image in shades of grey, colour commands are sent to the printer to change the colour of the ink used.

Threshold

This option is only applicable to black and white printing and as a rule seems to be ignored if you are printing either in colour or grey scales. The Threshold setting determines which colours on the screen are printed as white and which as black. The setting is made using a slider gadget which can be dragged to give settings from 1 to 15. The higher the Threshold setting the more colours are printed in black assuming that Image is set to Positive. Therefore with a low Threshold setting (say 1 or 2) only the darkest colours on the screen are printed as black.

If Image is set to negative then the reverse is the case.

Density

Density works on a scale of 1 to 7 and effectively sets how dark your printed image will be when printed. The lower the density setting, the faster the image will print as less dots are used, resulting in a lighter image. The higher the density setting, the more dots are used to create the image, the longer it takes to print and the darker – more dense – the image appears.

Note that there are many factors involved in using Density. For example, the EpsonX printer driver only supports six densities – therefore you can't use all seven settings! These and other subjects are more fully covered in Mastering Amiga Printers.

Graphic Dump

If you are looking to produce screen dumps from the Workbench then the easiest option is to use GraphicDump which can be found in the Tools drawer on the Extras disk. This program will print the front-most image on the screen, ie the window at the front, to the printer when you double-click on the icon. However, as the window at the front of the screen when you double-click on the GraphicDump icon will almost certainly be the one containing GraphicDump there is about a 10 second delay before the program seeks the front window to allow you to bring it to the front.

The print to the printer takes place in real-time. That is, GraphicDump does not, at the allocated time, take a look at the front most screen and record it to memory for subsequent downloading to the printer, instead it looks at the screen and prints it out one line at a time.

This basically means that, unless you want to get some weird and wonderful effects, you should leave the screen well alone until the image has been printed.

The type of image produced by GraphicDump is affected by the settings of the Printer and PrinterGfx Preference editors. Equally it is possible to define the size of the dump produced by assigning the correct Tool Type to the GraphicDump information window.

17:
Fonts

One of the major areas where the Amiga has developed considerably with the most recent software release is the important one of fonts – the various ways in which you can display typed characters on the screen and on printer output. This is a vast and complicated subject and an important one. But I can only begin to touch the surface of this huge topic here.

The study of fonts is a science in itself and comes under the heading of *typography*. With the increasing use of computers such as the Amiga in publishing, especially in the application of programs such as desktop publishing (DTP), typographical terms have wormed their way into the ever expanding world of computer jargon. More terms for you to learn!

Unless you are into typography you have probably never paid much attention to the style of the text (type) that you read. In fact, there are many hundreds (and probably thousands) of styles of type and these are called fonts. For instance, the very text you are reading now is typeset in a font called *Lucida*. For shorthand we might normally say: the text is set in Lucida. The two most common fonts in use are called *Times* and *Helvetica* and these are often seen in newspapers. Check out your daily! By default the Amiga uses a font called *Topaz*.

One thing you will have noticed is that the printed word comes in many sizes – type sizes are normally measured in their own system called points. A point is very fractionally over 1/72nd of an inch, although it is normally referred to as being 1/72nd of an inch. Therefore a font that is one inch high is said to be 72 points high. Samples of various point sizes are shown in Figure 17.1.

This is 12 point

This is 18 point

This is 24 point

This is 36 point

Figure 17.1. Point size examples.

Although there are many different fonts to choose from they can all be divided into two basic categories which are called *serif* and *sans serif* fonts and these are illustrated in Figure 17.2.

Times is a Serif font

Helvetica is a Sans Serif font

Figure 17.2. Samples of serif and sans serif fonts.

A serif font is one that is adorned with fancy edges, the most famous of which is Times. Helvetica does not have these extra bits and is an example of a sans (without) serif font. Although there are no hard and fast rules, by convention sans serif fonts are used for headlines and serif fonts for main text because they are easier on the eye. So, how do you know what fonts are serif and which are sans serif? Look at them!

The appearance of a font on your Amiga screen might well look very different to that which you get when you print out hard copy containing the same fonts. This is especially the case when printing from DTP style programs which have specialist printer drivers rather than those that simply dump the screen. The reason for this difference is that the Amiga's screen display does not correspond in a 1:1 ratio with the equivalent area on a printed page. The bottom line is that fonts on screen will appear about twice as high on the screen as they do in the printed copy.

In addition the resolution of your screen is about 25% that of a dot-matrix printer. As such the appearance of the font on screen looks very jagged and on larger type sizes takes on an almost pyramidic look. The printed font looks infinitely better. Bear these points in mind when you use fonts initially, with some experience you will get used to this.

Amiga Fonts

Your Amiga is supplied with a Fonts disk and this contains additional fonts – in fact it contains all your fonts except those built into the Amiga system, ie the font called Topaz. The original Commodore fonts are all named after semi-precious stones, for example, Emerald, Diamond and Garnet. These are all *bitmapped* fonts, that is to say, they are stored on disk in the form of pixels which are literally dumped to the printer when they are needed. This is efficient in the fact that it is relatively quick but it does not result in a nice looking font. This is especially the case when the font is scaled up. The software simply fills in the gaps which leads to a very jagged edged font – all the bits of the bitmap simply get bigger!

A new technology (to the Amiga) has been the introduction of outline fonts from Compugraphic called *Intellifont*. The data for these fonts are stored in the form of sets of coordinates which plot out the characters of each letter – a mathematical representation of the font if you like. The great thing about this is that they can be printed in any size without loss of quality. The outline mathematics are simply scaled accordingly. While the final output is massively improved, the overhead is that the fonts take longer to produce. The trade-off is your's to decide upon. Outline fonts on the Fonts disk include *CGTimes*, *CG Triumvirant* and *LetterGothic*.

You can use any of the standard Commodore fonts right away as they are already in position on the Fonts disk. If you are using a hard disk system then you will find that the fonts will be located in the Fonts drawer.

Because the Amiga uses bitmap fonts for the screen display you cannot use the Intellifonts straight off – you must create a bitmap set first using the Intellifont Tool in the System drawer of the Extras disk (AmigaDOS versions 2.1, and later).

Once you have installed a new set of fonts you must first run the FixFonts utility to ensure that the Amiga knows about them – more on this shortly.

If you anticipate using fonts on a regular basis them you should make a backup working copy of your Fonts disk and use this on a day-to-day basis.

Fonts 2.1

On the Workbench 2.1 disk there is plenty of room for you to add extra fonts simply by copying them across from the Fonts disk. With Workbench 2.0 (ie 2.04/2.05), if you have not added any extra files onto your Workbench disk you might just have enough room to copy an additional Amiga font onto it. If you are totally full – and you will need about 15K of free space to move a font such as Emerald across – you could try removing some of the less vital Workbench files.

You can copy any of the fonts supplied onto your Workbench disk, including the bitmap versions of the Intellifonts outlined above – once converted with Fountain that is. The limiting factor is the space available on your Workbench disk.

There are no icons associated with the fonts on the Fonts disk and therefore you will either need to use the Shell to move files or force icons to be displayed by using the Show All Files option from the Workbench menu. Files should be copied into the Fonts directory on the Workbench disk.

If you examine the Emerald directory you will find that it contains two files, both with numbers as names, 17 and 20. These are the font files and relate to their size. To install Emerald, copy the Emerald drawer across into the Fonts directory on the Workbench disk. You will also need to copy across the appropriate .font file. If you catalogue the Fonts disk you will see that there is a file called:

```
emerald.font
```

which is the one that must be copied into the Fonts directory on the Workbench disk. Once the fonts are in position you need to open the System drawer and double-click on the FixFonts to install them into the system and make them ready for use. Remember that for each font you need:

> The font directory

> The .font file

Fonts Preferences

In the Prefs drawer (Extras3.0 disk and Extras2.1 disk) you will find a preferences editor called Font. The Font editor has a simple role to play. It allows you to select the fonts that you wish to use on the Amiga, more specifically the font that is used to produce the menus, window names, icon names and so forth. Having said that, if you decide to change the system font, the results can be pretty awful. Topaz was designed for the job it does and it does it very well.

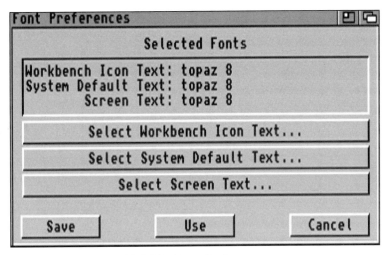

Figure 17.3. The Fonts Preferences screen.

When the Font Preferences editor window opens, it displays a simple screen – shown in Figure 17.3 – that defines the current settings and provides three button gadgets from which you can select either:

Workbench Icon Text

System Default Text

Screen Text

When one of these is selected a further window appears showing a list of the fonts installed in your system along with some text showing how the selected font looks.

The actual text affected by each of the three font window options is as follows:

Workbench icon text:
This is the text below the icons in Workbench windows.

Screen text:
This is the text that appears in menus, title bars, requesters and so forth.

System default text:
The text that is displayed in output windows.

So, for example, to set the Workbench icon text to Emerald 17, first select the Workbench text icon button and then locate and click on Emerald from the list of installed fonts. Finally select the size from the second list. Once you have selected these items from the lists you should get a preview of the text in the alphabet box. If you are happy select the OK button. You can use the menus provided to save font selections as Presets in the normal way.

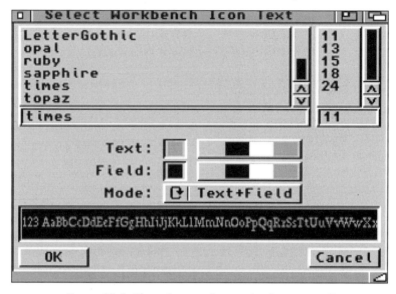

Figure 17.4. Changing text font and colours as well!

When dealing with Workbench icon text you can specify the colour of the text and also of the field, ie the space in which the text is displayed. You can then use the Text and Field colour palettes which are displayed with the font list to select the colours required.

Of course, it should go without saying that it's not a good idea to use text and field colours that are the same. Then again, if you want to confuse a friend who has an Amiga...

On a practical note – if you change any of the text settings on your Amiga from the system standard of Topaz then you will need to have the Fonts disk available each time you boot your Amiga so that it can read the font information when it needs it.

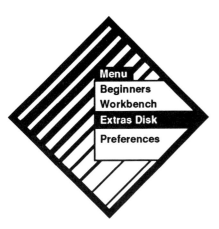

18: Graphics Galore

Graphics is what the Amiga was made for. It was originally designed as an arcade games machine, which explains the custom graphics chips. The Amiga was going to be a Sega or Nintendo until one day someone from Commodore thought it could be put to better use than just playing games, while still providing the best in games entertainment.

Just to prove the point and to launch the Amiga into the emerging world of computer graphics, Electronic Arts developed Deluxe Paint as the flagship program for this new computer and this program, which is constantly updated, still sets the standard when it comes to painting on the screen. From brushes to false perspective with blending and animation thrown in for good measure, this is one of the computer programs that has changed the world.

Deluxe Paint is a bitmap graphics program. The tools work on the individual pixels which appear on the screen to represent colour and shade. The pixels are moved around in clever patterns – the map of bits – to give the optimum effect. DPaint is often packaged with the Amiga so you may have a copy. If not, you'll want to know what it's like. Either way, you can refer to my quick guide at the end of this chapter.

Bits and Pieces

The bitmap-based program is the most common type of graphics program and it can encompass painting, processing, raytracing, animation, video captioning, presentation graphics and morphing. This is one of the most rapidly advancing areas in Amiga computing and you'll find much to excite the imagination.

Painting an original picture is usually only achieved at school for the majority of us but with an Amiga you can paint away to your heart's content, making mistakes and painting over them or making use of a very handy facility which places your latest actions into a backup store. This is usually called Undo and it means that you can go back and undo the most recent actions you have carried out on the picture. Brushes, shapes, fills, colours, tints, fonts and many other tools and features are available in a wide variety of painting programs.

All tend to display the tools as icons in an on screen toolkit which you click on with the mouse pointer to choose a method of drawing. The Menu Bar then reveals a host of special effects and options which can be selected to help create a picture. There are many shortcuts to impressive painting and, although daunting at first, it is worth mastering a paint program. After grappling with the jungle of features you'll suddenly find yourself on the other side, in a clearing and with a completely new skill at your command.

Graphics Processing

Processing graphics is the application of special effects to change the appearance of a picture. You choose the effect from a menu and then choose the area of the picture to which you want it to apply. For instance you might want to add a motion blur to the picture of a racing car so that it looks as though it is moving quickly. You'll either have to paint the racing car or get some existing clip art from a magazine disk or a PD library but you don't have to bother manually adding the look of motion. The processing program does this for you.

Processing graphics is closely related to digitising and scanning pictures into your computer and some processes are designed to improve these pictures for display on screen or for printing out. You can adjust the contrast and brightness, for example, of a picture, just like the controls on your TV. Processing also involves the swapping of pictures between different graphics formats. On different computers and even on the Amiga itself, there are different formats for pixel graphics and, as usual, they are incompatible with eachother. The processing program can recognise many different formats and can load in one format to save in another, acting as a kind of terminus for graphics traffic. This is increasingly useful because the Amiga can read MSDOS disks which can be used to import pictures from other programs. There's often a picture somewhere that you can use rather than do your own!

Pictures as Objects

There are other kinds of graphics programs which you should know about. Firstly there is the structured drawing program. The graphics which are created by the tools in this type of program are held in the computer's memory in a different way to the pixel-based Deluxe Paint. Each element of the drawing is held by the computer as a mathematical description, a bit like the grid reference used to pinpoint a spot on a map. Lines, curves, circles, text characters and other objects are remembered by the program in this way. This is why this type of program is also known as object-based or, because of the mathematical element of the object description, vector-based.

Vector graphics consist of lines rather than bits which means that you can do all sorts of interesting things to the graphics without having to do any drawing – always useful for us beginners! You can simply pick up a point on a drawing with the mouse pointer and move it around to change the shape, to stretch it or distort it. Objects in the drawing are said to have certain attributes. These attributes can be the thickness of a line or the colour of a rectangle and they all go to form the description of the picture.

Structured drawing is especially suited to printed output of a high quality because the better the printer, the better the appearance of the picture, something which can't always be said of bitmap pictures, which eventually run out of dots. Nor do structured pictures lose quality when enlarged, they just regenerate themselves at the appropriate scale. On the other hand they don't look any better on screen and they are, generally speaking, more awkward to create.

This is one of the big differences between an object based and a bit image picture made up of lots of tiny dots. The latter gets grainier the bigger it gets and the dots are magnified. Zooming (like using a magnifying glass) in onto this type of picture reveals the dots as coloured rectangles. Turning the telescope around and making the picture smaller (zooming out) results in the loss of some of the picture elements (pixels) and a consequent loss of detail.

Computer Aided Design (CAD)

Another branch of graphics on your Amiga is Computer Aided Design (CAD). This is a specialised area which has been overtaken by vector drawing programs a little in recent times. This is because full blown CAD is for designing buildings and aeroplanes rather than the patio in the backyard and more modest drawing programs do the latter job just as well and are perhaps easier to use.

CAD however has the edge when it comes to large designs and when precise measurements are needed, measurements which can be reproduced on paper at a later date for use in the real world. For reasons of accuracy, output from a CAD program is usually to a plotter rather than a printer. A plotter draws the lines from the description which the computer holds, much as described above, retaining the measurement attributes of the drawing on screen.

CAD programs provide drawing tools such as arc, polygon and rectangle and usually fill objects with patterns rather than solid fills which are difficult to plot. Grids can be employed to force the accuracy of these tools and measurements can be taken from the drawing. Another important aspect of a CAD program, and one shared by desktop publishing and drawing programs, is the ability to group objects together and to duplicate them. Grouping means that, once finished, a set of related objects can be glued together so that any subsequent operations are carried out on the group. For instance a single fence post can be drawn, duplicated 100 times and then the 100 posts grouped together so that the whole fence can be moved around and placed on a plan drawing.

Both object and CAD type drawing programs can change the size of the drawing without losing quality (except at the very limits) so that, for instance, a screenfull of a CAD drawing might show a leisure centre plan from above; moving in one step reveals the internal walls, doors and windows; moving in a second step reveals lockers, kiosk, poolside features; a third step shows the lines on the badminton court and the pattern of the tiles in the pool. Any amount of detail can be contained in the different layers of the drawing. Layers is a technical term which distinguishes between different parts of the drawing. Each layer can contain its own drawing elements and can be viewed individually or together with other layers. It's like drawing on an onion skin and then peeling off a layer to draw on the skin beneath.

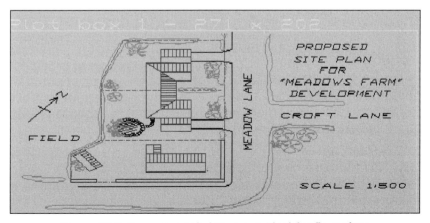

Figure 18.2. Computer Aided Design is ideal for floor plans,
maps and other two dimensional subjects.

3D Sculpture

Another design program which benefits from being object based is the three dimensional drawing program. This is a CAD program which adds the third dimension by offering different views onto the object in question and tools to move around the object. The shapes which can be generated are sometimes limited in this kind of program but sculpture on your Amiga can be great fun. The object is usually displayed as a wire frame, which means that you can see through the object. The surfaces can be added to the object but usually, and automatically, after the designing has been done.

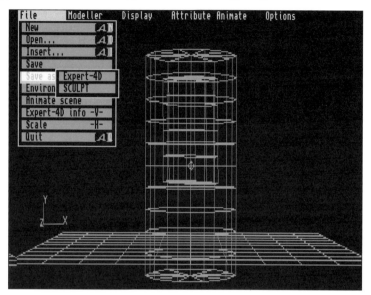

Figure 18.3. Three dimensional objects can be designed as wire frames and displayed from different viewpoints.

Toon Town

After painting and drawing comes animation. Animation on the Amiga consists of displaying lots of slightly different versions of a picture on the screen very quickly to simulate motion. This is done in a variety of ways and, in the 3D design type program, it is left pretty much up to the program to generate the frames which make up the animation. You tell the program which object to use, where it should start on the screen and where it should finish up and the program generates the animation.

More precise control over the finished item is available through Deluxe Paint and its frame-based system called cell animation. In the same way as cartoon artists using traditional techniques draw characters over and over again onto acetate to build up a cartoon sequence, the DPaint artist can paint onto a sequence of screens.

It's like the school child trick of drawing onto the corner of the pages in your exercise book and then flicking the pages. In Dpaint you can move backwards and forwards through the screens (pages) to edit the creation and you can load backgrounds over which the animation will take place.

A traditionally created cartoon is animated through the film camera capturing each cell in succession but the Amiga cartoon is animated through playback controls which more resemble the controls of a video player. And there are more sophisticated video creation programs for the Amiga which take a similar approach and provide all sorts of facilities to help you along with your creation. One of the most useful of these is called *inbetweening*. It does what it says, taking the first and last of something and automatically generating the frames in between. Inbetweening is restricted to short scenes, the movement of a limb, the trajectory of a ball through the air and that kind of thing. The rest is up to you and your director's imagination.

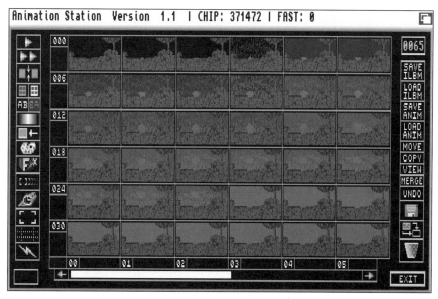

Figure 18.4. An Amiga animation is made up of many frames played back quick enough to fool the eye.

Desktop Video

The combination of video technology with the Amiga's graphics technology is discussed elsewhere but there is a phrase that was coined especially for the Amiga to tell the world that this computer could work with sound and graphics which is Desktop Video (DTV). Commodore saw multimedia on the horizon and placed the Amiga firmly in this vanguard and in the USA the Amiga is used in all sorts of creative and practical broadcast applications, practically running some small cable TV stations if we believe what we read in the magazines.

Ray Tracing

Reflections in limpid pools, metallic spheres and shadows cast across a desert landscape. These are just some of the static mathematical moments captured by a ray tracing program. Ray tracing has joined mandelbrots as one of the most sought after and hyped areas of pure computer graphics. Raytraced scenes are certainly computer-generated but the subjects of the pictures are chosen and positioned by the user. Some of the fascination is the mathematical modelling of something resembling the real world and this is one of the hottest topics in computing as the research labs target their workstations on virtual reality.

Figure 18.5. Spherical objects are favourites for raytracing.
You also need reflective surfaces and light sources. The Amiga does the rest.

The Amiga provides a variety of user interfaces for creating ray traced objects through manipulating objects on the screen in three dimensions. The most important choice is where to put the light sources. The program then works out how this effects shadows, reflections and light levels to lend the finished picture a feeling of reality. The other thing you need to know about ray tracing is that it usually takes a long time!

Fractals and Mandelbrots

The field of fractals is one where mathematicians can put substance to their claims about the beauty of mathematics. However, a deep understanding of the complexities of the number crunching involved is not necessary to appreciate the images that can be produced. These patterns and landscapes are not random but follow rules of mathematics and often reflect parallel rules which can be found in nature hence some of the *natural* features they contain.

Figure 18.6. A fractal landscape generated by the Amiga, following instructions on where various features of the landscape should appear.

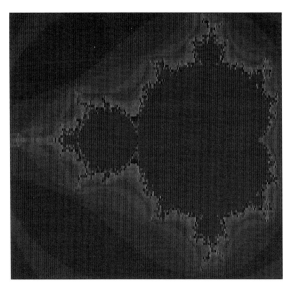

Figure 18.7. The classic Mandelbrot – a mathematical art form all of its own.

Getting to Know Deluxe Paint

Deluxe Paint is the premier graphics program for the Amiga and if you don't have a version, it probably won't be long before you get one. Even if you don't use DPaint, the following paragraphs will give you a good idea of how a bitmap paint program works.

DPaint's first screen is very useful for the beginner because it summarises the main graphics screen modes and demonstrates how you can have a different resolutions and numbers of colours in combination. Try out different combinations and click OK to see the effect. The colour palette in the bottom righthand corner shows the available colours. When a picture is loaded it often brings its own palette colours with it but these can be reset at any time.

To continue your screen mode experimentation press the righthand mouse button on the menu bar and choose Picture and then Screen Format to try a different selection.

Above the palette is the toolbox with its choice of brush shapes at the top, lines, curves and fills further down. Between the palette and the toolbox two colours are shown indicating foreground colour (in a circle) and background colour, the rectangle in which the circle sits. Click the lefthand mouse button in the palette to select the foreground colour, the righthand button to select the background. From now on pressing the lefthand button in the drawing area will result in the foreground colour appearing on screen, the righthand button will result in the background colour appearing.

As a quick demo of what DPaint can do, have a go at this:

- Press function key 7

- Select the airbrush tool – the watering can look-alike – by clicking on it with the lefthand mouse button

- Select the biggest circular brush (top right of the toolbox)

- Spray some colour by holding down the left mouse button while moving the mouse around.

In general this is how you use tools, pressing the left button and dragging the mouse. Drag quickly and there will be some gaps, drag slowly and the brush will fill in the gaps. Now some special effects. Press the Tab key (lefthand side of the keyboard) to animate the colours you are spraying. If this doesn't have much effect, look at the palette and you'll see that some of the colours are *cycling* and changing colour continuously. Click on one of these colours and then spray into the picture again. Press Tab to turn the cycling effect on and off.

For more fun, select other tools, such as fill (next to airbrush) and press the function keys F4, F5, F6 and F7 to see what happens! When you've selected a tool it stays selected until you positively deselect it. More than one tool can be selected at the same time so some can be used in combination if required. Clicking a tool with the righthand button pops up a box so that you can adjust its effects. Try it on the fill tool and change the dithering.

Flipping Great

From version III DPaint has supported animation and you get some examples with the program. If you get really interested in this black art then Real Things are animation *kits* which you can buy in sets to load into DPaint. They contain backgrounds and lots of anim brushes to create your own animation with. An anim brush is a brush like any other in DPaint and can be moved with the mouse and manipulated. The difference is that it consists of a sequence of pictures which, when flipped through, animate the brush. Using an anim brush it's a simple matter to use the mouse to place different stages of the animation at different points on the screen by pressing the mouse button, moving, pressing the mouse button for the next frame and so on. Then, when animated, the effect is of the animated object moving across the screen along the path traced out for it by your mouse movements.

DPaint has many cards up its sleeve, I'll leave you with just one last important trick. Press j on the keyboard and everything clears. But this is a new screen, a second screen, not a cleared screen. Paint something. Press j again and you are back in the first screen! You can load pictures and brushes into either screen, cut out bits from one and stick them down in the other!

DPaint is fun, challenging but forgiving of mistakes. Your first doodlings and loading of other people's completed pictures will entertain. Beyond are the skills of the graphic artist, made easy by a powerful tool. The documentation is very good so investigate the possibilities. You'll be happy you did.

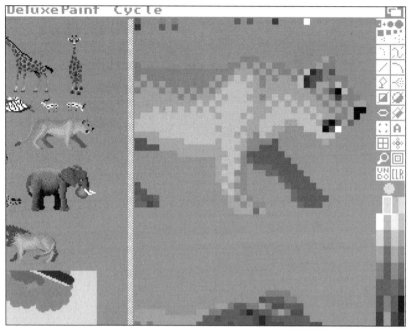

Figure 18.8. In Deluxe Paint you can zoom for painting in close-up. Note the jaggies, which don't look so bad at normal size.

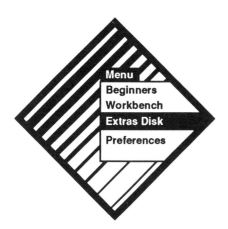

19:
Video
Link Up

When it comes to home video, the Amiga is the computer to own. It can play the part of video editor, titler, and effects generator. This chapter is about linking the equipment up and using it together with typical software.

Putting computer images onto video tape is much easier than getting them into the computer from video. It's cheap, quick to master and a videotape can run in any similar video machine, sidestepping all the different computer formats that are incompatible with each other.

Camcorder owners can benefit from using an Amiga which is thousands of times more capable of producing titles, captions, subtitles, borders and even animations, music and special effects. With a home computer along, the toy town tunes and flashing pictures can be replaced by professional-looking text characters, colourful artwork, smooth-moving graphics and near CD quality sound.

Linking Amiga with Home Video

There are three basic levels you can achieve when using an Amiga with your video equipment, each a little more sophisticated, and more expensive than the last. None are particularly difficult to achieve however and a standard Amiga setup is quite capable of adding greatly to the armoury of the VCR and camcorder owner.

The first level is to employ a convertor box which takes the computer's video output signal (the one that goes to the monitor or television) and turns it into something which your VCR or camcorder can happily record. This black box is known as a *PAL encoder* and, with one fitted, you can record anything that happens on your computer screen. You could record the course of a computer game, a slideshow of favourite pictures or a sales presentation. PAL is the TV display system used in the UK. *NTSC* is the system used in the USA.

Level two is the use of a more sophisticated interface between a computer/video player and video recorder. This time the black box is called a *genlock*, a circuit which combines two signals, one from a video player (a camcorder perhaps), one from a home computer, and sends them, happily synchronised, on their way to the video recorder. In this way titles can be placed over video footage.

The third level is about using a computer to take a hand in the editing of video tape. As well as combining the video signals, the computer controls the player and recorder, allowing you, acting as the film editor, to choose which scenes to use in the finished film and the sequence in which to use them. The computer takes care of assembling the scenes in the correct order on the final tape.

Sound can be recorded directly from the Amiga's headphone socket into the audio-in of a video recorder or, to combine with an existing video soundtrack, into the audio dub socket where available. Sound can also be added from other sources of course, a CDTV player for instance.

Desktop Video

When it comes to recording material directly from the Amiga then there are two approaches. Firstly you can use software to create pictures and/or music and then record them directly from the computer in realtime ie as they are replayed. Secondly you can create individual *frames* of pictures on the computer, recording them one by one onto video so that the sequence is animated by the playing of the video tape, not by the computer.

Some Amiga software generates animation frames like a stack of cards, each card with a slightly different version of an image. By flicking through the cards, movement results. This is called cell animation and it's based on the traditional method. In computer terms each cell is a screen of graphics. It needn't be a whole screen. The software often cuts down the screen size to avoid processing too many pixels so you record movement in a small window with a background coloured border around it. Clever software reduces the *overheads* of cell animation by maintaining only a record of differences between one cell and the next.

For three dimensional objects you can choose between combinations of geometrical shapes and ray-traced shapes. The former are easy to construct from building blocks like pyramids and cubes and the results remain obviously *blocky.* The latter start with similar building blocks but go on to take hours and days to produce, through mathematical calculation, smooth objects with reflective surfaces and shadows.

Figure 19.1. There are many programs and a wide range of fonts for creating titles.

Because of the overheads, an animation in three dimensions is limited to just two or three seconds of playback. You can loop back to prolong the scene and here the choice of subject and movement is important.The more complex the data, the longer it takes to generate each cell. Cells are saved to disk in a compressed format ready for uncrunching and display by a playback program.

Desktop video is the techie end of video and computing and you might not want to venture this far with the software side but you should be aware of its considerable potential when combined with video.

Soundtracks

Hi-fi video is now becoming an important part of the home entertainment system so cannot be ignored for Amiga video generation. Backing music can be played in realtime on the computer and recorded in stereo from the headphone socket. Dubbing music at a later stage is in the domain of the video recording equipment but the music could of course be generated by the computer via internal sounds or via sequencer software controlling a MIDI (Musical Instrument Digital Interface) instrument.

Locking On

Using a genlock, which will cost you upwards of £100, implies taking a new level of care with the post-production of the video footage you've shot. By joining forces with the Amiga you can now introduce professional-looking graphics, fades, dissolves, wipes and visual FX.

A genlock mixes the video and computer signals by *keying* on one of the colours in the computer's output so that wherever that colour appears, it is replaced by the live video. The keyed colour is usually that of the background. Some genlocks allow foreground keying which allows the live video to be masked off into a screen *window* by a block of graphics.

The Amiga has an especially good selection of special effects (SFX) programs and large text character fonts and symbols which are designed for subtitling and for scrolling text on screen. Border patterns such as widescreen cinema, binoculars and rifle sight can also be used to good effect.

Frame by Frame

The control you can get when you use a computer to edit tape to tape is equivalent of the best proprietory editing systems. Because you already have the Amiga you shouldn't need to buy an editing system but only the software and interface between the computer and video equipment. You do need to check that your brand of video equipment is supported by the computer editing suite you've got in mind.

There are a number of different systems including one specifically called an animation controller. This lets you prepare a sequence of cells before automatically recording them. The VCR is controlled via a cable running from the computer to its remote controller port.

The latest editing system is called Editman which supports Sony and Panasonic hardware. It works at video frame level, allows scene by scene editing and will assemble a video copy from a list of master scenes which you've entered.

Compact Video

The Amiga has its own CD player which you can add to your standard setup so that the Amiga can load digital pictures. What the Amiga can't quite do at the moment is to run digital TV on the screen although somewhere in California, and probably Germany too, the engineers are working on it. Commodore's CDTV animates using pictures loaded into the computer from a CD. It can also play music and display graphics at the same time (CD+G). CD Interactive, which is different from the Amiga CD format, promises full motion video and Commodore claim they will support it too.

Professional Pixels

As if to back me up and prove how capable it can be, Amigas are being used as the basis of some very powerful professional systems. It is being used for the weather maps you see on ITV weather bulletins and cable television stations in the USA use Amiga graphics for sports results and information pages.

20:
Comms

Computing is often portrayed as a solitary occupation, the haggard-looking hacker in a pool of light generated by a glowing monitor hitting the keys into the early hours of the morning. Certainly in the early hours of the morning it's off-peak for the telephone lines as well as for the electricity supply. You can save money and won't have to join a queue for the popular places to go. But using the telephone is a social act, as Beattie (BT), in the shape of actress Maureen Lipman, is always trying to point out. We are encouraged to lift the receiver at the slightest prompting.

Communicating via computer is no different and at the other end of the telephone line are groups of people waiting to welcome you onto their system, some for free, some for a fee. There are a wide variety of bulletin boards and commercial services, more of which later.

The main reasons for using telephone communications are to gain rapid access to information and to share information with others. The commercial services charge you for accessing their databases which are sourced from *information providers.* For instance *The Guardian* newspaper is a provider of news. The bulletin boards rely on users providing what they can to keep their databases fresh and interesting.

The other way that you share information is through the mail systems. These provide a personal mail box into which others on the system can post their messages to you. On some systems you can send your messages around the world via a *packet* system. All the mail is saved up and sent in data packets to a new destination, a *node*, where the packet picks up more mail before being dispatched once again. *Electronic mail* is used in business to send messages and memos and the text can be forwarded for sending by fax or *snailmail* (letter post).

What You Need

To communicate with another computer via the telephone system you'll need a *modem* and a cable to connect the modem to the serial port which you will find on the back of your Amiga. And you'll need some *comms* software to make the modem dial numbers for you and send and receive data in an intelligent manner.

The extra bit you have to buy is the modem which is a box of electronics which converts the data sent by the computer into (audible) signals which can be transmitted over a telephone line, and vice versa.

The speed at which information is transferred between your computer and the computer you have dialled is measured by a unit called *baud*. The larger the baud number quoted, the faster your modem can communicate. Line quality, data compression and other factors come into the equation but, in general, the larger the baud rate the better, and the more expensive, the modem.

Modems can be multi-purpose so make sure that the one you get is intended for the Amiga and that you are supplied with the correct cable for Amiga connection. Don't rush out of the shop or off the mail order phone line without checking these two vital points if you don't wish to be disappointed. If undecided this is also a good time to consider the comms software that you are going to use to tell the modem what to do.

Terminal Type

When it comes to comms, there are so many different permutations that you want a program which will deliver the standard systems like Prestel, ANSI BBSs (Bulletin Board Systems) and Telecom Gold without having to make lots of menu selections. At the same time you want to have all the options just in case you need to access a bulletin board which is a bit out of the ordinary.

ANSI is a *terminal* type which a lot of BBSs use so it's important to have this facility. You'll also want to be able to access *Prestel* type services. Prestel is a commercial system run by British Telecom which features the sort of blocky graphics you get on your TV if it has teletext. It has information about business, education, travel, weather, sport etc and you can pay for different levels of service. This is also true of *Telecom Gold*, a system which doesn't bother with graphics but is designed for business use and for accessing other information providers around the world.

Academic users need to get the most out of their systems through text or graphics terminal emulation (pretending to be like a university computer). Examples of text terminal emulations are VT320, VT102, VT52 and Teletype. An example of a graphics terminal is Tektronix, a number of versions of which you may encounter if you move in this world.

Macros (small programs that carry out a sequence of actions automatically) are handy in almost any application but in comms, when time is money, they are vital. A macro can be a small list of commands typed into a box or it can be complete script program. Typically a macro will set up the comms software, initialise the modem, dial a number, give personal details and take you to your favourite bit of a bulletin board. It can do all this faster than you can, thus saving time and money. If you are going to get serious about comms then you may wish to check that your choice of software can do this and whether it provides libraries of functions for you to use in your own programs.

Figure 20.1. The popular ANSI terminal emulation features blocky graphics.

Feature Phoning

Dialling up a service simply involves typing in the number, doesn't it? As we've come to expect however there are different ways you might want to use that number, tone dialling for instance or with an automatically-added prefix (often 9 to dial out of an office system), automatic redials and redial delay.

Call-logging and costing facilities can make it easy to keep track of costs expended on telephone time. A text file usually holds the unit costs so you can make your own amendments as the price of your calls changes (usually upwards!) or a new service is used.

Finally comms software usually has a mini database which can be edited, sorted and used to automatically configure each call through a card entry, a record card which keeps information about speeds and protocols together with texts which can act as prompts, responses and passwords. Keeping a password in this way means you can't forget it but also means someone else might be able to find it by using your comms software. You might want to password protect the record of your passwords!

Getting the Best from a BBS

The best bulletin boards and online services are now up to such a high standard that anyone with an Amiga should consider using them, not just comms enthusiasts. All you need is a 2400 baud modem and some comms software.

Apart from sharing information, the main reasons for using a bulletin board are downloadable files, technical help and discussion forums. Downloadable files consist of programs, pictures, text files and tunes. Downloading is the process of choosing a data file by keying a number or letter, followed by the activation of the downloading facility in your software. Your computer then accepts data via the modem, reporting back to the computer at the other end of the telephone if anything untoward occurs. Unless something dramatic happens the process is transparent ie you don't have to intervene. Although these files are *archived*, watch out for file sizes. Archiving reduces the size of files and is commonly used by bulletin boards to get more on the hard drivers which run the system. Pictures especially, and some programs, can be big, a fact which translates into many minutes of expensive download time. Software obtained in this way can work out expensive compared to ordering from a public domain library but downloading has the advantage of providing instant access to the file.

I mentioned that files are archived so you'll need a copy of any archiving/de-archiving software handy to unravel the file once it has been saved to a disk. A decent bulletin board will provide a copy of this software, or something like it, which can be downloaded so you are not left in the lurch. I have had the experience of not being able to de-archive the de-archiver but fortunately this is rare!

In comms there is little in the way of the graphical user interfaces we've got used to on the Workbench. You can dial up a bulletin board with a couple of clicks on a program icon but, once you are in touch with the board, the speed of data transfer down the 'phone line determines that text display and single keypress interaction is the most efficient manner of operation.

Be prepared then to struggle a little to begin with as you get familiar with the keypresses and how to move around menus. Some boards incite panic by restricting access to ten minutes at a time. But remember, you can always 'phone again.

The best way to familiarise yourself with this sort of bulletin board is to find the help files and to download them and write them into a file on your disk drive. They are text so the download doesn't take long and you can then read them in your text editor/wordprocessor or print them out. Another method to gain familiarity is to turn on the "logging" option in your comms software. This will make a recording of your session in a text file which you can scroll through later to see the routes you took and where you went wrong.

The other main aspect of any BBS is communicating with other users. You can do this in two ways. Firstly you can send electronic mail. You choose this option from a menu, fill in a form to say who you want to send the message to – an individual or group or even all users – and then type in your message and send it. Anyone you sent the message to is then warned when they next log on to the bulletin board that it awaits their attention.

The second way to communicate is more directly in a conference. In this situation you type in a message which then appears on the screens of others logged onto the conference and their messages appear on your screen. You're talking! There are conferences on many subjects, some are techie, some just chit chat or take on the guise of pub talk or a party atmosphere. Computer dating of a totally different kind is not unknown!

Forms of File

Because data is time and time is money, most files on a bulletin board are *compressed* in some way (the same as archived). Amiga files are usually in the ZOO, ARC or LZH format. Most PC files are in the ZIP format. Macintosh files are typically in the .SIT (Stuffit) or .CPT (Compact Pro) format. GIF graphics files are also often in a compressed format which can be unravelled in a graphic processing program. Once you've identified the form of compression, you can use the appropriate decompression utility.

There are a number of different methods of uploading (sending to an online service) and downloading (receiving from a service), most of which are supported by Amiga communications software. These are known as file transfer protocols and it is important that two computers communicating should be using the same protocols. Here are the main types summarised:

Xmodem   Xmodem is one of the most widely used file transfer protocols and can always be relied upon.

Xmodem-1K Xmodem 1K is essentially Xmodem with 1K (1024 byte) packets.

Ymodem   Ymodem is essentially Xmodem 1K that allows multiple batch file transfer.

Ymodem-g   Ymodem-g is a variant of Ymodem. It is designed to be used with modems that support error control. This protocol does not provide software error correction or recovery, but expects the modem to provide the service.

Zmodem   This is generally the best protocol to use if the electronic service you are calling supports it. Zmodem has two significant features: it is extremely efficient and it provides crash recovery.

Kermit   Kermit was developed at Columbia University. It was designed to facilitate the exchange of data among very different types of computers (mainly minicomputers and mainframes). You probably will not need to use Kermit unless you are calling a minicomputer or mainframe at an educational institution.

Sealink   Sealink is a variant of Xmodem.

Lots to choose from but which file transfer protocol should you use? In general, I recommend Zmodem if it's available on the system you are calling.

Where to Dial

There are hundreds of bulletin boards in the UK and many have Amiga dedicated sections. Even more cover areas of general interest which you might wish to access.

General Interest

When you begin to explore a bulletin board, or even to run your finger down a list of boards, it becomes obvious that these computer users have a wide range of other interests. More surprising is the range of subjects covered by more local and modest bulletin boards. Complete boards are dedicated to subjects such as astronomy, radio and sci-fi while large sections of others are dedicated to these and other items of general interest.

Most boards make an effort to be entertaining and interesting despite their computer bias, introducing distractions like the common list of events and births for the current date in history and the ritual taking of the fortune cookie. A typical example is a bulletin board called Chaos which has sections on science fiction and fantasy, Star Trek, international cookery, satellite TV, compact disc and music, vegetarian, home improvements, OU students, small business advice and chat about cars. Some subject areas are restricted to subscribers.

You may find that your local authority provides an online information service to local business and ordinary citizens. It can usually be accessed from terminals in local libraries but also from your Amiga at home. There's often information about services, about consumer rights, business into Europe, events and lots more.

Multi-user Games

Games playing over the telephone can be an addictive affair because you are taking part in a live game which changes its nature, according to rules laid down by a moderator, as the game progresses and other players make their moves. There are space adventures and fantasy role playing games involving trading, magic and battles. These worlds are negotiated through commands like NORTH, SOUTH, TRADE, ATTACK, CAST SPELL, SEND MESSAGE and suchlike.

Crossing the Divide

If a board is actually run on an Amiga, the facilities will be more appropriate and programs and data are also usually more abundant. However, on the other side of the coin, logging on to a bulletin board is a way of accessing data from other types of computer. On a board you are temporarily free from disk formats and file types and rub shoulder to shoulder with other computing environments such as PC and Mac, Atari and Acorn.

PC boards carry lots of data for printer users such as download fonts for the new Bubblejets, and of course there's the usual mass of pictures, usually in GIF format so you'll need to avail yourself of one of the graphics translator programs to turn them into IFF.

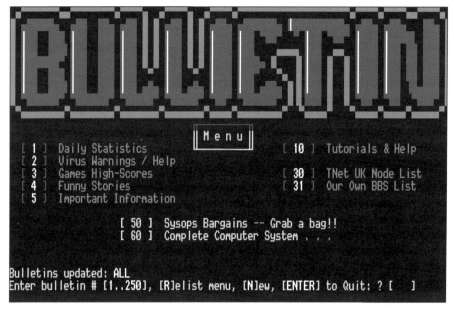

Figure 20.2. Bulletin boards don't care what computer you are using.

Pay Phones

Since the dawning of comms, there have been commercial services and at one time they promised to take over from your daily newspaper. It hasn't happened but there are still a number of services worth paying for. These may or may not include some of the 0898 type bulletin boards with games and other attractions which are being advertised. I'll confine myself to a small sample of the services available.

CompuServe

CompuServe is the biggest online network in the world with 760,000 subscribers, mainly in the USA, but now available in Europe and with an increasing relevance to UK users.

Getting on to CompuServe is a matter of sending off for your subscription and then going through a brief signing-on procedure on your first access. As part of your initial payment you get $25 worth of usage. In addition you can practice using the system with a guided tour and a practice forum free of charge. A free customer service voice line is available if you come across any problems.

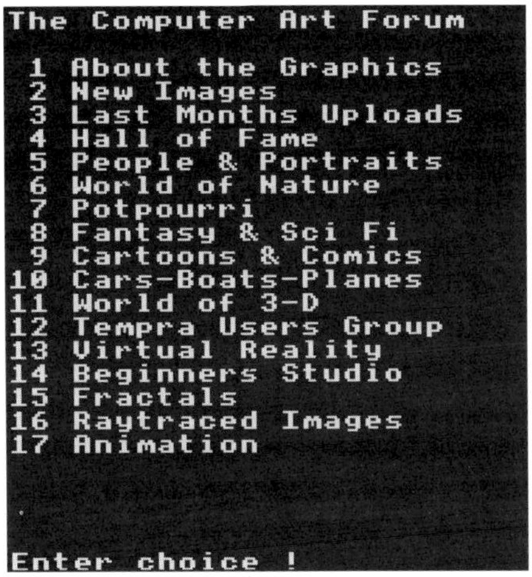

```
The Computer Art Forum
 1 About the Graphics
 2 New Images
 3 Last Months Uploads
 4 Hall of Fame
 5 People & Portraits
 6 World of Nature
 7 Potpourri
 8 Fantasy & Sci Fi
 9 Cartoons & Comics
10 Cars-Boats-Planes
11 World of 3-D
12 Tempra Users Group
13 Virtual Reality
14 Beginners Studio
15 Fractals
16 Raytraced Images
17 Animation

Enter choice !
```

Figure 20.3. CompuServe is the world's biggest online information service.

CompuServe is like most other on-line databases with a tree structure which you can plough through but with quick fixes to get you to known destinations. The GO command beams you up to a section or feature of your choice, GO INDEX for instance. GO COMMAND summarises useful commands, GO HELP gives a help menu and instructions, GO BILLING deals with your account. EXIT takes you up through the menus and finally out of the system.

Each of the areas has a mini menu of between three and nine items selected by pressing the appropriate number. There are messages, libraries, conferencing, announcements from the sysop, member directory and options – a list of relevant modes and commands available. A submenu of libraries usually deals with uploading and downloading.

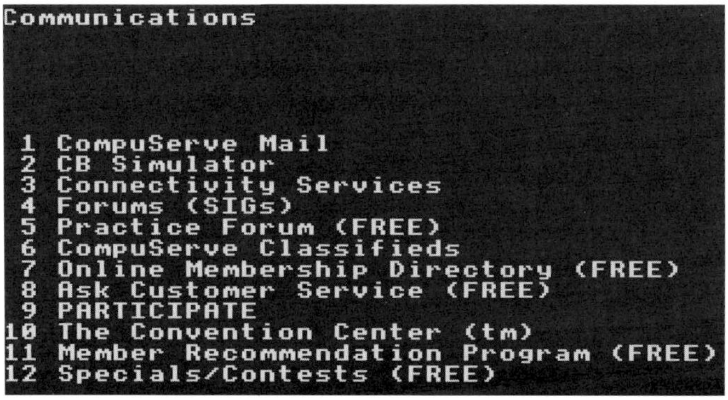

```
Communications




 1 CompuServe Mail
 2 CB Simulator
 3 Connectivity Services
 4 Forums (SIGs)
 5 Practice Forum (FREE)
 6 CompuServe Classifieds
 7 Online Membership Directory (FREE)
 8 Ask Customer Service (FREE)
 9 PARTICIPATE
10 The Convention Center (tm)
11 Member Recommendation Program (FREE)
12 Specials/Contests (FREE)
```

Figure 20.4. Online databases are more and more like magazines, covering a wide range of interests.

CompuServe is inclined towards the serious user. If you are serious about computers then you'll need to be broad-minded because the user groups, discussions and technical support areas are all geared towards the American favourites. However there are user groups on broad subjects for which your computer is irrelevant, for instance health, travel, weather, soap operas, rare diseases, aquaria, disabilities, photography etc.

Silicon Village

On entering the Village you discover those chunky viewdata style graphics which are familiar from teletext on your television. They also draw quickly so there's no waiting around. The guided tour doesn't hang about either, moving through the main features of the board and explaining the Village metaphor.

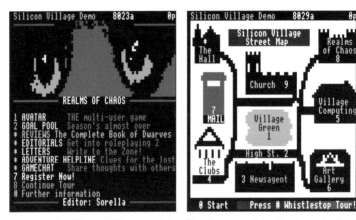

Figure 20.5. Silicon Village, a friendly place to visit via the telephone.

One part of the Village you do get to spend some time in is Avatar, a classic on-line game in which you take a part, communicating with other players, being beamed messages from the gods, finding your way around and discovering the purpose of your Avatar existence as you get lost in this world conjured up by a computer. It's easy to see how you might get addicted to this Limbo-land.

Numbers Game

When BT, the great provider, introduced charges for directory enquiries it did at least offer an olive branch to those of us with a modem. If you need to look up a fairly large quantity of numbers for business purposes – BT say upwards of 20 per week – then you might want to consider Phone Base. If you've already got the equipment then it is economic at even fewer enquiries although not as cheap as running out to the nearest call box!

Another BT service on-line is the Electronic Yellow Pages which can be found on Prestel where you can look up information supplied by Yellow Pages advertisers in and around London.

Hosting the Party

When you connect to a remote computer then you are dealing with a piece of bulletin board software in host mode. These programs provide the public and private mail areas, file transfer, user interaction and everything else which makes up a BBS. You can purchase these programs to create your own bulletin board but be aware that a certain level of hardware will be required and a lot of hard work and dedication.

Comms Turn-on

There are three main areas of telecommunications with a computer which are a turn-off, firstly the costs, secondly the differing standards and thirdly the jargon.

The first can be alleviated by cleverly preparing data beforehand so that sending it is the only thing you do while you are on the phone. Also make sure that you call at off-peak, make use of Mercury if appropriate and take advantage of special cheap rate holidays which BT periodically grants its customers.

The second should be taken care of by your software. Buying software and modem together and seeing it working first offers a level of protection against incompatibilities.

The third is a matter of experience and this chapter has started you on its way.

And Last, Safety First

If you belong to a commercial system then it is vital to keep your identity number and password separate from each other and apart from any reference to the system or system telephone number too. It's the same principle as keeping your cheque book and cheque card in different places so that they cannot both fall into the same hands.

The most tempting thing to do is to place your password and identity information into a script file or into a number directory entry in your comms software. If you are accessing lots of different boards which don't charge for subscriptions then this is OK but don't do it with numbers which can leave others free to use a commercial online system on your time and money.

Commercial Subscription Services

CompuServe   15/16 Lower Park Row, PO Box 676, Bristol, BS99 1YN. Tel: 0272 255111.

Your £22.95 gets you the European membership brochure, software and guide for PC or Mac (not Archimedes), $25.00 usage credit, $5.00 usage credit to be claimed on-line and a monthly CompuServe magazine.

Silicon Village   82 Byron Way, Ruislip Road, Northolt, Middlesex, UB5 6AZ. Tel: 0734 819399.

An enquiries voice line is available on 0734 819399. For a demonstration of Silicon Village, set up your communications software for viewdata, 7 bits, even parity, 1 stop bit and call 081 759 6996 (multispeed). Log in with customer identity 4444444444 and password 4444. Registration to the Silicon Village costs £10 and a month's subscription costs £6, both ex VAT. The subscription gives full access and two hours free usage, after which you pay 2.5p ex VAT per minute. You also pay for a local 'phone call as normal.

Campus 2000   214 Gray's Inn Road, London, WC1X 8EZ. Tel: 071 782 7104. A wide range of educational services.

A list bulletin boards to visit is given in Table 20.1.

Board	Telephone
Sharbrooks	0823 333471
Tug2	0905 775191
Enigma	0905 795002
Alternative Solution	0742 325232
Mission Impossible	0602 654329
Chaos BBS	0633 222475
South Lincs	0780 63954
Red Dwarf	0604 705744
ARCade	081 654 2212
Quercus (Denmark)	+45 31 679770
Icecube (Iceland)	+354 1 624677
Charon BBS	0420 63115
Atlantis	0273 696060
I.C.O.N.	0001 971660
HUCO_BBS	+31 1804 30785
StarNet	0603 507216
Nightingale	0272 535962
Microsurgery BBS	0223 416661
New Age BBS	0702 715025
Academics	021 705 2906
StarBase One	071 733 3992
Arcturus	0928 714460
MegaNet	0924 223456
Fields	0243 502492
Storehouse	0494 728094
DarkHaven	0604 413716
Cyclone	0603 260973
Psycho	0483 418467
Plasma Sphere	0925 757920

Table 20.1. Some Bulletin Boards for you to try.

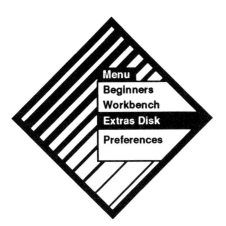

Menu
Beginners
Workbench
Extras Disk
Preferences

21: Music and Sound

For a lump of plastic with a bunch of silicon chips and electronics inside, the Amigas are capable of some pleasing sounds even in their basic configuration. You wouldn't exactly invite guests round for an evening with the Amiga but the many available sounds mean that a sensible range of musical software can be used without having to upgrade the hardware sound capabilities of the computer.

This range includes programs which show the musical score on screen and let you print it out. Others, known as trackers, show each sound as, for example, an A or E or F# which scroll vertically through a window as the tune is played. Finally there are programs which provide the features of a professional sequencer in which different tracks have their own characteristics and can be mixed, like in a music studio.

These programs can all play tunes using sounds held in the memory of your computer but many can also send the data to a musical instrument which is fitted with MIDI (Music Instrument Digital Interface). In this case the musical instrument plays the tune, not the computer's sound chips. Although a MIDI instrument was usually a keyboard in the past, now you'll find it possible to link up guitars, drums, saxaphones and all sorts. The most useful innovation perhaps for the computer musician is the MIDI box which provides all of the professionally sampled sounds but with no keyboard attached and intended purely for use with a sequencer.

So there's a wide variety of software to look at and you can get musical and find out more without delay because there are some very good music programs, like OctaMED, which are public domain or shareware.

Sound Production

The sounds which you hear from the your computer start off as software instructions which are interpreted by the electronics which drive the speakers - the same sort as you get in a cassette player or radio – to send the sound to your ears. The sound is in stereo and can come from any of four points (some software manages more) in the stereo field. Ideally you'll

Sound Sampling

Sound sampling is very much in vogue and is no longer just for musicians and games programmers. Sound can play an important part in making software more interesting and effective. Sounds themselves can also be interesting in their own right, put together to form music or their waveforms studied to understand their physical properties.

There is now a wide choice of sound sampling hardware and software. The hardware takes an input from a sound source such as a microphone or CD player and converts the sound into lots of small digital samples of the sound in progress which are held consecutively in the memory of the computer to make up the complete sound. The software controls this process and provides editing, file management and effects.

Recording is usually triggered from outside, either by the movement of a switch on the microphone or when a certain volume is exceeded.

You will come across the phrase *sampling rate* which means the number of digital samples which go to make up the sound you hear. The rate dictates the quality of the sample, the larger the number, the better the quality. Any setting always has to be a compromise between quality and length of sample and depends on available memory. You can actually get away with quite low sampling rates if necessary.

When you think that we find the telephone an acceptable level of quality then you needn't worry about CD sound when it comes to recording a set of instructions. Musical applications may need to raise the standards a bit but there is also a limit to the quality of sound that an Amiga can produce through its internal sound system. With some software you needn't play back at the same rate at which you recorded. Varying the rate can have strange effects and these are worth experimenting with.

The other important specification to watch out for is the number of bits which are used to hold the sample, 8 or 16. In theory 16 bits can hold more data than 8 bits so samples can be of a higher quality.

The sort of effects which you will come across in software are echo – including slap back and reverb – randomize, Q-filter, Q-emphasis, scale, interpolate, pitch, and the more conventional fade in and out, reverse and wipe. You don't need to know what they mean at first, you soon find out what they achieve through experimentation. It isn't long before you realise how most of today's pop songs are put together.

As well as sampling from the real world, you can generate sounds from scratch by combining waveforms made by mathematical or graphical processes. The waveforms are created by editing the characteristics of a raw sound, by typing in numbers or dragging points on a graph to create new values for *parts* of the sound. The Amiga plays the sound back so you know when you've hit upon something you like.

Using Samples

Once you've got a sound you like what do you do with it? Well, here are some suggestions. Use it in a sequencers, rhythm composer, or soundtracker to give a tune a personal touch. Use sound effects in a multimedia presentation to keep the audience's attention. Sample some animal and other *real world* sounds for use in some educational programs put together in AMOS. Sample voice messages to leave audible notes on your hard drive to remind you what you have stored and where.

Hints and Tips

- Use looping to save memory. Take a three second sample, put in two loop markers at say 0.25 and 0.75 second, and if you're careful, this 0.5 second section will loop continuously and smoothly. Suddenly your three second sample is just 0.75 second but will continue to sound as long as you've the patience to hold down a key! With care you may get sample lengths even shorter and save even more memory. But it's worth noting certain sounds defy looping while others loop almost anywhere.

- Use a manual or time elapse trigger in noisy environments.

- Invest in a quality microphone to sample from the outside world. It can make all the difference. If you've got a camcorder you may be able to use its microphone, if separately attached.

- If you are sampling from an amplifier, why not use it to also playback the sample by connecting the Amiga's microphone output to the amplifier's phono in.

- Get some of the CDs which have sound effects and background mood music on them which is copyright free (once you've bought the CD) and can therefore be used in your AMOS games or as background to your latest video production.

Trackers and Sequencers

The tracker is a type of music editor which didn't exist before computers. A tracker loads instrument sounds which can then be used by the composer to create a rendition of an original, or well-known, song. This is done by typing in note values for each instrument which results in four parallel sequences (tracks) of notes. When played back, these notes sound together to create chords. One track is often used for percussive sounds. The tracker controls the speed of playing, the tempo, too, and shows the notes of any tune that is being played as coloured characters scrolling vertically through a screen window.

Most people use a tracker to play back a preprepared tune, thousands of which are available. What you can do of course is play back some of the tracks and enter notes from the computer keyboard *live* on a spare track, editing the results afterwards. Trackers have come a long way in recent years, always under development and growing features such as new graphical views of the music and MIDI control.

Sequencers offer more than the tracker family in the way of looping and professional features which a studio musician would need. The editing of soundtracks is done with wordprocessor-style cut and paste tools. Music can be played directly from a MIDI instrument into the sequencer, which registers the notes as they are played. The notes can then be edited and arranged and other instruments and effects added. All you need to do is make a video and you've got a top 30 hit!

Real Music

Real music comes in the form of a sequencer but with conventional music notation. The notes and rests are displayed on screen as you'd expect to see them in a book of sheet music. This makes it easier, if you can read music, to type in your favourite tunes. The professional software can produce a high quality printout too so you can create multiple copies of your first orchestral work, beautifully transcribed for the individual players by your Amiga. Poor old Beethoven and Bartok had to do their own scores or get their wives to help!

MIDI

MIDI is no minor subject when it comes to music on computers but it is for the advanced musician and computer user, not the beginner. It is a standard method of sending data between MIDI instruments, which includes your Amiga. One instrument can take details of a song – MIDI data – and then pass them on to another instrument. The instruments are connected together by cables. If you enjoy making music on your Amiga then you will probably end up learning much more about this subject.

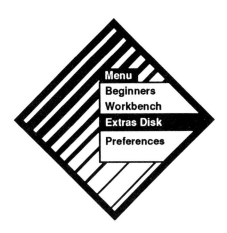

Menu
Beginners
Workbench
Extras Disk
Preferences

22:
The Offices:
Home and
Business

Amigas have always been a bit ahead of their time to make it into the world of corporate IT. They get in through the back door, into design and media environments which love the graphics, into research departments which need the speed and into home offices where they are also entertainment boxes par excellence.

An office setup implies at least one add-on for your Amiga, a printer. It probably means that you are spending a lot of time in front of your Amiga so it should also mean a monitor rather than a TV if possible. It could just be a mono monitor if games playing at lunchtime is not involved!

The Big Three

What are the software tools which the Amiga can provide to deliver productivity? The big three applications on any computer are wordprocessor, spreadsheet and database. The wordprocessor and database are often linked through the merging of name and address data and form letters. Writing to your MP has never been easier. The spreadsheet is a less well-understood tool but is becoming equally significant, linking its numerical data with graphics presentation software so that the less numerate can also understand what's going on. I'll take a look at these main applications in turn.

Wordprocessing

More than any other application software, the wordprocessor has to be the most versatile of programs. On the Amiga a wordprocessor can be expected to perform the main tasks of editing text but also to spell check it, incorporate graphics and produce an attractive layout on the available printer.

Hopefully a wordprocessor will take advantage of the advanced features of the Amiga such as mouse click control, different fonts and printing via the available drivers. It should also conform to the standard methods laid down for working with applications, such as mouse clicking and dialogue boxes. Or should it? What about the good old keypress combinations and function keys? Fortunately, whatever your preference, there is probably a wordprocessor to suit you.

What's in a Word?

Wordprocessing means different things to different people. You could use a wordprocessor for preparing an essay or article which needs to have page numbering and the same heading on all the pages. You could prepare a letter to customers telling them about a new product, ready for personalising by mail merging the letter with individual names and addresses from a database. You could have a picture and twenty carefully devised words to create an effective advert for your next rave!

Different tasks, different requirements. And I'd choose a different wordprocessor for each of the above. The way a page is printed from your wordprocessor is fundamental to how you go about any wordy job and you have two choices: character based printing and graphics printing.

Depending on your printer, graphics printing can be a joy or a liability. Graphics, including fancy fonts, take time to form up in memory ready for printing so a single page of text can take some considerable time and each page has to be formed in the same way. When a printer has no on-board memory to hold the page image, ie when it's not a laser printer, second and subsequent copies of a page also take the same long form-up times. A long document can take a very long time to print. A single A4 letter in 13 point can take up to five minutes on a modern dot-matrix. A good sized printer buffer on the printer itself or a print buffer utility at the Amiga end can come in handy here.

If you are doing big mailmerges with hundreds of letters you aren't going to wait around for outline font printing unless you've got a laser printer. On the other hand, the combination of graphics fonts and the new bubblejet printers is very attractive.

The other major issue is that of the user interface. Here a program like *Protext* is the champion of the old style keyboard-based interface with lots of keypress commands available. This, together with the style of its menus and its long list of printer drivers, is a reflection of its PC pedigree and a certain way of doing things. The use of the mouse with menus is the one concession to the desktop approach.

On the other hand you've got a wordprocessor like *ProWrite* which has supported graphics and fonts from the start and has gradually become more sophisticated to the stage where it can now print to a PostScript printer. The interface is mouse and menu, click and drag. I'm not saying which I prefer but you can choose the one to suit your way of working.

Selecting a Wordpro

Because the wordprocessor is such an important tool, I've drawn up a list of specifications which you should check when choosing your wordprocessor. Try to think of what you are going to use it for, today and in a year's time. The list is given in Table 22.1.

One of the areas in which the Amiga can be confusing is that of text and graphics printing and, because your wordprocessor's natural output is to a printer, read the chapters on printers before choosing your wordprocessor.

Editing and Checking

Using a wordprocessor can be great fun. Whatever the standard of your typing, you can always get it right eventually! Firstly you can edit the text by selecting it and choosing to delete it, move it elsewhere in the document or copy it.

Moving text is also known as cut and paste. The cut action removes the text and stores it out of sight temporarily until you position the cursor where you want the text to go and paste it in. The term comes from the design industry where, before computers, the artist would use a knife to cut out the paper with the text on and glue it into position somewhere else.

Ease of file setup – do you just save?...❏

Line lengths...❏

Indentation ....❏

Tabbing ....❏

Justification styles ....❏

Type styles ....❏

Superscript/subscript ....❏

Selection by word, sentence, paragraph etc.....................................❏

Cursor movement around document...❏

Time to move through a document..❏

How many keystrokes/button presses for block operations ....❏

Undo function..❏

Inter program data transfer ....❏

Search and replace options, style sensitive?....................................❏

On-screen formatting...❏

Headers and footers ....❏

Multi-column ....❏

Intelligent page breaks...❏

Flexible page numbering ....❏

Book (left and right) numbering..❏

Footnotes..❏

Table of contents ....❏

Bibliography ....❏

Indexing ....❏

Line spacing...❏

Foreign language support ....❏

Prefs printing ....❏

Background printing ....❏

Print queuing..❏

Cut sheet handling ....❏

Merging with name/address data ....❏

Automatic file backup...❏

Spelling checker ....❏

Import/export options...❏

Math functions..❏

Configurable defaults ....❏

Special characters available from keyboard/utility ....❏

Table 22.1. Choosing a wordprocessor. Check these specifications.

To make sure everything is correct you can spell check your document. The spellchecker is a program which works together with a couple of dictionaries which are held on disk. It's pretty stupid really and only knows words which are in these dictionaries. Therefore the bigger the dictionary, generally the better at spelling it is. Each word in your document is checked to see if it identical to a dictionary entry. If the word is not found, you are informed and you can change it if it obviously wrong, look up a similar word if it is an awkward spelling or teach the spellchecker the word because it is correct but not in the dictionary.

There are even grammar checkers which will analyse your sentence structures, word frequencies and style. These are fun but not much use unless you are a professional writer and then they just make you feel small! Search and replace is another useful standard tool on a wp. For instance I've just written this piece using "wp" to denote wordprocessor, that's two characters I had to type every time I wanted wordprocessor in my text, not 13. I've then chosen to search for "wp" and to replace it with "wordprocessor" and I chose to do so selectively so that I could keep the "wp"s above.

Search and replace can be used to do individual versions of a form letter. For instance you can send the same letter to all your relations at Christmas but search and replace their names! There is another way that wordprocessors let you do this and it is called merging. Merging involves writing just one letter and typing a special code into the letter where you want the merged data to appear. When you print, the data is imported automatically to where the code appears and the letter is printed. When finished, the next item of data is merged and another letter printed and so on. Very productive these wordprocessors!

Presentation

As well as the words themselves, a wordprocessor also handles the layout of your document. Presentation these days is very important and the wp takes care of your margins around the page, the number of lines and the text styles such as bold and italic. You can define a header and a footer which is text which appears above or below the main body of the document, sometimes a page number or heading which is required on every printed sheet. You can also set the justification of the text, which effects its appearance and readability.

Wordprocessors also handle the setting up of a document so that the printed version is correctly positioned and looks the part. The more up to date wordprocessors will show you what your document looks like while you are editing it but some have a print preview which displays a screen version of what will appear from your printer. This is especially useful for checking page breaks so that you don't find yourself printing over the perforations in the printer paper.

This text is left justified, also known as ragged right.

This text is fully justified across the width of the document. Small invisible spaces are introduced to fill out the line length.

This text is centred.

This text is right justified.

| This | text | has | tab |
| stops | at | regular | intervals. |

Figure 22.1. Wordprocessors provide control over text justification and should be able to show you beforehand how your text will appear on paper.

Choosing and Using a Database

All applications handle data of some sort or another but databases have the job of organising it for a useful life in your computer. Useful is the operative word here. However much data you can collect, it's not much use if you can't access it in the way you wish. And so the first piece of advice when considering data handling on the Amiga is to think through how you will want to access any information you gather. The sort of questions that are relevant are: how quickly do I want the information? In what form do I want it, printed as a report, graphically on screen, ready for export to another application? How much data can I store on my system? Do I want to protect my data from inspection by others?

Make a checklist if you are at all serious about this operation and then check it against the available commercial software. As an example consider the requirements of a picture editor/librarian on a football magazine. He or she gets in plenty of pictures, it's what to do with them that counts. A record card can be designed to hold information about each photograph, containing a *field* to indicate the type of photo – action shot, team photo, football ground, player portrait etc. A field is a box on a record card into which information can be typed or imported. Further details would include the name of the football club concerned and the league they play in. An important field would allow a *flag* to be set to indicate whether the photograph has been used and, if so, when. A flag is a computer term for a yes (the flag is set) or a no (the flag remains unset). The field containing the information about when the picture was used will be a date field and a field to show how much was paid for the photo will be a money field. These *field types* are used to make it possible for the database to calculate, for instance, money spent on photographs between one date and another.

Once the record card has been designed, information can be typed into many cards and all of them saved as part of a single data file. You might want to keep track of a collection, to keep club records, to track subscriptions or print name and address labels. All can be carried out by a database. Some other programs are specialist databases hiding behind another name, eg a family tree program.

What Do You Need?

Keep in mind that the first question to ask is: what do you need from a database?

As an absolute minimum every computer database needs a card index structure, which is the ability to store data in tabular form, with fields (possibly of different lengths and data types) representing columns in the table and each row in the table representing a separate record.

An important feature is the size of table that can be manipulated, how many fields, how big can they be and how many records can be contained in the data file before it becomes too large for the program to manipulate it. Also important is the number of data types available. Are you going to enter large numbers? Do you need precision mathematics? For historical or payroll purposes you may need a date type from which you can calculate periods of time.

To get information to and from the tabular file you need a form. Conventionally this is designed like an index card, with the various fields positioned conveniently and helpful text labels and headings added so that the information is meaningful. You should be able to design a form on screen without too much difficulty.

More important you should be able to flick from one record to another (often achieved with video style controls), scroll around the card form or move to second and subsequent pages if it is too large for the screen, edit and add data.

Searching and Reporting

A screen form usually displays only a single record although very sophisticated programs offer *scroll zones* in the form, which can display multiple values.

To examine several records or produce a selected set of records requires a report generator. This can select a specified subset of records, sort them into a given order and format the fields to suit a document across the page, in columns, in separate blocks for mailing labels or as continuous paragraphs. You should be able to add titles, subheadings, headers and footers and page numbers and to intersperse the records with text. You should be able to print reports out directly or to export them to another program such as a wordprocessor.

The available range of mathematical and allied functions (statistics, financial analysis, trigonometry, etc) determines whether or not you can perform more complex calculations. For answering immediate queries you'll need a quick search facility, preferably with wildcards for finding entries you are not quite sure of. Wildcards are characters which can represent any other character as far as the program is concerned and learning to use them is a skill in itself. For example you might use:

**burgh*

for a town ending in burgh but you aren't sure which one, and:

Ma???

to find all the names starting with Ma

Logical operators, which are ways of comparing one item of data with another, are also useful to find entries based on other factors, for instance:

Martin AND designer

to find all the Martins who are designers and:

Martin AND (designer OR postman)

to find all the Martins who are designers or postmen. The above examples would have different information in different fields.

Transferability

You may be lucky enough to run your database on one computer all your life but the chances are that someone will want to share it or buy information from you. You might upgrade to more powerful hardware or, if you work for a stone-age company, you may want to use the data on an IBM PC at work, then return it to your Amiga at home. You may need to feed it into a wordprocessor for final editing or into a spreadsheet for more convenient calculation.

Relationships

You may also need to relate one file on your database to another: given three files: of video tape, shelf number and orders, can you look up a given order, find which video tape is required and which shelf it's on for picking?

If a customer rings with a complaint, can you find them in your database, extract all related orders, identify the goods they contained, then find who supplied you with them? At the very minimum you may want to have two database forms open at the same time so that you can compare and exchange data between them. The ability to relate one data table to another is what differentiates a *relational* database from a mere card index. Relational databases are more complex and more expensive by far.

One advantage of related data files is that, having created a database structure, you need not worry if it later proves inadequate. Instead of rebuilding the structure you simply create a secondary table which you join to the original one.

Collecting Data

What a database, however good, won't do for you is type in the data. But data is available in forms other than on paper. You can collect data from bulletin boards and from the TV teletext services via teletext adaptors.

There's a mass of data already around on disk too, from bits and pieces, such as UK telephone dialling codes, to massive files such as the complete Bible on PC format disks or on CDTV disks.

Once you've got text then a database can import the files in various formats but it'll need to know what text should go into what field and when to stop filling one record and to begin filling the next. This it does by recognising markers in the text. A common file format is comma separated value (CSV) which marks fields with commas and the records with a return character. As it meets a comma, the importing utility moves to the next field and reads more text before encountering another comma. On encountering a return character it closes the record and moves onto the next, filling each field again in turn.

Hypermedia

Many Amiga databases are not restricted to text and number data. The record card can contain a picture or even a sound (a voice instruction for instance) or piece of music. The word *hypermedia* is often used in the context of databases which interact with other programs and can be used to trigger other processes. Multimedia presentations, which are becoming popular on CDTV, are also huge databases holding these many types of data.

Spreadsheet Selection and Use

The third program in the holy trinity of computing is the spreadsheet. Because we've all only got quite small monitor or TV screens to view the data inside our computers, it is difficult to describe a spreadsheet. In the same way that a platform game has many different screens, above, below and side by side each other but only one screen is displayed at a time, so the spreadsheet is a large sheet of ruled paper which can only be viewed one screenfull at a time.

The blank sheet can usually be as big as you'll ever need, certainly big enough for home accounts, a work schedule, even a small business accounts. The sheet is ruled vertically and horizontally, usually with about 10 text characters between each line. The squares enclosed by these lines are known as *cells* and it is in the cell that you place information, either text or numbers.

Manipulating Numbers

A spreadsheet is a program designed to manipulate numbers. You input a number by activating a cell and typing the number into it. Usually you type into a line editor at the top of the screen and then enter the number into the cell at the cursor by pressing Return. As well as a number, you can type in a formula for instance:

4+3

will appear in the cell as 7 and:

4*3

will appear in the cell as 12.

The * (asterisk) is usually used to mean multiply in spreadsheet formulae. The value in the cell is then available for use in another formula, for example:

C3-5

where C3 means the cell which appears three in from the left – A, B, C – and three down from the top. This is the grid reference method which is used to refer to any cell in the sheet. When a large sheet gets to Z, it continues with AA, AB, AC etc.

As well as numbers and formulae typed in by yourself, the spreadsheet program works with its own built-in functions. The number and type of functions depends on the program you are using. The simplest involve adding up columns and rows of cells. For instance:

sum(A1:A50)

might add all the values in the first 50 cells in column A. The way in which you enter these functions (the syntax) depends on the program but spreadsheets adopt broadly similar approaches. More complex functions might calculate the percentage APR on a loan, the depreciation of a piece of equipment or the time it will take for a chemical process to occur.

Typical categories of functions are time, trigonometry, maths, financial, database lookup, statistics and finally control functions which glue together the others with ifs, thens and gotos, just like a programming language.

Text Labels and Reports

Text entries are more important than you might think in a numbers program because they are needed to describe and document the numbers, whose meaning you would soon forget if they were left on their own, unlabelled. Imagine a colleague at work finding a sheet full of figures on your desk. The figures wouldn't mean much unless there were quite detailed descriptions. Text can also be used to present the numbers in the spreadsheet in the form of a report. Some spreadsheets are better at this than others and it may be that you will export (save in a standard format) the numbers for use in a wordprocessor.

Spreadsheets are also commonly used for project management and for testing out *what if* scenarios in business.

Integrating Software

A particularly difficult product to get right is integrated business software. Often useful if you are on a budget, or RAM space is tight, integration means a degree of compromise on functionality but has the tremendous advantage of sharing data efficiently, in theory. Many home office products feature integration. For instance some wordprocessors, spreadsheets and databases incorporate the ability to incorporate or generate charts and graphs.

Presentation Graphics

Not for the home office necessarily but important for the Amiga using businessman and an area where the Amiga can score over other less graphical computers. Graphs and charts can be generated from business software and then used, together with backgrounds from a paint program. The Amiga itself can be used to make a slideshow presentation using a program like Scala, which also provides fades and other special effects between screens.

Desktop Publishing

Desktop Publishing is included here because all businesses need to produce literature. If you produce office stationery, proposals and letters to clients then I refer you back to wordprocessors. The DTP programs for the Amiga are for real design and print purposes. Product catalogues, newsletters and advertisements are among the documents which can benefit from the typographical and design features offered by these programs.

One of the most important considerations when embarking on DTP on your Amiga is to match your hardware to the program you choose to use. There is no point using a fully featured program which redraws slowly on your screen or which doesn't support your printer. DTP involves working with page sizes that are bigger than your monitor can display so the program will need to redisplay the screen quickly to make it usable. Large or lengthy documents require extra hardware such as multisync monitors and hard drives so take it easy. For a modest newsletter you can get away with a basic hardware setup.

When using DTP you are creating a document which will have to be printed. Is it going to be in black and white (and grey) or in colour? How many copies are going to be printed and how? Is a colour printout going to form an original for colour photocopying (hundreds) or are you going to use a typesetting bureau to prepare the document for commercial printing (thousands).

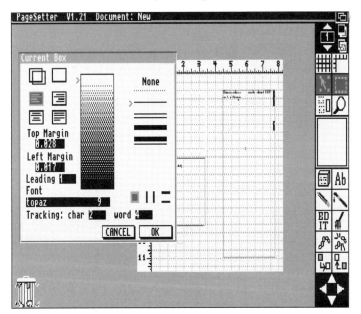

*Figure 22.1. Desktop publishing is ideal
for designing newsletters and flyers.*

More Figure Work

Accounts programs are naturally considered boring and unusable but they are sometimes a necessity. Not to take advantage of your Amiga if you are self-employed or run a small business is to waste an opportunity. An accounts program may be a daunting prospect but it is usually less so than a flexible tool such as a spreadsheet because the accounts program is set up ready to use, with forms on the screen to fill in and lists and categories already defined. You enter the data about your business and the program sorts out the figures. A printer is an important add-on for this kind of work because someone, eg your accountant or bank manager, will want to see the results and he may not have an Amiga!

Databases can also be used for running business affairs such as stock control, if they can handle the right type of data such as dates and money values. Programs like Superbase are suitable and are especially good at producing reports which you can design yourself on screen.

Home accounts is a different matter and can be handled by a simple spreadsheet model or by a specially written program which lets you manage different accounts. Home banking is possible using your computer as a terminal but the only bank offering this service is the Bank of Scotland and it doesn't seem to have caught on as yet for the home user. For a small business wishing to keep track of funds, it has considerable potential.

Figure 22.2. Microdeal's home accounts program.

Menu
Beginners
Workbench
Extras Disk
Preferences

23:
Programming
Languages

This may sound dramatic but your Amiga is a mere heap of silicon and metal without programs. Programs tell the components what to do.

The basic unit of a program is a single instruction. A program is made up from building blocks known as routines, procedures and functions, each of which are made up of instructions. The instructions are carried out under the control of structures such as loops, which repeat groups of instructions. Decision making commands send the program down particular paths depending on the state of the computer.

The programs don't grow on trees but are typed into the computer by a programmer into a text editor. Editors are important things for programmers. They are a special kind of wordprocessor designed to look after the layout of the program, to make it more understandable, to aid the productive entry of code through special key presses etc, and to check the program for errors, reporting them sensibly back to the programmer. The Amiga has its own editor in ED, described in detail elsewhere in this book. Modern programming can also involve describing the program in diagrammatic or graphical terms, which are then converted automatically into code of a more conventional nature.

High level – which means near English language – program instructions need to be converted to something the computer can understand. This is carried out by an *interpreter* or *compiler*.

A human interpreter at the European Parliament listens to what is being said in one language, for a few words, a few sentences at a time, and then passes the information on in a different language. This is also what a computer language interpreter does, in fact interpreting each command line at a time and passing on its interpretation to the computer's electronics.

A compiler is a more like a human language translator, though a bit quicker. It takes in the complete document (the program) and translates it all, making more than one pass over it if necessary, looking up bits in its dictionary (libraries) and, only when finished, sending the complete translation to the Amiga's processor.

The main consequences for programmers are usually to do with the speed of the finished program. An interpreter is held up when running a program by having to go to and from the processor and program. A compiler takes longer to translate the program but only when it is compiling a new faster version of the program (*compile time*). When this faster version is run (*run time*) there is no hold up to speak of.

AmigaDOS

AmigaDOS is an everyday part of using your Amiga and, as such, you'll find many practical examples for you to try in this book. AmigaDOS has few of the structures of a high level language but it offers direct control over the devices which make up your Amiga. It is interpreted line by line. If you wish to learn how to program in AmigaDOS then get a copy of Mastering AmigaDOS Volume One from Bruce Smith Books.

ARexx

I mention ARexx next because it appears as part of the system software on all new models of the Amiga. It can also be obtained as a complete package from its author Bill Hawes. The language is attracting attention because it fits in with the Amiga's ability to have more than one program running at the same time. Once you've got a couple of programs running side by side, the obvious question is: how can I get data from one to the other? In many cases ARexx will be the answer and many commercial programs have what is called *ARexx support*. Bruce Smith Books' Mastering Amiga ARexx is a complete tutorial on programming in ARexx.

BASIC and AMOS

The BASIC computer language, a standard way of programming on so many of the world's personal computers, has had a chequered history on the Amiga. What might have been if Microsoft's early AmigaBasic had been half good? Now there is no BASIC language bundled with the Amiga but there are a number of commercially available BASICs to choose from such as HiSoft, GFA and True BASIC. However none have captured the imagination of programmers wanting to show what they can do with the Amiga's strong points.

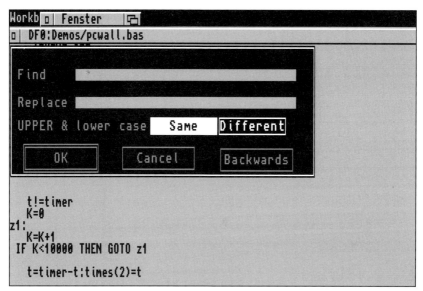

Figure 23.1. HiSoft BASIC provides an editor and a compiler which turns the instructions into a new program containing machine code.

The gap has been filled by the advent of AMOS, a programming environment which provides a set of commands familiar to BASIC users and with many additional features to bring both the programming facilities and its ability to drive the Amiga, up to date. AMOS is widely owned and there are many libraries of add-on utilities and programs written in the language. I've therefore devoted a couple of complete chapters to AMOS and what it can do and provided you with an introduction to the art of programming to give you an idea of what is involved.

Don't skip the next bit on the other languages but, if you are new to programming, AMOS may be the place to start your coding career on the Amiga. Get a copy of the Bruce Smith Books title *Mastering Amiga AMOS* to point you in the right direction.

Assembly Language

Something fundamental to the operation of the Amiga is the flow of instructions from the user to the chips which do the work. At our end, there's the press of a key or the click of a mouse button. At the chip's end there's a binary instruction, a string of 0s and 1s which carry the off and on switches for the electronics. This is called *machine code* and the level just above this is termed *assembly language* – half human, half Amiga, entirely unintelligible!

Actually the bias is heavily on the side of the machine so assembly language is the most difficult of computer languages to learn. The commands are typed into an editor, which has some checking functions built into it. The commands are then assembled – by running the assembler – into machine code.

Constructing routines in assembly language is very difficult and it is easy to forget what a piece of code is supposed to do. Programmers therefore add copious comments to their code to remind them what it does. Routines can be saved and merged into a new program when useful and some code can be generated automatically at *assembly time*. A bit of assembly language can be viewed in Figure 23.2:

START	move.w X, a0	copy X to lowest 16 bits of a0
	move.w a0, Y	copy lowest 16 bits of a0 to Y
	rts	
X	dc.w	10 allocate one word and initialise it to 10
Y	ds.w 1	allocate one word but do NOT initialise it

Figure 23.2. Some assembly language instructions.

Development Languages

You'll see references to many computer languages such as Forth, Logo, Cobol, Prolog, Fortran etc but, unless programming as study or a career is your aim, then you can go through life happily ignorant of what they are. If anything, the C family is the most interesting for the layman because it is in C that most of the Amiga's own operating instructions are written.

C is therefore the language of development of serious applications for the Amiga while Assembler is the natural language for games and other speed dependent programs. There's an example of C code in Figure 23.3.

Note that there are no line numbers in a C program and that the indented layout is designed to reflect the program operation. The code is developed inside a text editor and is then sent to a compiler which turns it into machine code which the processor chip in your Amiga can understand.

```c
#include <stdio.h>

#define maxint 5000
#define true   1
#define false  0

main ()
{ int i;
for (i = 2; i <= maxint; i++)
  {
  if (prime(i))
    {
    printf ("%5d",i);
    }
  }
}
```

Figure 23.3. C is a high-level language, in other words it has some recognisable words in it! The Amiga's own operating instructions are written in C.

Tools are available to link new code with libraries which perform standard tasks and which create different kinds of useful code – for instance to send data to the screen – without the programmer having to do any extra work. "Why reinvent the wheel?" is an important principle in programming. Commodore's own libraries of C code are available to serious programmers, at a price.

There aren't really any other languages being used for serious development on the Amiga but there are versions of other languages available for study and practice, such as Pascal and Modula 2. C++ is the likely successor to C because it is especially suited to the graphical elements of Amiga operation. Full versions of C++ are now available so look out for more talk of *object oriented* programming, which refers to the way in which compilers are now providing programming building blocks which can be linked together to create all the common elements of the graphical user interface (GUI) – our beloved Workbench.

For the beginner to programming, high level development tools such as *3D Construction Set* can be used as an alternative to writing code. They give the same sort of creative satisfaction and are worth investigating.

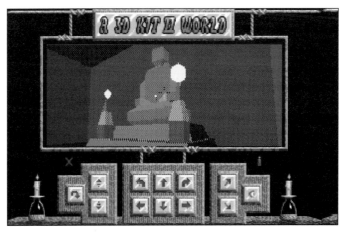

Figure 23.4. Why write code when you can move blocks.
Graphical environments can be created in programs like
3D Construction Set as this adventure screen shows.

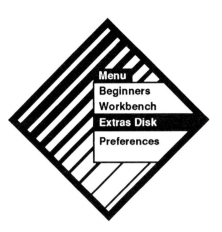

24:
The
Art of
Programming

If I softly utter the word *programming*, promise not to thumb past the next couple of chapters muttering to yourself, "Programming's for techies. I'd never be able to get into that."

Instead, just bear with us for the next chunkette of pages, as I try to persuade you how even the most basic mastery of programming can add enormously to the pleasure of owning your Amiga. Thanks to AMOS – one of the best pieces of software written for any computer, ever – you can bring your own imagination to creating, with almost indecent ease, a limitless variety of games, serious software, utilities, and a whole treasure chest of other programs that will look and perform as well as (and often better) than commercial titles.

Taking the Lid Off

Owning an Amiga without ever trying your hand at programming it to do things your way is like driving a Testarossa without ever changing up from first gear. There's nothing wrong in thinking of your Amiga primarily as a state-of-the-art games console-cum-PC and using it as just that most of the time, but to start enjoying the real rewards of owning the world's most powerful home computer, bring yourself to jettison the notion that programming is something that requires an IQ running into four figures or a grasp of conceptual mathematics that would make Blaise Pascal look like an abacus with a few beads missing.

Anything and everything that your Amiga generates on the screen of your TV or monitor is a just a response to a series of 0s and 1s – in essence, they're signalling yes or no – electronically interpreted and processed in a particular pattern and sequence. That principle (known as binary code), was behind the world's first computer, for which Charles Babbage pirated the concept of the punched cards used by 19th century English weavers – who themselves filched the idea from a French genius, Jacques Jacquard – to produce patterned cloth of previously undreamt of complexity. The punched sheets of music that drive a traditional pianola work the same way. And when you catch an old movie on late-night TV, you'll often see that even IBM computers were still using punched cards into the late 1960s, until someone came up with the idea of recording those streams of 0s and 1s on spools of magnetic tape – and software (which in those times meant the medium rather than the information that it carried) was born.

Mind Your Language

Writing sophisticated, task-specific software must have been a real pain in those early days, with only 0s and 1s to work with – imagine trying to write a book like this one using just a two-letter alphabet. Life got better with the creation of assembly language (aka machine language), which allowed the programmer to write software using a much more user-friendly set of *mnemonics*, such as JMP and LD – meaning jump to another part of the program, and load a certain value into the computer's memory.

Better was yet to come. In the 1960s, some clever clogs at Dartmouth College in the USA dreamt up something called the Beginner's All-purpose Symbolic Instruction Code – BASIC – which allowed anyone with it to write software which consisted of a series of instructions taking the form of ordinary English words and phrases, such as IF, AND, GOTO, and END. This series of instructions was called a program (a program of events if you like). To be able to run a BASIC program you needed some software that could recognise each instruction of the program and then act on it accordingly. This became known as the BASIC interpreter and down the years versions of this have become very sophisticated and quite clever.

BASIC – of which there are many versions – used to be supplied with the early Amigas but was finally dropped around the launch of the Amiga A500 Plus. However, there are some other versions of

BASIC around and I particularly recommend HiSoft BASIC. However, in 1988 AMOS was released and Amiga programming entered a completely new realm.

AMOS is a BASIC-type programming language that is geared towards writing games software and which takes advantage of, and fully exploits, the full potential of the Amiga. What is more it is available in several flavours and is cheap!

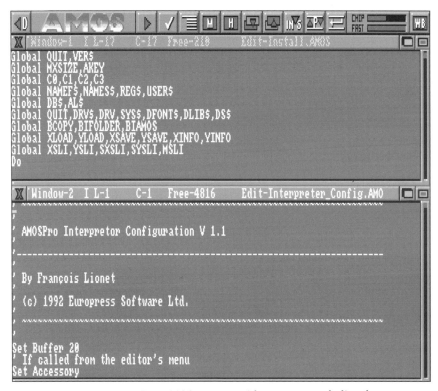

Figure 24.1. Two AMOS screens with program code listed.

Despite being a mainly games orientated language you can do virtually anything you want with AMOS (well, within reason). And learning AMOS will provide you with a very sound grounding in programming languages because, whether you are writing a shoot-em-up or a serious application, all programs have the same logical and straightforward structure. The rest of this chapter will explain that structure, and in the next you can find out more about AMOS and how it makes it easy to look after the twiddly bits.

Almost without exception, a program has three and only three working parts. It is easier to think of them as a trio of self-contained modules. The first is the equivalent of a prologue to a play in that it serves to set the scene by telling your Amiga how the screen will look, what will be displayed on it and how it is going to be managed when it's actually running. The second is the program loop, the third is the library of procedures that do individual things in the program.

The three key building blocks of any program are variables, statements, and commands. First things first. A variable is just that – something that can constantly change its value while the program is running, usually to reflect something that's happened. So one of the first lines in your program might be

SCORE=0

In this example, SCORE is the name that I've given the variable, and 0 is its initial value. Later in the game, when your Astrocruiser hits a Klingon, or whatever, you can introduce a statement – an instruction – to record your victory, like this:

SCORE=SCORE+10

Here SCORE is assigned the old value of SCORE plus 10. If SCORE was 0 then after this action it will be 10, because 0+10=10!

You can name a variable with just one or two letters if you like, such as:

SC=0

but, believe me, giving variables appropriate, unambiguous names will make life much easier for you later.

Incidentally, AMOS comes with a lot of invaluable, ready-made variables ready to go – such as JOY, which automatically detects joystick movement, and MOUSE, which locates exactly the whereabouts on the screen of the mouse pointer's hot spot.

String Serenade

Things like SCORE are known as numeric variables – they can only identify numbers. But there will be plenty of times when you want a variable to take the form of proper text that will be displayed on screen or used as part of the program's logic, such as in an adventure game. Text variables are called strings, and whatever name you choose for them must be rounded off with a dollar sign to distinguish them from numeric variables, like this:

TITLE$

PLAYAGAIN$

You can fill each string with whatever letters, words or numerals that you choose:

START$="Are you ready to play?"

RESULT$="Your score was"

Then you can use another word in BASIC's vocabulary, Print, to display the contents of a string on screen:

> **Print RESULT$+SCORE**

As you see, numeric variables and string variables can be chained together or to each other using simply the plus sign, so the result would be a screen message reading

> **Your score was 500**

where 500 was the value held by SCORE when the game finished.

The first module, then, is used to declare any variables you'll want to call up and modify, determine the look of the screen (which you can turn into a shimmering tapestry of pixels by loading up a ready-made design that you have created in Deluxe Paint or using a brilliant AMOS accessory called TOME), and even start music playing in the background.

Going Slightly Loopy

The second module, known as the *program loop*, is where all the action is. Here's where you stake out what will happen if, for example, the joystick is moved forward, your Pacman clone comes up against a dead end, or your Tetris-style coloured blocks don't fall in the right order. You can think of it just like a child's train set, where the loco runs round and round but stops when a signal is set against it or branches off in a new direction when it comes to a set of points.

Once you've started trying your hand at programming, you'll soon realise that certain routines, several lines making up a particular set of instructions, will crop up time and time again in the main loop – such as checking the joystick or mouse pointer location, creating a satisfying apocalyptic explosion when a baddie sprite is hit, or producing drop-down menus like those on Workbench.

Proper Procedures

If you were to bolt together all the routines that you want to in the main loop, one after another, it would slow everything down considerably, because the program would have to run through lots of bits it doesn't want next (such as a scoreboard, which it will usually only need last of all) to get to the one that it does. That might not be so important if you're writing something like a text adventure or database, but the effect on a fast-moving arcade-style game would be disastrous. It would be slowed down!

Helpfully, you can instead group the lines that make up a specific routine together as if they were little anterooms, and open the doors into them only when they're really needed. Together, they make up a program's third module. In BASIC they're called subroutines and in AMOS, Procedures. You give them each a unique name, and call them up from the main loop, like this:

If LIVES=0 then Procedure Scoreboard

Then tucked away at the end of the program you could have

SCOREBOARD

Print RESULT\$+SCORE

In this case, if the value of the variable called LIVES was equal to 0 then the Procedure called SCOREBOARD would be executed. Simple.

The nice thing about AMOS Procedures is that you can save them on their own to disk, just like a full-blown program. In that way you can build up a library of useful routines that you can import into any future programs that can make use of them, perhaps just changing the Procedure and variable names to something more appropriate. That saves a lot of time, because you don't have to keep writing the same routines over and over again!

Believe it or not, if you've managed to come to grips with that introduction to programming, even if you have to read through it a couple more times, you've mastered all the fundamentals of the art. All you need now is an easy way to apply them, and that's where AMOS comes in.

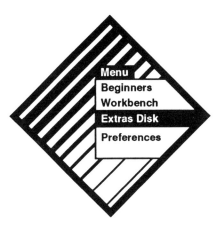

25: Access to AMOS

First choose your weapon. AMOS is available in three quite distinct flavours, and it is worth giving thought to the one that is just right for you at this stage in your programming career. AMOS pure and simple (which Phil South, author of *Mastering Amiga AMOS*, eloquently defines as *classic* AMOS) was the first to be hatched, back in 1990. From the first, its creator, François Lionet, and the program's publisher, Europress Software, adopted a policy of frequent updates and improvements, so the actual version of AMOS that you'll find on the shelf today will be v1.34 or an even later offing.

Ahead of the Game

Europress deliberately added a subtitle, making it *AMOS – The Creator*, because they did not want it to be thought of as just a sophisticated version of SEUCK or any other games creator. After all, AMOS is packed with enough advanced features to allow the user to create a wordprocessor, database, or any other sophisticated application, from scratch.

Open the box and you'll be greeted by a quartet of disks containing AMOS itself, demos, some useful accessories that can live alongside AMOS in memory, a library of ready-made sprites and other graphics that you can play around with in learning to use the language (and even incorporate, copyright free, in any program you create), and RAMOS – a special utility that allows you to produce stand-alone versions of your programs that will run on any Amiga 500, 600 or 1200, without having AMOS in memory.

Paging M. Lionet

The kit also contains a chunky manual describing AMOS's 500 commands in some 300 pages. The manual, it must be said, left something to be desired – at least in its earliest forms. It is doubtful whether anyone could have bettered Stephen Hill's valiant attempt to explain such a powerful new subset of BASIC – especially given the fact that he had to compile it at more than arm's length from AMOS's creator, and zat krazy Frenchman was busy fine-tuning certain features way after Stephen had already been committed to print. However, the manual also was subsequently corrected and revised, and you should find that the one that you get today is all present and correct.

Not so Basic

Although AMOS was marketed very much as an answer to a novice programmer's prayer, the truth is that it was very much more accessible and immediately usable to those who already had a fair amount of BASIC programming experience. AMOS was, in short, too much, too soon – and I dare say that not a few copies of it are living a lonely existence in some far-flung disk boxes, their owners having been discouraged from making any further use of it after a voyeuristic peek at the demos.

Getting a Move On

Part of the reason for that may have been the inclusion of AMAL – virtually a language within a language, which allows stupendously fast manipulation of sprites and other graphic elements without the slowdown that occurs – as I explained earlier – when, typically, the main program loop is stuffed with instructions for moving a large number of animated sprites. AMAL commands hit straight at the heart of the Amiga's blitter chip and others at the same time that the rest of the program is running. Using it is almost like bolting two Amigas together and piping their output to the same monitor. Stupendously powerful, but not for the faint-hearted, let alone the programming newcomer. I know, I was that faint-heart.

Back to the Drawing Board

Europress, who seem to be one of the most customer-conscious software houses around, must soon have realised that something was *not quite right*. Not that classic AMOS wasn't a success – it was the first programming language ever to hit the charts – but I suspect that a lot of feedback from purchasers was on the lines of, "I know that this is brilliant, but I just can't seem to get into it."

AMOS hadn't turned out to be quite the smooth segue into BASIC programming that novices – perhaps a little over-optimistically – had expected, and while the integrity of the image was unquestionable, it must have become clear that a fresh approach was needed if AMOS was to grab the hearts and minds of what was undoubtedly, and encouragingly, a veritable horde of would-be programmers.

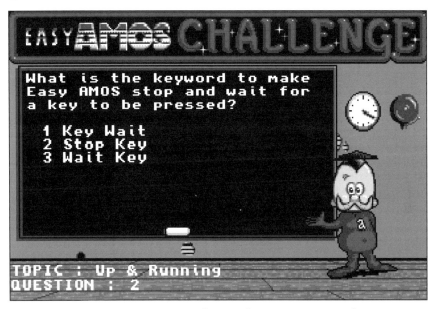

Figure 25.1. Easy AMOS teaches you how to program and even prints out a certificate at the end of your training session.

Now You See It

Enter, in 1992, son of AMOS in the form of (to give it Europress's full title) *First Steps to Programming – Easy AMOS*. Gone was Stephen Hill's studious manual in favour of a jokey, reader-friendly primer scripted by Mel Croucher, peppered with cartoons, and designed fairly and squarely to take the mystique out of programming.

Gone was AMAL, its place taken by a host of new goodies that make Easy AMOS absolutely irresistible. Chief among them is the on-screen tutor, an innovative and phenomenally useful helpmate that allows you to watch your program run in a miniature screen – rather like one of those clever digital picture-in-picture TVs – either at full speed or step-by-step, while simultaneously displaying the relevant lines from your AMOS program.

That makes it possible for you to write a few lines and immediately see what they do, then improve or amend the result as you like. And it's invaluable in hunting down the bugs that haunt even the most experienced programmer, because running the program a line at a time lets you easily identify any problem and correct it.

Another welcome feature is a series of built-in tutorial mini-programs that take your hand and gently guide you through all the concepts in the manual, but live on screen, so that you can see exactly how everything is meant to work. Work your way through that lot, answer the quiz that wraps the whole thing up, and AMOS will print out your own graduation certificate!

Definitely a First

If that brief round-up of Easy AMOS makes it sound over-simplistic and lacking in sophistication, I haven't done it justice. True, it doesn't offer AMAL, but bearing in mind the added speed that compiling a program brings (about which, more later), it's not likely that you'll find it stopping short of your needs for a long time to come. And when it does, you can update to Professional Amos at a discount. If you have never programmed before, or even if you had a stab at AMOS and lost heart, I cannot recommend too strongly the choice of Easy AMOS to really get you on the road.

Heavyweight Professional

Not content with hatching a duo that ostensibly appeals to programmers new and gnarled, Europress went on listening to the purchasers of their products and only a few months after launching Easy AMOS, unleashed Professional AMOS, which combines the very best features or its predecessors and then heaps on even more.

The invaluable tutor is still there, AMAL is back, Arexx control (a powerful interprocess communications language) makes its debut, it will run IFF ANIM files of the kind generated by Deluxe Paint – but even faster. Noisetracker and Soundtracker music files (such as those produced by MED) will now pipe up, and you can define your own macros to cut down on the amount of keyboard hammering that you have to do.

The tutorial concept is taken one step further with immediate on-line help. Position the cursor over a keyword, such as Procedure, and up pops an explanation and an example of how it should be used correctly. Brilliant.

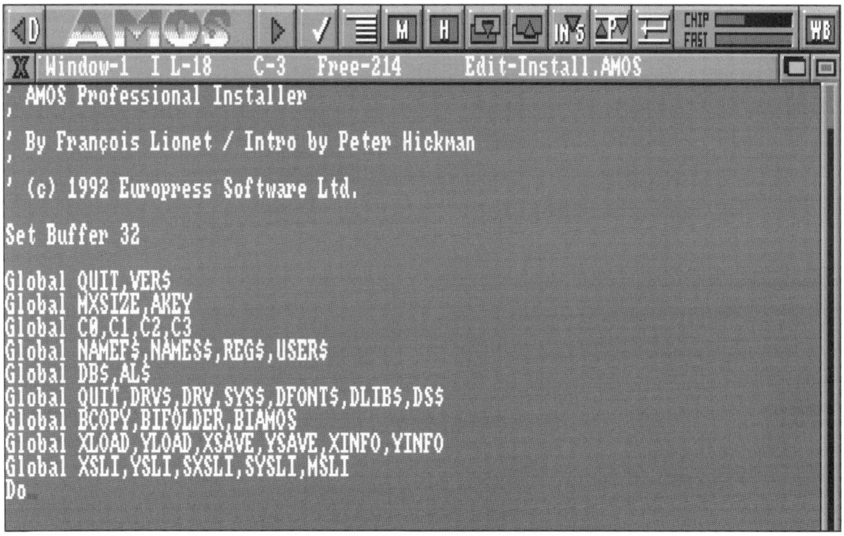

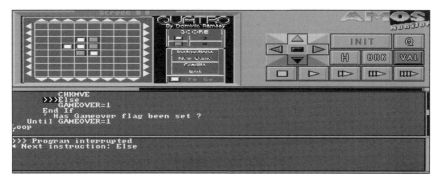

Figure 25.2. AMOS Professional's program editor.

Professional AMOS also sports a much smarter, Workbench 2-type editor, and more than 40 new commands to control your Amiga's device ports – useful for controlling that Robocop look-alike you've been constructing in the garden shed.

The new boy on the block also offers a couple of novelty features, such as an animated mouth that moves in sync to the synthesised speech that AMOS's Say command can generate. It is difficult to imagine what more any programmer could want, but no doubt Europress will add it if there is enough demand.

Figure 25.3. AMOS Pro's monitor with its picture-in-picture display showing simultaneously what appears on screen and the program code that creates it.

Bells and Whistles

I mentioned earlier that RAMOS – one of the accessories that comes with AMOS and Easy AMOS – lets you create stand-alone versions of your program that other Amiga owners can run independently. However, an even better option is to save up your pennies and buy the AMOS Compiler. This idiot-proof utility painlessly strips away all the bits of AMOS and other code that isn't really needed to create a new version of your program that may not only run considerably faster – important if you're interest is writing arcade-style games – but is more compact and pry-proof (your compiled BASIC program can't be listed, so no one can nick your lovingly crafted routines).

TOME of Your Own

Another invaluable bolt-on is Shadow Software's TOME, or total map editor. It allows you effortlessly to create scrollable memory-saving backgrounds or playfields stretching across hundreds of screens by building them up from a series of tiles, just like professional software writers do. The latest version, TOME 4, adds animated tiles, an improved editor, and a single command to permit eight-way scrolling! If your ambition is to write multi-platform or dungeon and dragon-type games, for example, TOME is a must and it will save you hours of preparation.

Sprites and Types

Once you really get going with AMOS, you'll find two other tailor-made utilities of particular value. Although all versions of AMOS come with their own sprite editor, it is not the best in the world, and SpriteX 2.0, a low-cost licenseware title, is a great improvement. Of equal value if you anticipate using lots of fancy display fonts in your programs or utilities (such as a video titler) is CText, also from Shadow Software. It makes light work of creating multicolour fonts of your own design, or you can load in, alter and enhance any of the hundreds of ready-made fonts that are available for next to nothing from PD libraries.

Joining the Club

One of the nice things you'll discover when you acquire any version of AMOS is that you're not just buying a product but joining a fraternity. For a start, there's the AMOS Club, run by Aaron Fothergill, who was closely involved in some aspects of AMOS from its earliest days and is the author of TOME and CText. The club regularly publishes a small magazine packed with helpful articles and sample programs, and offers a discount on Shadow Software products. The popularity of AMOS is also reflected by the coverage it receives in leading Amiga-specific magazines, such as *Amiga Shopper*, *Amiga Computing*, and *CU Amiga*. *Totally Amiga* is a magazine on disk, each edition of which is crammed full of articles, demos, graphics, and music. Well worth checking out.

Library Steps

AMOS users also benefit from one of the best PD/licenseware libraries on the Amiga scene. The Déja Vu Software collection, which is added to virtually daily by AMOS programmers happy to share their efforts with others, comprises hundreds of games, educational programs, utilities, music and sound samples, and goodness knows what else, all at bargain basement prices. A large proportion of the programs on offer can be loaded into AMOS and listed, so that you can see exactly how they were created and, needless to say, save yourself hours of toil by snaffling other people's ingenious routines.

Another source of AMOS-specific PD is the AMOS PD Library, and 17 Bit Software also stock a good selection of AMOS public domain software and licenseware titles.

Contacts

Europress Software
Europa House, Adlington Park, Macclesfield, SK10 4NP
Tel: (0625) 859333

Shadow Software/AMOS Club
1 Lower Moor, Whiddon Valley, Barnstaple, North Devon
EX32 8NW

Déja Vu Software
7 Holling Brook, Beech Hill, Wigan, WN6 7SG
Tel: (0942) 495261

Totally AMOS/AMOS PD Library
1 Penmynydd Road, Penlan, Swansea, SA5 7EH

26:
Virus
Menace

For some time I held out the hope that commonsense might inoculate Amigas against the new threat of computer viruses. But the phenomenon could not be kept at bay and there are now a large number in circulation. The task of every Amiga owner is to put them out of circulation and a number of utilities have been devised to achieve this.

A virus is a computer program, usually small, often disguised as something else. Its primary purpose is to reproduce itself in the memory of an Amiga and on floppy disks put into that Amiga. It may also have a secondary purpose, more of which below.

Viruses first caused panic in the world of business computing when rumours were spread about their destructive capabilities and the issue of data security remains a large one in constructing computer systems of any size. Even a personal computer like the Amiga can command vast amounts of data and any virus with evil intent can result in the loss of some, or all, of that data.

Viruses originate with a programmer who mistakenly believes it is clever to invade other people's computers. He or she saves a virus program onto a floppy disk and gives that disk to another Amiga user who puts it into their computer. This is the point of infection when the virus copies itself into the memory of the computer and from there onto other floppy or hard disks. This process of infection is repeated over and over again as disks are passed between computers.

A virus need not be malevolent, it could just be designed to reproduce itself, but the actual installation of a virus without your say so means that it is changing your system without permission. Viruses are not the only programs to do this so the reproduction element is what tells them apart.

Viruses don't usually tell you that they are infecting your disks but hide themselves in the nooks and crannies of computer memory and camouflage themselves as other types of file. Viruses do make themselves known through messages and strange goings-on such as malformed mouse pointers and wobbly Workbenches and these can be annoying. The worst can do damage to data and that's the very best reason to learn about them and do your best to prevent them. Killing and preventing viruses is therefore a matter for a professional hit man, a utility which knows about them, seeks them out and permanently deletes them.

Strains of Virus

The problem with viruses is that, despite the headaches they can cause, they also have a certain fascination for computer users, possibly because they represent one of those new aspects of computing which results in computer code which can regenerate itself, the beginnings of life? So I'll give way to this fascination and take a look at the main viruses which might infect your Amiga and how you might get rid of them.

Limpet

Often called the bootblock or boot sector virus. The term Limpet derives from the way the virus adheres to the bootblock of infected disks. These are the simplest viruses of them all – and usually the easiest to catch. These were also the first viruses to appear on the Amiga.

The very first Amiga Limpet came courtesy of Swiss Crackers Association or SCA – no prizes for guessing: pirates! Bootblock viruses consist of a small section of code which loads a disk's boot sectors when the computer is booted from an infected disk. Every time a new (write-enabled) disk, is inserted, the virus writes itself back to the new disk thus infecting it. Depending on the type of Limpet, some write themselves back during soft resets, others to every uninfected disk inserted.

Doppleganger

This works by replacing the code of an original program completely with its own. Next it moves the code of the original program somewhere else on the same disk and gives it a blank name. When the original program is called, the virus runs (doing its dirty work) then exits by launching the real program. Sounds complex? Not at all – three simple AmigaDOS calls can be used to do this. BSG9 was an early example of this type and can be identified by the tell-tale blank file it leaves in the DEVS directory of the infected disk. The AmigaDOS' LIST command shows it up – DIR does not. If found, BSG9 is usually the first command in the S:Startup-sequence and has a bytesize of 2608 when listed.

Trojan Horse

Sometimes just called a Trojan, this type has yet to crop up on the Amiga in large numbers for reasons which will shortly be revealed. Trojans get their name from the Greek fable of the Trojan (or wooden) horse.

As the story goes, the Greeks tricked the Trojans by leaving a wooden horse outside the gates of Troy. The Trojans dragged the horse inside, and at nightfall the Greeks hidden inside the beast crept in under cover of darkness and killed the Trojans in their beds.

In the same way, a Trojan virus is a computer program, usually placed in the Public Domain not by Greeks, but still with a very sharp sting in its belly. The reason why real Trojans are rare is because they take some skill to implement. The only way they will spread is if the program hiding the stinger is useful enough for lots of people to use. And once the Trojan is uncovered, everyone stops using it. For this reason Trojans use a time-bomb technique whereby they only activate after they have been used a set number of times or, sometimes, on a certain date. Most Amiga Trojans are genuine programs infected by a Parasite – see below.

Parasite or Linkvirus

Also called Worm, Zombie, Lycanthrope, and Vampire. These bloodsuckers are the scourge of utility software and generally a real pain in the Startup-sequence. Like real vampires they duplicate by attaching themselves to other programs. The problem with parasites is they turn genuine software into Trojans by locking onto their code and transferring across onto all and sundry. Like Trojans, Parasites are tricky to implement so there are less around. Unlike the Limpets, they multiply between disks and across directories at an alarming rate. Also they're very tricky to catch without software specifically designed for the purpose – Peter Cushing never had it this tough.

Signs of Infection

There are two mainstream effects of virus infection: destructive and nuisance. Neither are very pleasant – some viruses exhibit both.

Nuisance Effects

Silly messages

"Software piracy is theft...", "AmigaDOS presents: The IRQ Virus", "Something wonderful has happened" and so on. The only wonderful thing that could happen to the persons responsible for these gems would be the spontaneous combustion of their Amigas.

Reversed keys

The two Amiga keys, for example, suddenly become transposed.

Lock outs

The whole machine stops accepting keyboard input – but everything else appears to be working normally.

Obscene mouse Pointers

I kid you not – is nothing sacred?

Nasty Effects

Random trashing of files

Has the effect of causing programs to suddenly crash without warning, corrupts data in pictures, music and text. Lamer Exterminator is known to have this effect.

Random trashing of disk block checksums

Difficult one to pin to a virus because it can also happen through wear and tear, badly stored disks and a whole host of other things. Likely sign of a virus if it starts suddenly.

Random guru meditations

As above, this can happen through poorly written software so might happen quite innocently. It is possible to *guru* AmigaDOS at a pinch.

Protecting Against Them

It only takes one slip to catch a virus because once the little beggars get onto a disk, they spread very quickly. This checklist covers the most important points.

1. No known virus can get past the write protection notch on a floppy. Never insert a write enabled disk unless something has to write to it. Better still keep data disks separate from program disks. If a virus gets into memory it can only be kept off disks which are either (a) never booted or (b) don't contain any executable files.

2. Keep a Canary disk. This is a freshly formatted disk with a couple of commands and a Startup-sequence. If a Limpet tries to attach itself this disk will suddenly become bootable. A suite of programs to make Canary disks (and a lot more) is included with Mastering AmigaDOS 2 Volume One.

3. Get a disk of Virus killers from your friendly PD library and check every file and bootblock of every disk you get before attempting to boot them or run any of the programs contained therein.

4. Never, ever, use pirated software. This includes games, utilities and applications – it's a sure-fire way to catch a virus.

Killing Viruses

The only sure way to be virus free in this day of over 100 known viruses is to use a virus killer program. If you don't have a virus killer (and I strongly urge you to get one) then there is something you can do, although it is a little fiddly and doesn't help with all types of virus.

Virus Killers

There are a great many virus killers on the market, and all of them are freely distributable. PD houses stock them, and usually you can guarantee that a virus killer disk at least will be free of viruses. (Obviously the guy who programmed the killer would take the trouble to kill the viruses on his own system!) There are many different types, and all of them are pretty good by now, having undergone many different revisions since the virus problem became apparent on the Amiga in around 1987.

However, at the time of writing two of the best available are ZeroVirus and Master Virus Killer, which both cover over 100 viruses and seem to be the most intelligent about which bootblocks and files they kill. As well as these programs to detect and kill a virus, if you think you have a problem, I'd recommend having a small killer in the C directory on your bootdisk, with a command to run it in your startup-sequence. I'd suggest CV, because it seems small enough to fit on a floppy as well as a hard drive. Check out our chapter on using AmigaDOS which will help you install such a program.

Note: Most of the above killers are available on 17 Bit Software PD disk number 949. Master Virus Killer v2.1 is on 17 Bit disk 894.

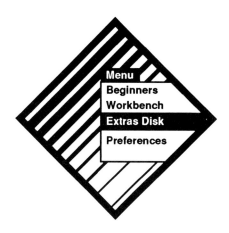

27:
Upgrading

Hardware is expensive and you've already got a lot of high technology under your belt with the Amiga itself so you might not be intending to get the bonnet up on your micro for some time yet. Although it rather depends on which computer you do have. If you have a model which takes add-in cards then you probably bought it with the intention of increasing performance in some way. All of us however are in the market for the more interesting add-ons in life, even if it's just window shopping part of the time.

This pocket guide to hardware extensions to your computing repertoire skims the surface of what is available. Technology changes constantly so check your magazines and local dealers to see what's new.

The computer software which Commodore provide with their Amiga computers has a sophisticated look about it, with icons and menus etc. But this user-interface is sitting on top of AmigaDOS which is a set of programs which glues together parts of the computer system such as the monitor and the disk drives.

When AmigaDOS can handle a new type of monitor then you can go out and buy one, and not before. If AmigaDOS doesn't know what an IDE hard drive is then it will do you little good to purchase one. So take advice on which hardware can be sensibly added to your Amiga and the version of AmigaDOS which you have running on it. You may need to upgrade the version of AmigaDOS together with your hardware, which shouldn't be a problem.

The Importance of RAM

RAM (Random Access Memory) is where the computer remembers the information you have put into it. But your Amiga has a short (volatile) memory and forgets almost everything when you turn it off. I say "almost" because it does remember what to do when you turn it on, which is to look for a Workbench (or Kickstart on early models) disk.

This simple fact about computer memory determines a lot about how you go about upgrading your Amiga. If you find the Amiga is so useful that you use it all the time and use lots of different programs then you'll notice that you have to load a program and any data it's working on from disk every time you want to use it. And, although in theory you can have many programs operating in your Amiga at the same time, you'll find that the practical limit is quickly reached.

The solutions to these problems is to upgrade your Amiga, which means buying additional bits of electronics to plug into your computer to improve its performance. If you have lots of programs but you use them separately, for example a wordprocessor and a game, then you should look first at disk storage, an extra floppy, or more likely a hard drive.

If you use programs with a common aim, for example a DTP program, a drawing program and an image processing program, then keeping these together in the computer's memory may have added benefits (eg data can be quickly transferred between them) and so you should look first at extra memory. Heavy users of such programs will also gain productivity from improving their Amiga's sped through a new or additional processor and storage, through a hard drive.

Adding On

A common term when talking about upgrading is *add-on* and this more properly describes boxed units which plug onto external connectors of your Amiga, units such as a cased hard drive, a sound sampler, a MIDI interface etc. The add-on is sometimes secured to the side of the Amiga with some kind of bolt-on assembly.

Extra memory is usually an *add-in* and so too are IDE hard drives. The electronics on these *boards* (from printed circuit *board* – PCB) is so compact that they can be fitted onto connectors provided for this purpose on the Amiga's main board.

Those models of Amiga which come in metal cases with separate keyboards can be upgraded through the purchase of *cards*. These Amigas are suitable for those who wish to have PC (MSDOS compatible) capability, extra processors or interfaces to specialised equipment. These extras are not denied to other Amiga owners but can come more expensive because the electronics to connect them has to be provided by the add-on.

Returning to RAM to round up our thoughts on upgrading, memory boards can be purchased in two ways: populated and unpopulated. The latter contains no memory at all, just the connecting electronics. It's then up to you to buy the cheapest RAM chips and to plug them in. When populated, a board has RAM installed – although it needn't be all the possible RAM it can hold. For instance you might buy a 8 megabyte (Mb) RAM upgrade board but you can only afford to buy 2Mb worth of RAM chips. Later you can buy and install the extra 6Mb. The potential problem here is that every year or so a new bigger capacity, smaller size, cheaper chip is designed and made, at which point the older chips tend to become less available and therefore more expensive. So preferably buy populated boards.

Adding an Extra Floppy

It might be that you've decided on a second floppy disk drive on grounds of cost and this is a sensible, but usually temporary, course to take. This is an exercise which all Amiga owners can carry out and merely involves purchasing a second drive which can be plugged into the back of the Amiga. AmigaDOS then recognises any Amiga formatted disk placed into the drive in the same way it recognises the internal drive. A second drive allows you to leave the Workbench disk in one drive while using the other as a data disk.

Adding a Hard Drive

What is a hard drive? Often referred to as a fixed disk, the hard drive is a magnetic disk spinning very fast inside a sealed container. Drives are mass manufactured and have a low level format placed on them. When a hard drive is prepared for use on an Amiga, a second format is placed on top, one which AmigaDOS can recognise.

The main points to consider when buying a hard drive are: how much storage will you need next year, not now? Will you want to use the drive interface as a route to further expansion? Have you an expansion port free or will you need an expansion system? Watch out for: old technology, small capacity drives; potential noise in a school classroom or home environment; external drives take up valuable desk space; you'll need utility software to backup a hard drive.

After extra memory, the hard drive is the most useful general add-on you can buy for your computer. The first productivity gain is the simple fact that everything happens very much faster. Secondly you can much more easily employ the filing cabinet metaphor of the disk filing system without having to search for the correct floppy disk every time you want to use a file.

AmigaDOS itself can also benefit from having a hard drive. The reason for this is that AmigaDOS needs to access a number of resources from disk storage so the faster the storage the better the response time of the system. When operating with large files such as screendumps or scans, you'll see an immediate benefit.

Programs will load more quickly into memory and, if RAM is short, you can swiftly quit one program and load another. Day to day activities on the Workbench such as booting up, file copying and archiving, take up much less time. Making backups becomes less of a chore and so you do it more often, thus avoiding loss of data and more time recovering it.

When files are copied between applications, there is often some hidden disk activity as temporary files are created by the system. If the storage device is slow, ie a floppy drive, the process takes longer. Some applications use overlaying techniques so they need the program disk to hand, on a hard drive this action does not demand your intervention. Other applications, like databases, run out of space on a floppy disk and thus restrict you to a certain number of records, on a hard drive this is unlikely to occur.

A hard drive is also a sensible first add-on purchase because the amount of data that an Amiga program sometimes generates in RAM can exceed the floppy storage of a disk. A new high density disk format may be a response to this growing problem but for existing owners a hard drive should be considered first. Clip art, sound samples, multimedia databases and even games are getting fatter all the time.

There's no reason why you shouldn't have two hard drives and you can mix the types of drives. Perhaps you can afford an IDE drive now but will look to an additional SCSI interface and drive in the future. You can choose to have an internal drive or external, cased and with its own power supply and possibly fan for cooling.

Different Technologies

There are several hard drive upgrade possibilities. Third party add-on drives can be added to the expansion port of an Amiga. Amigas such as the A600 and A1200 can be upgrade with IDE drives fitted internally. Amigas which can be upgraded by installing cards can have a SCSI card and drive(s) fitted. Others have the drives attached via an expansion port.

The IDE (Integrated Drive Electronics) concept brings together both interface and drive mechanism on one plug-in card. AmigaDOS handles all the communication with the mechanism and you just see and manage the files on the Workbench.

IDE supports two drives, the master and slave, so it's worth checking to see what the manufacturer offers in the way of second drives so that you are prepared for future upgrades should they become necessary.

With SCSI (Small Computer Systems Interface) you are dealing with a much more general standard which can support up to seven daisychained devices. In other words, the first SCSI device can pass the interface through to a second device and so on down the line. One of the advantages of the SCSI standard is that it is device independent so, with the advent of SCSI-based CD ROM drives, tape backup systems, optical drives and even SCSI printers, this has many advantages for future expansion.

Hard Drive Speeds

What do you want from our hard drive? Reliability, speed and ease of use seem reasonable criteria for purchase. Reliability may come from the mass manufacture of the hardware but you should look for guarantees and the reputation of the supplier.

Quoted speeds for average access time and are given in milliseconds, say 10 m/s. The average of writing to and reading from the hard disk (not necessarily in equal number) gives the average access time. The smaller the quoted time, the better the performance. You will also find references to transfer rates and sustained transfer rates, given in both kilobytes and megabytes per second so watch your Ks and Ms. Speeds are also sometimes quoted for different hardware eg A1200 operation.

The main experience you get when you upgrade to a hard drive is one of speed. Everything happens many times faster than on floppy disk. Check on speed if the product has been around for more than 12 months because it may be old technology. Only if you want hard drive speed for a particular purpose, such as heavy duty sampling from instruments (scientific or musical) direct to disk, will you need to make speed your main criterium. Normally you will probably find other parameters equally important in making your choice.

Hard Drive Backup

As affordable hard disks get bigger, you commit more and more data to this storage and, although hard drives are getting more reliable, crashes are not unknown.

Nor need it be a hard disk error which loses all your data, it could simply be a mistaken use of the delete or copy facilities. It is not that difficult in the Workbench to select multiple files without really knowing it. So, instead of deleting the one file you've finished with, a second also mysteriously disappears.

Another easy trap to fall into is to load an old file as the basis of a new piece of work. You load it with the intention of using it as a template and you are going to save the new document under another name. Then, following the habits of a computing lifetime, you choose save from the file menu without changing the filename and in that instant the original file is lost.

It can't be stated too often or too strongly: back up your data regularly and thoroughly. Because your hard disk will begin to contain important system files and your resources will be ordered as you want them, it is important to backup the complete hard disk on a regular basis. How regular might depend on your hardware. A 20Mb hard disk to floppies is boring but acceptable. One hundred Mb to floppies is going to become a bit of a chore. If you are looking at big disk sizes then you will also need to look at backup systems, perhaps to tape which is automatic and doesn't need you to keep popping back to insert another floppy disk.

As well as regular complete backups, it's not a bad idea to backup specific work in progress. If you have just completed a day's work in front of the computer, say a DTP document or a C program, then a few minutes backing up the file or the relevant directory is excellent value in terms of insurance.

File Management

Creating a directory structure, especially on a hard disk, is an exercise worth taking some time over. Think about where programs should belong. Does the form printing utility go into a utilities directory or in with the printer drivers. Do you like to group programs under their function, perhaps together with the data files with which they work, or by category, so that you put all the programs into one directory and all the data files into another.

Matching up with a Monitor

Since you spend most of your time observing the output from your Amiga through a monitor screen of some kind, it makes sense that you should match this viewing device with your precise requirements. The Amiga range is very flexible when it comes to display devices and different models support anything from an ordinary television to a 19" big screen monitor.

To view output on a television your computer will have to have a modulator but it has to be said that even the best modulator cannot do justice to true quality of the graphics display. However it is an easy way to use your Amiga without breaking the bank. The latest models of the Amiga have a modulator built into them but earlier models may need a modulator add-on which fits between the monitor output on the back of the Amiga and the television.

A quick tip if you use a television is to use any spare video input socket on the back of the TV in preference to the aerial socket. If you do have a video input then buy a cable to make the connection from the video output (yellow). Connect the sound outputs (red and blue) too if you have a stereo TV. All three will go into a single SCART plug for connection to the most modern TVs.

Another tip, if you are plugging in and unplugging your Amiga regularly is to use any video and audio connections on the front of your TV or VCR. Many TVs and VCRs now have connections on the front intended for camcorders but also ideal for your Amiga!

A monochrome monitor can be used for wordprocessing or other text based work but it hardly does the graphic chips' capabilities justice. The Amiga's special video controller chips mean that you can have a choice of numbers of colours and a choice of resolution. The display you look at is usually a compromise between these two elements. A standard colour monitor is the most popular choice of display, fine for anything from games to DTP. Becoming more popular but still relatively expensive are VGA and multisync monitors, which can display more of the Amiga's screen modes.

A screen mode is a definition of how the screen should appear, how many pixels should be used horizontally and vertically and how many colours should be available for display. Because the pixels you can see on your monitor are held in the computer's memory, each one takes up a bit more valuable RAM. More colours take up more RAM because, to make up each colour you see, the computer needs to mix a number of red, green and blue pixels.

The Workbench, the most familiar of screens on the Amiga, is made up of 600 pixels across, 200 pixels down – its resolution – and four colours. At this resolution, the screen can have up to 256 colours (16 in early Amigas). The resolution of the screen can be increased to 600 x 400 pixels. A common lower resolution screen is 320 pixels across and 200 pixels down with 256 colours (32 in early Amigas). Hold And Modify (HAM) and other variations are available to increase both resolution and colour and these are reliant on there being appropriate software to display the pictures. For instance, there are paint programs which work specifically in HAM mode. DCTV, IFF24 and other improvements have been introduced as add-ons to the basic Amiga, so if you need higher quality for DTP or video work then it's available.

The latest Amigas can handle more colours and higher resolutions and some of these cannot be viewed on standard monitors, which brings VGA and multisync into the frame. VGA is a standard type of monitor for PCs so the prices are good but the range of display is still limited. Multisync monitors do what their name suggests, they synchronise their display with a range of output from the Amiga and can thus handle all the available screen modes. Watch out however for multisync monitors which have overtaken the Amiga and cannot cope with the lower resolution modes anymore!

Input Devices

The main input devices you already have: keyboard and mouse. Next on the list for games playing is the joystick and there's a good crop to choose from, some with highly entertaining shapes, some in the shape of cartoon characters etc. There are even special sticks and wheels for flight simulators and car racing.

Touch screens are useful for young children or children with special needs but are not for mainstream consumption. Touch tablets are cheaper and also very appropriate for young children who can't handle a keyboard. A cheaper option is the light pen which lets you point at the screen with a pen-like device. Graphic tablets – often called digitisers in the USA – are a different matter. They are highly sensitive pads set up to represent co-ordinates on the screen, used with a pen and for detailed graphics work.

A popular input device for CAD work is a tracker ball, an upside down mouse with a large ball on top and buttons beside. Finally, if your mouse cable gets caught up on the furniture, you can get a cordless mouse which works like the infra-red control on your video.

Digitisers

Perhaps the most exciting of all the add-ons for the Amiga, a digitiser captures real |life and stores it in window a few centimetres square on your desktop, from where you can drag it to disk storage or to a paint program, database or desktop publisher.

Digitising is the process of transferring video images into the Amiga's memory for editing, rerecording or printing out. The digitiser is perhaps the best-known add-on for a computer after the disk drive and the printer. You simply run a cable from your VCR or camcorder to an input socket on the digitiser. You calibrate the system from a screen menu and click a mouse button to capture or grab a frame of video. Some systems let you automatically capture frame sequences and perform effects such as reversing out, contrast adjustment and colour enhancement.

The description above is how most pictures are captured but there are some different techniques you should know about. the most important distinction to make is between realtime and non-realtime digitising. In realtime digitising you view a constantly changing version of live video playback in a window on your computer. You choose the moment you wish to capture and press the button. The digitiser holds the video frame in memory (often on its own card) and converts it to the appropriate picture format so you can use it.

Non-realtime digitising means that the subject to be captured needs to be still ie when using a VCR, you'll need to use the VCR's freeze frame facility and when using a camera, you'll need to stick to still life. You've heard about the downside but there is an upside. Because the digitiser electronics needn't be in a hurry, it can take longer to scan the subject, can scan it more than once and can compare scans to iron out any problems. For this reason non-realtime digitised pictures are often of a very high quality.

The video signal needs to split up into red, green and blue components if you are to view it on your monitor and this is usually done by electronics on board the digitiser card or sometimes in a separate splitter box. Some pictures however can be painstakingly captured through RGB filters with the old monochrome digitisers and a monochrome camera.

It's surprising the number of times that digitising involves trying to capture a sequence of pictures. Good digitising software addresses this requirement and thus overcomes a bunch of frustration trying to accurately position video tape. The number of frames between grabs can usually be set by the software, providing frames for animation and even a form of time-lapse photography. It could be used to instantly summarise a long documentary film or to show a flower opening in the morning sun (via a video camera). Individual frames can be edited out or saved if required.

Scanners

You use a scanner with an existing picture, or artwork, of some sort. The scanner device is cabled up to your Amiga via an add-on box. It passes some light sensitive electronics over the picture and captures it as a pattern of dots.

There are two main categories of scanners: handheld and flatbed. There are also drum scanners but they tend to be very expensive indeed and needn't concern us. Handheld scanners are generally the same width as a piece of A4 paper. You pull them across the artwork you wish to scan. A flatbed scanner looks a bit like a desktop photocopier. You lay the artwork face down on a glass panel and drop the lid down on top to secure it. The scan takes place under software control.

The number of dots in the scanned picture depends on the resolution setting of the scanner – normally from 75 dots per inch (dpi) to 400 dpi for handhelds, up to 600 dpi for flatbeds. Different scanning modes are usually provided for scanning photographs and line art (mono). The pattern (or screen) used to group the dots to represent the tones in the original picture is also an important factor in how the picture will come out on screen. These dot arrangements can be modified to change values such as contrast and brightness.

A black and white scanner costs considerably less than a colour scanner and you can't upgrade from one to the other. A colour scanner can be used to scan black and white material. Colour scans are very attractive but they tend to result in large picture files.

Think of scanning text as scanning a picture of some text. That's how the scanner software thinks about it! It scans a page of text as a page of graphics, not much use if you want to use your favourite font design. Enter another acronym: OCR. Optical Character Recognition has turned out to be one of the more difficult things for a computer to do, but the boffins are beginning to get the hang of it. More, and better, OCR software is beginning to appear.

An OCR program looks at the graphical shapes of the text and guesses which letters or numbers the shapes represent. It uses dictionaries of shapes and applies contextual rules to guide its interpretation so, for instance, it shouldn't put an I in the middle of a telephone number but should know that a 1 is required.

MIDI

Musicians need to know about this bit of hardware which connects, via a cable, music software running in your Amiga, with professional musical instruments. I refer budding Beethovens to our chapter on sound and music.

Control

The Amiga's printer and serial ports can be put to good use in this area. Computer control of the outside world involves interfacing the computer in some way with the devices to be controlled. For instance, a program to control a robot arm will take instructions in the form of *up, down* and angle of rotation and interpret these into binary (on and off) codes. These codes are sent, via the serial or printer port, to the interface electronics (usually in the traditional black box) which turn the on/off instructions into electrical impulses to drive motors a certain number of steps, causing the robot arm to move as instructed.

Lights can be turned on and off, model railways can be made to run to time under computer control and the computer's clock can be used to provide delays and to trigger events when you are not around. It's a fun area to get into and, if computers and electronics are a potential career, it's the first step on the ladder.

Networking

This is a growing area in the wider world of computers, especially in big offices. It involves laying cable between the desktop computers so that people can send messages to each other and share equipment, such as laser printers and CD ROM drives. As a truly personal computer, the Amiga is rarely called upon to take part in such group activities.

Genlocks

A vital part of the desktop videographer's repertoire, the genlock mixes the two, formally incompatible, signals from the Amiga and the video device. It locks the two signals together so that they cAn be displayed together on a monitor. There's no more physical space in the picture area so the video and computer graphics are combined in ways determined by the genlock and any software control it may be under. For instance, the video picture might fill the whole screen with any computer graphics overlaid, either solid or see-through. On the other hand the computer graphics might fill the screen with the video action only showing through a window, which might be programmed to move along a predetermined path.

As well as creative control, you should consider signal quality when choosing a genlock. You pay more for better electronics which provide a better signal for more professional results, especially if you have already invested in semi-pro S-VHS and Hi-8 video equipment.

Fax Modems

Definitely the in thing, fax modems are the logical development of the modem, which is used for sending computer data, to incorporate the bleeps and squeals which a fax will understand. A fax machine is in fact a combination of modem, scanner and printer – all everyday Amiga peripherals. The great thing about sending a fax directly from your keyboard is that you don't have to wait for it to be printed out, you don't have to rely on the substandard scan of your lovely printed document and you don't waste any more trees. Unless of course you are sending it to a fax machine rather than another fax modem!

Receiving faxes directly to disk and on to screen is just as good. You can look at your incoming messages and print out only those that interest you. If you wish to use any text from a fax then you'll need fax software which has built-in optical character recognition (see OCR) to do the interpreting for you.

Accelerator Cards

The chips inside your Amiga are members of a family of chips designed to work together. Some are unique to the Amiga, others are widely available on the open market and so talented electronics designers are always coming up with ways of matching the Amiga up with them.

The questions you always have to ask about an accelerator card are: will my software work with it? and can I upgrade the model of my Amiga to get the same performance at a similar cost? The answer to the latter is usually no but there are moments in the Amiga product cycle when a new machine becomes available with, for instance, a new processor.

The chip family I am talking about is the 680x0 family from American manufacturer Motorola. Your Amiga will have a 680x0 processor of one kind or another in it and you may want to improve on its performance by upgrading to a later version, for instance from a 68000 to a 68030. You can do this by getting an accelerator board which contains the 68030 chip and the electronics to divert your Amiga's attention away from the old chip and over to the new one. You will often find that, in making this kind of upgrade, you get a combined upgrade of processor chip – the 68030 in this case – and of a support chip called a maths processor which handles certain software instructions more efficiently than the processor itself. This chip is only useful if your software knows how to send the appropriate instructions to this new chip.

The sort of processor chips I've been talking about run at a speed determined by a number of factors in the design of the accelerator card. The speed is quoted as Mhz and a 68030 at 25Mhz goes slower than a 68030 at 33Mhz.

CD

CDs can carry computer data as well as musical sounds. The Amiga can connect to a special CD player – Commodore's own make – and can load games, pictures, Public Domain software, whatever is being published on CD, as long as the CD itself is in Commodore's own format. The Amiga can't read CDs made for other computers. The Amiga can also be used to control the playback of audio CDs from a control panel on the screen.

The phenomenal thing about a single CD is its capacity. To give you an idea: In 1986 Fred Fish started his PD library, issuing new disks on a regular basis and with increasing frequency. By late 1992 he had issued some 660 disks. With the advent of CD, you can buy them all on one shiny disc, and for a fraction of the price of the equivalent floppies.

The CD is best suited to providing these large amounts of data, such as picture libraries and encyclopedias although reading information from a CD isn't as fast as reading from a hard drive. Recordable CDs are now available for commercial use and, given faster access times, perhaps the CD could become as common as the floppy disc is now.

Serial Communications

Assuming you've got the telephone, the modem (MOdulator/DEModulator) is the only add-on required to get into comms. See the separate chapter on this subject for a full run down on what can be achieved.

Card Sharp

The introduction of a PCMCIA card slot into some models of Amiga caused a bit of a stir amongst games players who saw it as the route to cartridge games on the Amiga. Although this may be so, the PCMCIA is a standard connection to the outside world which can be used for adding extra memory in a convenient, credit card sized, plug-in, form. New types of memory will make bigger and bigger RAM sizes possible. Another useful type of memory is powered by a battery which means that you can remove the PCMCIA card and the information in the memory will be retained. You could then put the card into another computer and it could read the information. All sorts of add-on are likely to become available in this handy format, from memory to modems and beyond.

Emulation

Love it or hate it, the inescapable fact of life is that MSDOS is the world standard operating system. It, or a clone of it, is run on just about every PC on this planet. For this reason one of the major obstacles any manufacturer comes across when it produces a non-standard computer (that's one that doesn't use MSDOS) is that most people want to use DOS at some point or another.

There are two routes to MSDOS use on an Amiga. Firstly, if your Amiga can accept upgrade cards then you can install the PC electronics and operating software and switch between being "in" the Amiga and "in" the PC. Secondly, a software emulator, a program which creates a "virtual PC", can be run. The Amiga then takes on the appearance of a slow running PC. The emulator program intercepts your input or the commands of a PC program which you run and converts it all into something that the Amiga electronics can act upon.

A number of attempts have been made to turn the Amiga into an Apple Macintosh. Although the two computers use similar processor chips the task is complicated by the fact that all the Mac operating software is in chip form and Apple do not make these chips widely available. With computer prices falling everywhere, I have to point out that emulation can offer little advantage over actual purchase of the computer in question.

Although it is difficult to recommend using an emulator for extra productivity unless you really have to. More useful is the ability to copy data files onto a disk which has been formatted for another computer. The most useful format, because most computers can read it, is that of MS-DOS, the 720K size. Our chapter on CrossDOS will help you out on this subject. If you don't have CrossDOS on your Amiga then you can purchase a utility to format a disk as MS-DOS in your Amiga floppy drive, and to copy files to it from your Amiga disks, often via the Ram Disk.

Possible exceptions to the above warning about emulations are those which provide the operating environment of old computers such as the Commodore 64, Sinclair Spectrum and BBC Micro. These offer budget access to the vast libraries of software for these computers, much of which may still be useful.

PC Software

The business software available on the Amiga is of a high standard but the number of programs is small compared to the PC world, which is where a PC add-on board or emulator might come in. The cost of PC business software is quite prohibitive for general home consumption and the copyright laws mean that you shouldn't be using an office copy of software on you machine at home. However, there is a vast range of shareware software which offers clone facilities of the major packages at a fraction of the cost and these are worth considering.

Shareware programs are widely available for MS-DOS and some programs offer a range of features which you would normally expect to pay hundreds of pounds for. Documentation is usually provided on the discs and most offer on-line help when in use. As always complete compatibility cannot be guaranteed but if you use PC programs such as Wordstar, Lotus or Dbase, there are operationally similar and data compatible programs available as Shareware. This is also a source of material such as picture and CAD files.

Compatibility

One word of warning. Although emulators can offer full working DOS environments they are not 100% compatible with all PC software. Thus you should avoid buying PC software on spec and expecting it to run. There are no hard and fast rules as to ensuring compatibility but if you bear in mind the following points you should not go far wrong.

*   A lot of DOS software expects to run off of a hard disc. This is because the software is often large in size and will often run as modules which load automatically when required. Look to see if the software requires a hard disc. If you don't have one avoid the software.

- Most large programs require 640K of memory to run (eg dBASE IV) so to accommodate these you will need an Amiga with enough memory fitted to accomodate the emulator and the program.

- Software that expects propriety hardware and extra memory in the form of expanded or extended memory will not work.

- Software that does not access the components of the PC through the DOS routines will not work – this typically includes games and any protected software.

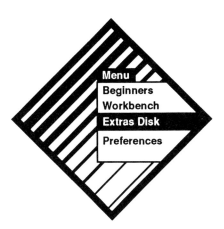

28: Software Choice

Washed ashore on a desert island with, coincidentally, your Amiga and a disk box, what would you choose to find in the box? Which software would you consider essential? It is an impossible task to take you through the huge range of software available for your Amiga, so let's take a brief look at the sort of software you might need as you progress with your new computer at home.

Everyone has a restricted access to software, through ignorance of its existence, through the restrictions placed upon all of us by a financial budget, and in some cases through inadequate hardware. Therefore we all have to make important choices about what software will be particularly appropriate to our requirements.

Home Entertainment

With few exceptions we all enjoy using our computers and one man's entertainment is another's late night slog with assembly language programming. Games cannot be mistaken for anything other than great fun and there are many games of various types to choose from.

There are many categories of game and designers keep coming up with original ideas to challenge and entertain. But there are some classic formats you can look out for. Arcade games include shoot-em-ups when you control a craft or character which has to fight its way through different obstacles using weapons, from fists to bazookas. The fight games pitch fighters with different strengths and attributes against each other and demand dexterous keyboard performances from the players.

The adventure game introduces a strong story element and quite complicated puzzles and, recently, stunning pictures to add atmosphere to the exotic locations of many of these games. The arcade adventure brings together both elements, offering tasks to perform and puzzles to solve but in an arcade environment with animated characters and action.

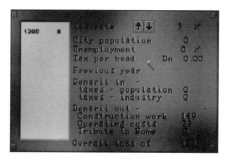 

Figure 28.1. Caesar is an example of the popular strategy game format, sometimes historical, sometimes sci-fi.

Mind games and word games are also very popular and block puzzles, crosswords, Scrabble, Trivial Pursuit, Cluedo and many others are available in computer form. Sports simulations are a whole different ball game and football is number one by far with games based on and off the pitch. Car racing, tennis, basketball, the list is endless and they are all on disk these days. Baseball and American Football are especially popular imports.

Figure 28.2. Car racing games are always popular. Left Lotus and right Crazy Cars.

Games can be played from the keyboard and/or mouse and a joystick is still an important add-on for the avid player, especially for action games and flight simulators. Sometimes games offer a two player option which means that two joysticks or two sets of keys are activated for use.

From a budget point of view, the asking price of a game depends on if it's an original full price title, a full price conversion from an existing game or a budget price title.

One thing to watch with all software is compatibility and this can be especially the case with games because their programmers are always trying to get every last ounce out of the machine they are in at the time. Amiga A1200 owners are using new hardware – some of the components under the bonnet have changed – so compatibility is a real issue. If you do encounter problems then make sure that you've tried the tweaks which Commodore have built into the startup procedure. The instructions are not that clear so here's how you go about it.

Tweaking the A1200

The normal sequence of events which take place when turning on your Amiga can be interrupted by holding down the two mouse buttons when switching on the computer. After a short delay, the screen clears and, instead of the normal disk prompt, you are presented with a grey screen with three main options on it. This is the Amiga Early Startup Control. This program has seemingly come from nowhere and is in fact permanently inside your computer ready to be called up by the genie of the mouse!

The three options given are Boot Options, Display Options and Expansion Board Diagnostics. We'll leave this last one to the dealer.

The first two options could help you run software if you have encountered a problem. Commodore estimate a high propor-tion of software produced prior to the A1200 will work without a hiccup but that means that some won't!

The simple procedure to follow is to try the different settings possible in these two Options screens. When you click on Boo t Options, look at Disable CPU Caches, which is a gadget situated under the Control Active Devices window. If empty, selecting this box will put a tick into it and turn the CPU caches off. If ticked, selecting the box will remove the tick and turn the CPU caches on. You don't need to know what this means, only that it could make a difference.

Back to the Amiga Early Startup screen and Display Options This brings up five gadgets in two groups, Display Type and Chip Type. We are interested in the Chip Type buttons. Only one of these buttons can be selected at any one time. Selection is indicated by the button turning blue from background grey, and you can choose from Original, Enhanced and Best Available. Best Available should be selected as your default (ie factory) setting.

Now it's a matter of experimentation. Deal with the Display and Boot Options separately and try changing the Chip Type settings before moving on to turning CPU Caches on and off (through Display Options).

This is the sequence of actions you should carry out to try out different settings with a troublesome piece of software. We'll change the CPU setting as an example:

1. Hold down both mouse buttons and turn on the A1200.

2. Select Boot Options.

3. Select Disable CPU Caches.

4. Select Use.

5. Select Boot.

The A1200 will boot from its Workbench disk as normal with the new settings in place. You can select Boot With No Startup-Sequence to boot from the Workbench disk into a Shell window.

Creative Classes

Home entertainment for me can also span messing about with pictures and music. Graphics can be an entertainment in themselves and there are many paint packages and image processors to make them your own. If you can afford to input with digitiser or scanner at one end and output to a colour printer at the other then you are in for an exciting time.

If you haven't got the hardware then pictures are available in profusion through public domain sources and budget priced art collections. Make sure you are aware of the difference between vector type and pixel type (IFF) graphics. These are the two types of graphics representation available for the Amiga and they are, generally speaking, incompatible. However they can be used side by side in desktop publishing programs.

*Figure 28.3. A paint program is a great way for
a young child to learn about the Amiga.*

If it's all the family using the computer and that means younger children then don't be frightened to look at some of the paint programs advertised as educational. These are designed for ease of use and provide excellent experience for the youthful artist.

If you like messing around with a camcorder then a profusion of programs to add captions, backgrounds and special effects can be purchased. Go for the biggest available fonts because computer characters disappear into insignificance on a TV screen.

Learning Fast

A large range of quality software is available to the parent and software can be purchased in consultation with teachers so that it complements school work. Some are question and answer trivia type programs which don't offer much in the way of motivation. Look for more creative use of the computer's sound and graphics with nursery rhymes as rewards and use of the mouse or keyboard overlays which children find easier to use than the conventional keyboard.

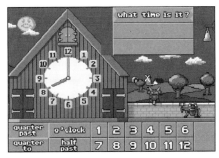

*Figure 28.4. The Fun School series of educational programs
offer motivation through sound and graphics.*

Of course many programs are educational without being designed that way for instance the many astronomy simulations, the NASA pictures of the solar system, the databases of plants and animals. CDTV prices are no longer out of this world and new developments such as PhotoCD are going to tempt those of us wavering on the edge of this new home entertainment/education phenomenon. These systems are based on compact disc players which can play back computer data into the computer's memory and can be controlled from the computer's keyboard or from an infra-red handset.

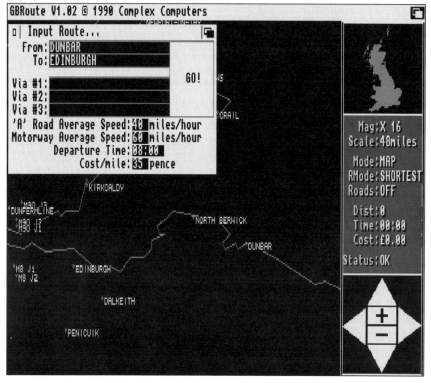

Figure 28.5. GBRoute helps you plan your journey by car.

Other useful programs for the home help out with travel planning and home-budgeting, room planning, garden design, putting a bet on the horses and dreaming up a recipe for dinner!

Is it for Me?

There's plenty of it then, but how do you get the software you want? Magazine reviews can help point you in the right direction but there's nothing like using the software in your local dealer before you buy. Here is a brief checklist of phrases used on the packaging and advertisements for you to bear in mind when purchasing software:

- *Memory required* – does it do everything in 1Mb?

- *Minimum hardware* – does it really run from floppies?

- *Technical support* – is there a help line?

- *Update policy* – does this company continue to develop its products or is this it?

- *Documentation* – is the manual of a decent size or is it a scrap of photocopied paper?

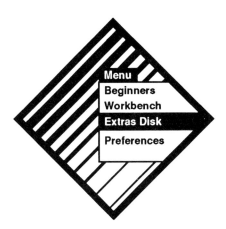

Menu
Beginners
Workbench
Extras Disk
Preferences

29: Software on the Cheap

Everyone reacts positively when they see FREE displayed in a shop window or in a magazine advert. But there's always a sneaking suspicion that nothing in life is free! This applies to the world of public domain and shareware on the Amiga.

Public domain (PD) programs are made freely available to all Amiga owners by their authors. They are passed on through personal contact and through PD libraries. Shareware programs are made available by their authors for free trial but the programs must be paid for if used for any longer than a specified period.

So many programs are swimming about in the PD and Shareware software ocean, just waiting to be fished out. But there are two costs: firstly you have to pay a PD library to duplicate the programs onto a disk and to send it out properly packaged and with the correct postage; secondly you have to spend time searching the columns of magazines to find the program you want. The actual program is free but the extras are not.

Nevertheless PD and Shareware is very good value for all Amiga owners and is an excellent way to start your interest in computing. You will be receiving programs proudly submitted to the PD libraries by programmers who have created an application or a utility which they feel is good enough for public exposure.

The PD librarian plays an important role in sieving the material available and it is common for a library to specialise in a particular type of PD, music files for instance, and a library will have a demonstration disk to give a flavour of what it offers.

Another excellent source of software if you are on a budget is the magazine cover disk. Although much of the material on these disks is designed to advertise products to you, there are some which contain useful PD and shareware as well as original programs and programs which, although a few years old, still stand up very well and are worth having.

Definitions

There are two fundamental types of free software available for the Amiga. These are the definitions so you know what you are dealing with when ordering and it is important, especially when purchasing Shareware, to follow the etiquette.

Public Domain/Freeware

This software carries the copyright of the author. The author has given his/her permission for you to freely copy the software and pass it on to other users as long as:

• No files that it contains are deleted or changed.

• No files are added.

Further wishes of the author may be contained in a text file and these should be adhered too. If you wish to use or change any part of a public domain program it best to write to the author and ask for permission. If no address is contained within the program, make sure that you give the original author credit.

Shareware

The standard rules of shareware are:

• You may freely distribute copies of the software to other users.

• You have a 30 day trial period to evaluate the software.

• If, after this time limit, you are still using the software or intend to use it in the future then you must register with the author and pay any registration fee due. You are breaking the law if you fail to do so.

- If you do not intend using the software then you must delete it from your floppy/hard disk.

So now you know where you stand. You may well find more conditions within the program itself or in a help/text file. This is increasingly the case as Shareware is more and more used as a legitimate method of software distribution. I haven't heard of any Shareware millionaires yet but you never know, the time may come.

There are other wares in the market, such as Licenceware but these don't come free or on trial but rather you have to pay up front as with any other commercial product.

How to Get PD Software

PD software is about quantity not quality but at the same time you can discover miniature masterpieces amongst the thousands of disks which are advertised through the Amiga magazines. PD comes directly from its authors who place a program, picture or music file onto a bulletin board or send it to a PD library once they think it's good enough for the world to use.

There are a number of easy ways of getting hold of public domain and shareware software:

- By copying colleagues' disks.
- By sending off to a PD/shareware distributor or library.
- From magazine disks.
- From a bulletin board via the telephone.

Copying from friends and colleagues is the quickest and cheapest way of obtaining material. Unlike normal commercial software, for which passing between parties is illegal, you are positively encouraged to copy them. Shareware authors desire the widest possible distribution, as this increases the number of people who may possibly register.

Choosing PD is a matter of scouring the magazine adverts or sending off to the PD libraries for their sampler or library disk, possibly for a nominal fee. This disk may contain some actual PD or it may be packed with lists of PD programs. The more ambitious catalogue disks have quite sophisticated presentations and the most useful have full descriptions of the programs. Your aim, as far as possible, is to find out what you are buying. Each disk in the catalogue has an identification number which you use when ordering so note down the numbers of any disks that interest you.

Watch out for duplication of material because some libraries compile their own collections, of utilities, pictures etc, which are taken from existing disks in the catalogue. If you are dealing with more than one library then this becomes more difficult to check. Most libraries don't do a pick and mix service so you have to buy the disk with 20 printer programs on it because it's got the one you want even though you will immediately delete the other 19 because you've already got them.

MODE Execute	** Goldstar Computers (EC) Ltd **	
About Goldstar Computers Catalogue	The Amos Public Domain Library	A
Utilitie's	The A.M.I.G.O.S. Collection	U
Demo's	The S.N.A.G. Collection	D
Animations		A
Picture's and Slideshow's	Amos Licenceware	P
Business and Serious		B
Education & Games		E
Music,Audio,Modules & more	The Slipped Disk Collection	M
	want to turn the stars back on ?	
New Zealand Amiga User Group(NZaug)	A Different Game (stop music first)	N
TOPIK Collection	The Original Computer Game!!!!!	T
PANARAMA Collection	D Copy Backup Utility	P
	Directory Util to Move/Copy files	
	Boot Block Scroller writer	
Want to restart the music ?	New Commercial Software & Hardware	W
Wanna turn the stars off ?	Menumaster & how to modify it!!	W

Figure 29.1. A typical catalogue disk puts PD into various categories, by subject and by user group/club collection.

The most popular forms of PD are pictures, music and sampled sounds and demos. The demo is a completely new art form unique to computers and is the creation of an individual programmer or group of programmers to show off their skills through pushing the Amiga's sound and graphics to their limits. A basic demo involves a long text message moving across the screen with multicoloured effects, Star Trek type backgrounds and loud music. A different type of demo is the commercial demo which is placed into the public domain to show off the features of a commercial program.

A lot of PD comes from the USA and Europe as well as the UK but nearly all of it is available though UK libraries. A number of US user groups put their names to PD collections which are similar in presentation to disk magazines with friendly menu systems from the Workbench. Real disk magazines sometimes carry PD items but be careful because it is often mixed in with copyright material which you cannot copy.

Shareware distributors come in all shapes and sizes, from hobbyists doing it for fun, to highly professional firms with large and detailed catalogues. Naturally, a professional firm employing staff and printing catalogues will have more overheads, so you might expect to pay a little more per disk for the material. Costs range from about £1.50 to £10 per disk, although virtually all the distributors at the higher price bracket reduce the unit price if you order several disks at once. In practice, the cost of blank media plus duplication is usually the smaller part of the distributors' overheads, the larger part being staff to fulfil orders and answer telephone calls, and advertising and printing.

There is, incidentally, no law preventing anyone actually making a profit from shareware distribution, but natural competition has brought the charges to a very fair level. Some distributors have a club system, whereby as a member, you obtain better prices.

Many authors have actually specified a maximum charge (usually $10) to be made for the distribution of their disk, and shareware distributors generally have charges which are below these levels. Some authors even go as far as to specify that no charge whatsoever may be made – you will normally only find these programs on bulletin boards, or bundled on disks with other programs, as even blank floppies cost money!

Most shareware distributors have no involvement with the author registration process, and once you have purchased disks from them, that is the end of it – if you want to obtain updates, you have to contact the author direct.

Using PD

PD Software is often distributed in a compressed format so you may have to run a decompressor utility before you can use it. Although it's cheap, it's still annoying if a disk corrupts during this process, so take a copy beforehand. When decompressed you can take the programs that you really need and put them onto your working disks by copying them via the Ram Disk or straight onto floppy or hard disk. If there's an option to decompress onto another disk then choose this. Copying the compressed program to another disk and then trying to decompress it may not work because the distribution disk contains the decompression utility required.

It's usual for PD disks to provide access to the programs on them via the Workbench but on some occasions you may come across a disk which will not boot directly or needs you to enter a Shell to use AmigaDOS to access the software. Our beginners guide to AmigaDOS in this book will prove ideal for this purpose.

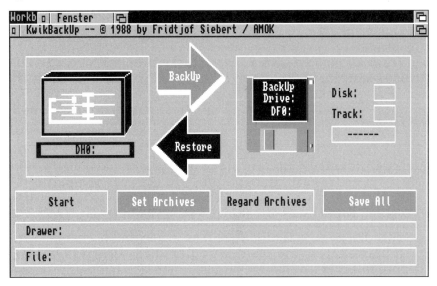

Figure 29.2. Hard drive owners will love this example of excellent Shareware.

PD provides lots of ways to make your micro that bit different through startup screens, screen-savers – animated graphics to entertain and stop your screen being damaged at the same time – special mouse pointers, clocks, Mac style window opening, pop-up menus etc. You get the idea. For real fun you can run programs which dissolve your Workbench or make your mouse pointer act in a drunken manner!

More useful are utilities for compressing files to save space on your disks, backing up files, recovering accidental deletions and so on. Some PD is very specialised, eg a houseplant finder which can choose a suitable houseplant for your lighting and temperature conditions. This kind of PD can prove a fantastic find if it suits your interests, but is otherwise meaningless.

Song files for trackers, sound samples, graphics conversion utilities, slideshow programs, these are among the favourite topics of PD authors. Some small business shareware looks like very good value but make sure dates and money are in British, not US, format if that's what you want. Beware good looking programs which have either no documentation or documentation in a language you don't understand.

Magazine Disks and Disks on Magazines

A popular form of entertainment on the Amiga is the disk magazine, a floppy version of the full-blown magazine format you buy in your newsagent. Well, not quite. These electronic newsletters carry articles, reviews, hints and tips and news as well as programs and pictures. The level of presentation varies enormously, most having their own *reader* which presents the text and pictures. Magazine disks provide an outlet for some of the most creative programmers, musicians and artists on the Amiga and so are well worth trying.

A different beast, and a publishing phenomenon, is the magazine cover disk. One or even two floppy disks appear on the front cover of your favourite computer magazine these days. These disks carry anything from PD/shareware to a complete commercial program with demo programs in between.

The demo program is usually a full version of the commercial program but with one or two vital functions, such as save and print, disabled. A game might let you play only one level of many in the real thing. These demos are useful in showing you what a program can do. Magazine disks have now gone a further step forward in providing full commercial programs on their cover disks. These are usually only barely documented inside the magazine and you are encouraged to purchase the full manual, usually at a very reasonable price.

When you rip your disk from the magazine cover, hang fire for a few moments and do two things: make a backup and find the instructions in the magazine on how to use the disk. The data on many disks is compressed and in order to carry out decompression it is often necessary to boot from the disk in question. You can do this from Workbench by pressing <Ctrl-Amiga-Amiga>.

To copy onto another floppy disk or hard disk can sometimes be awkward because the programs need decompression routines which are tucked away out of sight. Use the Show All menu option to find these and copy them with the files you want to use elsewhere. Game demos tend to need a preliminary session decompressing and saving themselves onto either one or two blank disks, so stock up on floppies.

Write-protect your disk unless otherwise instructed. Some disks do demand that you leave them write-enabled while decompression takes place. Take a backup just in case, then run the de-archiver and, when successfully completed, you can use the backup disk for something new, nothing lost. If a disk error is encountered then the disk can be returned to the duplication company for a free replacement.

Decompressing from the Shell is mostly via a utility such as lharc which needs to have a source and destination file specified, with other optional parameters. You may find pictures are compressed in a different format, such as JPEG and need a specific utility, usually provided, to access them.

Fish Disks

A PD publishing phenomenon has to be Fred Fish and his disks. Fred was a great source of technical material, accessed from the Shell, in the Amiga's early days and has gone on to provide, now under Workbench, a massive mixture of programs. Often the place for pioneering ideas in code, the collection is available from a number of libraries, is documented in a number of magazines and has been compiled onto CDTV format.

```
R B 1 2 3 4 5 6 7 8 9 0 fred-fish                    S:17664  L:339
       Fred Fish section
       U=Utility F=Graphics D=Games DD=Game demo
       FF038 Csquared (U) Fixobj (U) HP-10c (U) IFFDump (U)
             Jsh (U) Newstat (U) Reversi (D) UUdecode (U)
             Vdraw (U) Voice filter (U) Window (U)
       FF090 Amigazer (U) Cardfile (U) Conman (U) Imandlevroom (U)
             Newdemos (U) Othello (D) Printext (U) Prtdrvgen (U)
             Rainbench (U) Shortcut (U) Showprint (U) Sizzlers (U)
             Spaceace (U) Timer (U)
       FF105 Asmprogs (U) Amiga basic programs (MIXED) Bison (U)
             Drunken mouse (U) Flankey (U) Gravity wars (D)
             IPO2C (U) Pere-et-fils (U) Record-play (U)
       FF135 TEXF
       FF164 C-Functions (U) Newton (U) Poylroot (U) Disksalv (U)
             Newzap (U) Prtdrivers (U) HED (U) PCview (U) ZOO (U)
       FF223 Chs (U) Fixdisk (U) Gravitysim (U) IFF2SUN (U)
             Paccer (D) Popinfo (U) Setcpu (U)
       FF228 AZ (U) Glib (U) Jazzbench (U) Xoper (U)
       FF232 Bally III (D) Dbug (U) Resourcedemo (U)
       FF240 Crossdos (UD) Memlib (U) Dis (U) DM-Maps (U)
             Runback (U) Xprlib (U)
       FF251 Disksalve (U) Diskspeed (U) Linstrom (U) Monopoly (G)
             Roadroute (U)
       FF252 Crossdos (UD) Trektrivia (D) Zerg (D)
       FF273 Battleforce (D) Pennywise (U)
       FF295 Gnugrep (U) LHWarp (U) Mandlemountains (F)
       FF301 Aquarium (Fish Directory utility)
       FF302 Chop ( ) Disktalk (U) MiscUtils (U) PPMore (U)
             ProgUtils (U) Quickhelp (U) RollON (D)
```

Figure 29.3. The Fish collection is legendary and a fascinating body of software for any PD collector.

Shareware

Shareware is a software distribution system which originates from the USA, and which works on a principle of honour. The software is distributed by the author to the computer-using community at large, through specialised shareware distributors and bulletin boards. Shareware distributors make charges to cover the cost of disks, postage and packaging and so on, but these are small compared with the true value of the software. If you like what you have tried, you can then register, and again the costs are small in comparison with a similar commercial product. For example, a small disk management utility might have a registration cost of $5 (£3), against say, a cost of £20 for a commercial product. A full-blown wordprocessor may cost $75 (£50) to register, whereas the commercial equivalent would be several hundred pounds. The price you pay – often to an American or German software author – could depend on the exchange rate at the time!

When initially distributed, the idea is that the software is on approval, effectively a free trial. Each program will contain information about registration and a disk based text file providing enough documentation to allow you to use it effectively. Registration means that you pay a more realistic price for the software, by sending payment to the author. In return, you will receive the benefits of a normal, commercially available package, such as updates, printed manuals, extra facilities and so on. If you don't like the software and therefore don't use it you don't have to part with any cash. A true case of the software author putting his mouth where is money is.

Because you, the customer, are dealing directly with the author, the registration fee is much lower than the cost of similar commercial packages. Even major packages cost only about £30-£40, and small ones may be as little as £3. It is even reported that (some) shareware authors are often better at providing customer service than (some) commercial firms. Naturally, registration is a matter of trust, and no-one is going to know if you don't register. However, if you are serious about a particular shareware program, you are likely to want the full documentation and extras that are available, so there is a natural incentive to register. Indeed the products are often so good that you want to register to receive future updates.

Payment is not the problem. Most of the authors will accept Access and Visa card payments, or have European agents. International Money Orders and Eurocheques are readily available for a small charge at your local bank.

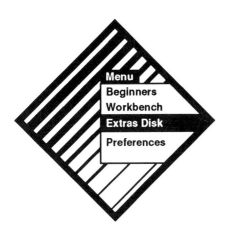

30:
Multimedia

Multimedia is being heralded as the means by which computers will lure the next generation of user by putting television like pictures on our screens, CD like sounds in our speakers and interactive control of masses of information in electronic *books.*

The theory is that the current systems are the early stages of this technology and that, like desktop publishing in the 1980s, multimedia will develop into a fully fledged industry that scarcely existed before the computer made it possible. Another theory says that multimedia is a nothing word, covering a host of possibilities but without real meaning or a real use.

What Is It?

Multimedia is indeed a coverall term which takes in the combined use of different media, usually delivered by different technologies, tied together by a computer. Resources, such as music, sound effects, speech, video footage, photographs, text and graphics are combined to deliver a message to the user. As the processing power of the Amiga computers increases, the more these resources are turned into digital form, the less they are delivered by separate hardware.

Thus you have a situation where software can playback a movie in a screen window with sound to match, with no hardware strings attached. Where hardware is playing a part is in the increasingly sophisticated way that we can *capture* the real world through digitisers, samplers and scanners. Perhaps one day all multimedia will be software based but for the moment even the Amiga needs the injection of specialised extras on add-on cards to capture and manipulate video footage. The combination of video and computer graphics – including text fonts – is one such area. Grabbing images into a framestore for digital processing is another. There's more on this in the chapters on upgrading and graphics and sound.

Sometimes the forced combination of different technologies doesn't come off but the amalgam of home computer and compact disc has resulted in a brand new home-entertainment medium. The CD can provide the storage capacity for all these other media. In CDTV, Commodore have created a whole which is greater than the sum of its two parts. More of which later.

Authoring Programs

Anyone can write a multimedia program and save it to a floppy disk. What you need from a multimedia authoring program is the ability to use any of the standard resources of your Amiga, for instance pictures, sounds and fancy fonts, to create a presentation. A program such as CanDo provides tools to present these resources in a controlled manner by positioning them, timing their use and the way that one screen moves on to another. It keeps track of the resources and can generate a stand-alone program to run the presentation.

CanDo is also an example of a program which controls events through a script language which can be edited or written from scratch as well as being generated automatically by the program when you use its graphics tools. Because of the Amiga's heavy involvement with video, most authoring software tends towards the presentation of pictures etc at the expense of database like features such as searching.

An authoring program like CanDo requires absolutely no programming skills to use since the user interacts directly with the objects on screen. Therefore the emphasis is on design and planning rather than programming. You will hear more and more about Object Orientated Programming (OOP) if you stick with computers. Scala, a profressional graphics presentation program, is also turning into a full-blown multimedia presenter in its most recent versions, even controlling CD, video tape and video disc players. It too has its own script programming language.

Dynamic Total Vision

The competition for the few sockets on the back of your television got much hotter when Commodore launched CDTV (Commodore Dynamic Total Vision), an Amiga with a difference. By a neat coincidence CDTV is based on a CD player and a TV so you can remember it both ways.

If you feel that you've got enough in the way of TV channels and film releases, CDTV will let you branch out into some competitive fun and take the weight off the bookshelves with a wealth of easily accessible information. And all of this is available to all Amiga owners through an add-on CDTV compact disc drive.

The compact disc player reads digital information from the now familiar CD. If it's computer data it's sent for processing. Special computer chips display and animate the graphics and produce sound effects. If it's audio information then the CD player sends it through the audio system, so getting the best of both worlds.

The CDTV is controlled from a remote console which is not dissimilar in purpose to a video remote control. However it's crescent-shaped with the buttons fairly widely spaced with a horizontal rather than vertical layout. A cluster of up/down/right/left keys are on the lefthand side. Items are selected from screen menus by moving up and down and highlighting the choice. Two action buttons A(dvance) and B(ack) are on the righthand side. The headphones' volume can also be controlled from the handset. Other infrared devices are available, including a joystick, keyboard, a trackerball (a static brick with a ball in it) and a two-player interface.

Typical CDTV discs are Hutchinsons Encyclopedia, Lemmings – a humourous and addictive game – and Barney Bear. The latter is an educational story book with a typically gentle Tom Baker voice over. Pointing at objects on screen brings amusing results, a willow weeps, a balloon carries a mouse up into the air, a snail slides from beneath a log. The narrative is written up on screen and can even be broken down by child or parent into individual words and phrases.

This is a new medium but a great deal of expertise has been built up by creative companies on both sides of the Atlantic. These production companies are often associated with or offshoots from large organisations like the BBC and their output has been for training and educational purposes. There is also a pool of sophisticated computer software publishers who employ artists and musicians amongst their staff.

Designing interactive *books* is both an art and a science and involves second-guessing the user. An *user interface* designer usually has experience of both computer software and psychology. Commodore have laid down no strict rules for the design but all the titles I have played turned out to be very easy to use.

An excellent example of the education/information titles available is the Hutchinson Encyclopedia which can be accessed in the traditional alphabetical method except you move through a list of subjects on screen rather than flicking through the pages.

Selecting a subject produces a full clarification in whatever is the most appropriate form. An obscure animal might just have a text description but a well-known historical event will benefit from pictures and sound. I looked up Moseley and got a text description, a picture of the British brownshirts from the '30s and a speech by Moseley himself. The sound recordist could never have imagined at the time where the recording would end up. In all, there are 25,000 entries, 7,000 biographies and 250 tables.

A world atlas title contains maps and detailed statistics. You can just as easily listen to the local music of a South American region as view a street map of Moscow or learn to say "where is the toilet" in Japanese. Information can be compared and graphs displayed so doing geography homework is going to get a lot easier all of a sudden.

The other titles available can be placed into the categories of home interest – medical, gardening, language learning; child-centred – storybooks and educational activities; and games – arcade/reaction and intellectual/strategy types.

The scope that CDTV can cover is indicated by Virgin's announcement of a role-playing version of part of Sir Ranulph Fiennes' Transglobe expedition, North Polar Expedition. And soon to be released is a CDTV version of the Guinness Book of Records. You can also choose from the Complete Works of Shakespeare, the illustrated Old and New Testaments and the Grolier Encyclopedia.

Commodore feel that CDTV will have a role to play in education in schools as well as the home. The ambitious Japan World disc has been created for Derbyshire schools whose pupils will soon be applying for jobs at the local Toyota factory.

The Compact Disc player is also a piece of hi-fi which plays conventional CDs. The player is programmable with time, track and volume information on the front panel. You can get 10 second sampling, looping, randomising (mix), CD+G and, interesting for musicians who want to do advanced Karaoke, CD+MIDI. CD+G is a record company format for displaying pictures with music. The player also supports ISO 9660, the standard for CD ROM.

Movies and PhotoCD

Commodore plan to make the CDTV player compatible with the Moving Picture Expert Group full-screen, full-motion standard once established and available. Full motion video means digital video with each frame of the video being drawn on the screen in quick succession, resulting in something fast enough to fool the human eye, just like a real film or video.

You will also be able to play back your family photos via PhotoCD. This technology has been developed by Kodak and is designed as an alternative way of taking home your photographs from the high street (or mail order) processing shops. You take your film in as usual but, instead of prints or slides, you take home a CD with digital versions of your pictures ready to be played back on your television. Undoubtedly there will be programs to catalogue and manage your photo collections.

31: PCs and Amigas

As popular as the Amiga is it is only one of many hundreds, and probably thousands, of types of computer available to users around the world. While it is certainly one of the most popular computers in the world, it isn't *the* most popular in terms of units installed. That claim to fame goes to the ubiquitous PC, of which there are literally tens of millions on desks in every corner of Planet Earth.

Because of this, the particular disk format it supports is very important. You will recall from earlier chapters that the the Amiga disk system is effectively AmigaDOS and this is the format used. Well, on the PC the disk system is called DOS – Disk Operating System – of which MS-DOS is the most popular. This format – as with most formats used on other computers – is incompatible with AmigaDOS. Thus, if you insert a disk from a PC into your Amiga disk drive you will find that it responds as if you have just inserted a brand new unformatted disk into the disk drive. Similarly, if you take an Amiga formatted disk and place it into a PC disk drive then the PC will be unable to read it.

This incompatibility can often be a source of great frustration. An Amiga in the home, a PC in the school or office – it seems a shame that you can't swap work between the two especially as they support software in common –

for example, the wordprocessor *Protext*. Well, there is a simple answer to the problem which means that you can swap data without too much effort.

The incompatibility problem referred to above is not a physical one (hardware), it is simply because the software which controls each relevant disk reading exercise is not aware of the format used by other, alien, disks. Therefore, all you need to be able to read a PC format disk in an Amiga disk drive is some specifically written software. Prior to the launch of Workbench 2.1 there were several DOS-reading programs available. However, with the launch of Workbench 2.1 Commodore started to supply the popular CrossDOS software as part of its Workbench entourage of software. Thus if you have Workbench 2.1 or later you will already have the means to read PC disks. If you are using a version of Workbench prior to this you will need to purchase a copy – or better still, upgrade your Workbench!

CrossDOS

CrossDOS is a *commodity* (more on which in Chapter 32) which allows you to use your Amiga to read and write MS-DOS format disks. It is a simple transfer platform for moving files between the disk systems. It will not allow you to take a file created in, for example, Word on the PC and load it into ED on the Amiga. However, there are ways around this which I will point out a bit later. It is important though that you grasp just what CrossDOS is and what it cannot do. A Sealink ferry will transfer you from England to France, but it will not enable you to speak French if you can't already do so!

Before you can use CrossDOS you must first install it and this involves a simple decision – what floppy disk drive are you going to use. The decision may be made for you if you only have an internal drive. If you have an extra external drive you could use this. At the end of the day your choice is only one of convenience because even after you have designated a disk drive as the MS-DOS disk drive you can still use it as an Amiga disk drive.

You will need to have your Workbench and Extras disks available. Copy the DOS Driver from the Storage/DOSDrivers drawer to the Workbench:Devs/DOSDrivers drawer. There are two associated icons in the drawer labelled PC0 and PC1. PC0 is the icon for the Amiga internal disk drive and PC1 the icon for the external disk drive. To give your Amiga the ability to read PC disks in the internal disk drive at any time copy the PC0 icon across as illustrated in Figures 30.1 and 30.2 opposite.

Once there, every time your Amiga is booted it will automatically allow the disk drive to be used to read a MS-DOS disk. Note that you will need to perform at least a soft reboot (Ctrl-Amiga-Amiga)on your Amiga the first time you copy the file across.

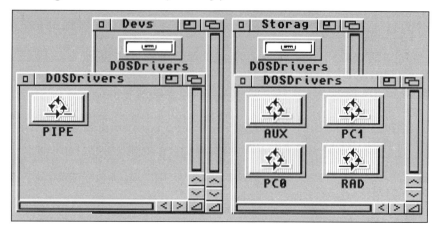

Figure 31.1. Open the DOSDrivers drawers in the Devs and Storage drawers of the Workbench and Extras disks respectively. WB3.0 users have a separate storage disk.

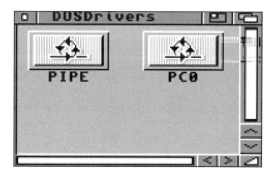

Figure 31.2. To set the internal disk drive to read MS-DOS disks,
copy the PC0 icon across into the DOSDrivers drawer in Devs.

DOS Access

When a MS-DOS disk is inserted into the drive it will first appear as a bad disk icon but will then be duplicated on the Workbench, showing its MS-DOS volume name. You can then open the disk window as normal simply by clicking on it. Files and folders will be displayed in the normal fashion and you can use it for all intents and purposes as an AmigaDOS disk to select, copy and move files get information and delete.

MS-DOS format disks can be accessed from the AmigaShell using most of the standard AmigaDOS commands. The disk may be referred to by its volume name using the normal convention or by use of the device name.

For example, if the internal disk drive was made MS-DOS compatible and a disk called PCDISK was inserted you could catalogue its directory in one of two ways:

        DIR PCDISK:

or:

        DIR PC0:

File Compatibility

If you are using Protext on the Amiga and have access to Protext on the PC then as far as wordprocessing goes you are totally compatible and simply moving your files from one disk format to another should be enough. However, life is never that simple! If you are not using similar software then the files will be largely incompatible. In these cases you need to find a happy medium and this is best achieved by saving files in Text or ASCII format. All wordprocessors have this ability and, although you may need to reformat a document when you reload it into the new software, the technique works well.

Wordprocessed files are straightforward, as should be data files from programs such as the such as a spreadsheet as these allow you to save in a a variety of standard formats. More of a problem is databases and you would need to investigate this further to see if there is a format which your database has in common with a database on the target computer.

Graphics files create further problems as there are so many standards. However, in recent times the Amiga has gained a reputation as a serious graphics system and as such most new software supports its ILBM or IFF format. Look out for this. There are plenty of utilities to convert from common PC formats such as GIF and TIFF to Amiga IFF.

One thing you will not be able to use if you manage to transfer it, is the software itself as this is always very specific to the machine type it is written for!

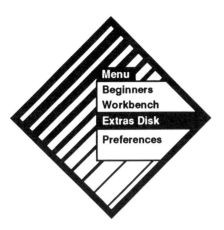

32:
Startup
Commodities

We're coming close to the end of our tour of the Amiga for beginners now and hopefully you are well on your way to being a Mastering Beginner. To bring us just about full circle these last couple of chapters are devoted back to the Workbench aspects of the machine and some of the other hidden goodies supplied with it. Some of the most useful of these are the Amiga Commodities.

The Commodities drawer is found in the Tools drawer of the Extras disk and this contains the tools that can alter the way in which your Amiga works. For example, if you have several windows on the desktop you have to physically select the one you wish to access by clicking in it. There is a tool in the Commodities drawer that does this automatically for you each time you move the Pointer over it. To see those which are on offer, open the Commodities drawer.

AutoPoint

This is one of those tools that you'll either love or hate. Personally I love it! Basically it selects and activates the window over which the Pointer sits. There is no need for you to have to physically select the window by clicking the mouse select button.

To launch the tool, double-click on the icon. Don't be fooled. This tool, like a few others in the Commodity drawer, does not open a window. It simply loads in as – in the jargon – a *background task*. In other words, it beavers away in the background.

You can test to see if it is working simply by opening a few windows and moving the Pointer over them. If you wish to stop AutoPoint you can do so by double-clicking on the AutoPoint icon again – it works like a switch. Alternatively you can kill the program by using the Commodities Exchange window which I'll deal with in due course.

ClickToFront

This tool – like AutoPoint – does not open a window and is run simply by double-clicking on its icon. It allows you to bring any window to the front simply by clicking the Pointer in the selected window whilst depressing the lefthand Alt key. This solves what can be an annoying problem when you have several windows open and have to sort through their depth gadgets. Used in conjunction with AutoPoint this is a very worthwhile utility.

When up and running ClickToFront can be removed by double-clicking on the ClickToFront icon.

Blanker

This is a screen blanker which turns-off the screen display if there has been no keyboard and/or mouse activity in a specified period of time.

When you double-click on the Blanker icon a small window appears on the screen. The window displays the default blanking time which is normally 60 seconds. So if a period of 60 seconds passes without a keyboard and/or mouse button being pressed, Blanker will black out the screen. You can change the blanking period simply by changing the Seconds setting. To set a period of two minutes delete 60 and type 120. Select the Hide button to run the Commodity but remove the window.

If both the Cycle Colors and Animation gadgets are checked then the screen will display an animated graphic which continually changes colour when the screen is blanked out.

The original display can be restored by pressing a key on the keyboard or the mouse. The Quit button can be used to remove the Blanker operation.

Although at first sight Blanker may appear to have no real value, in many respects it is an essential accessory if you leave your Amiga idle for more than a few minutes at a time. The idea is to prevent burn-in on the monitor. Burn-in is the etching of characters into the screen phosphor. Although this affects mainly monochrome monitors, it can affect colour monitors as well.

As it runs in the background without any real hindrance, it is worth running it, though you may find it more convenient to increase the blanking period to 180 seconds or so, by editing the 60 seconds figure in the string gadget in the window when it is displayed.

There is a hot-key associated with Blanker, which is <Ctrl-Alt-b>. If Blanker is running and you press the hot-key combination, its window will be displayed, allowing you to either edit the blanking time or to kill it off altogether. Note that double-clicking on the Blanker icon again will not turn the accessory off but simply bring the Blanker window to the forefront again.

The above three Commodities are the ones I personally find the most useful. As such I tend to have them running all the time. So, to that end I ensure that they are firmly in place in the WBStartup drawer on the Workbench disk.

Exchange

All Commodities can be controlled by a tool called Exchange – using this you can control each of the Commodities in use, allowing you to disable, kill or launch new ones through a simple window with standard gadgets.

The Exchange program is located in the Commodities drawer. Double-clicking on Exchange displays the Commodities Exchange window.

You can run and add any of the other Commodities programs simply by double-clicking on the relevant icon. They will be added to the Exchange list and, should you open the Commodities Exchange control panel again, you will see them listed.

We'll come back to the use of the Commodities Exchange program when we have had a look at what the Commodities programs supplied on the Extras disk do. These are located in the Commodities drawer which is to be found inside the Tools drawer.

The Exchange control program window may well be self-explanatory to you at this stage. Certainly it is no more complex than any other Workbench orientated window we have encountered to date.

Each Commodity that is running is listed in the Available Commodities window which is positioned roughly centrally in the Exchange window itself. If none are listed then none are running.

You can select any Commodity in the Available Commodities window simply by clicking on it once. When you do this the Information panel relating to the selected Commodity will show some detail about its function.

When a Commodity is run it will be enabled and therefore be fully functional. It can be disabled by clicking on the Active/Inactive cycle gadget on the righthand window. This is useful when you want to stop the functionality of the Commodity but anticipate needing to use it again shortly, in which case you can select it in the Available Commodities window and select Active again. To kill off a Commodity totally you select the Commodity in the Available Commodities window and then select the Remove gadget.

The Show Interface gadget brings the window for the selected Commodity to the front of the screen. If the window is closed Show Interface opens it. This gadget is only applicable therefore to the Commodities that have windows available to them, namely Blanker, and FKey. Once displayed the window can be hidden by selecting the Hide Interface gadget.

In the Project menu in the menu bar you'll find Hide and Quit which affect Exchange itself. Hide removes the Exchange window from the screen – it can be recalled again by pressing <Ctrl-Alt-Help>. Quit removes the Exchange program from memory, however any resident Commodities already in use will still be available. The net effect of Quit is that you cannot hot-key the Exchange window into life with the <Ctrl-Alt-Help> combination, you have to run the Exchange program by double-clicking on its icon in the Commodities Drawer of the Extras disk.

FKey

FKey allows you to assign a string of characters to a specific function key. It is intended to make repetitive tasks, like entering AmigaDOS commands, easier by assigning them to function keys – the grey numbered keys across the top of the keyboard.

When you double-click on the FKey icon its window is displayed. You can assign strings to every function key and shifted function key (that is the same function key pressed in combination with the Shift key), thus providing up to 20 functions for definition.

There is a cycle gadget which allows you to select from a series of functions available from the function keys, these include Run program and Insert Text. For instance you could run your favourite program directly simply by pressing a function key. For example, to run DPAINT or a similar program by pressing Alt-F1 you would take the four simple steps:

- Click on New Key gadget

- Enter the following into the string gadget:

  alt f1

- Select the Run Program option from the Cycle cycle gadget.

- Enter the name (including path if any) of the program into the Command Parameters string gadget, ie:

  DPAINT

This and any further definitions can be saved using the Save Define Keys option from FKeys Project menu. When Alt-F1 is pressed the function defined is carried out.

If you terminate a command with \n then this is interpreted as Return and has the same effect as pressing the Return key. If it is missed off then you will have to physically press the Return key after selecting the desired function key to implement the command.

When you have entered your desired strings, select the Hide gadget to remove the FKey window. To use a key to issue an AmigaDOS command, first either select Execute Command from the Workbench menu or open an AmigaDOS Shell. Then press the desired function key. If the command is assigned to a shifted function key remember to hold down the Shift key as you press the required function key.

You are not limited to using AmigaDOS commands, you can assign any text you require to the keys. Thus, if you are using ED or similar and have trouble spelling certain words, you could assign each to a function key and simply select the required function key at each point. In such a circumstance there would be no need for you to include the \n Return character at the end of each line.

The FKey strings that you enter into the text gadgets are not, by default, saved. Thus when you turn off or reboot your Amiga any FKey settings will be lost. To retain your definitions you can Save from the Project menu.

This Commodity does not open a window. When run it effectively disables the Caps Lock key on the keyboard. Other keys such as the Shift key remain functional. When pressed and turned on Caps Lock forces all keystrokes to capital letters, thus if an a is typed, A will be produced.

NoCapsLock

With NoCapsLock in force capital letters can still be produced, by holding the Shift key down when pressing the appropriate letter on the keyboard. Double-click on its icon again to disable NoCapsLock.

33: Bits and Bobs

WBStartup

WBStartup stands for Workbench Startup and any files that are stored in here will be executed automatically when you turn on or reboot your machine. Normally, on a standard vanilla Workbench disk, the WBStartup folder is empty and is located in the Workbench disk window.

To use the automatic startup facility you simply drag the tool or tools you want to run at startup into the WBStartup folder – in this case some Commodities – as required. However the snag here is that there will probably not be enough room on the Workbench disk to accommodate them all.

If you have a hard disk system then you can simply drag them into the WBStartup folder without too many problems. On a copy of your Workbench disk you may find that you will have to rid yourself of a few of the tools that you are not using. Ensure you do this on the backup, working copy, not the master copy!

If you do not wish to do this but would like to see how WBStartup works, copy a useful tool into the drawer that is already on the Workbench disk – Clock for instance.

To see the tool or tools auto-launch, press Amiga-Amiga-Ctrl. If you wish to remove a file from the drawer that has originated from the Workbench disk, do remember to do so by copying it back to its source drawer.

If you find that you are using any of the Commodities on a regular basis, for example, Blanker or AutoPoint, then you can launch them automatically every time you turn your Amiga on by copying them into the WBStartup drawer.

MultiView

MultiView – which made its debut with the release of Workbench 3.0 – does exactly what its name suggests – it is a utility that gives you the ability to view all types of Amiga files that follow standard Amiga formats. There are several formats in all but the two most obvious are text and graphics. Text files should be just that – not wordprocessor files – and graphics files should be in the ILBM format. If this is a little bit two much jargon for you don't be put off. Look at it this way: if someone gives you a text file or a graphics file that is for the Amiga, MultiView should allow you to look at it and examine it! MultiView also allows you to look at AmigaGuide documents (these are Hypertext database files – but we're getting a bit ahead of ourselves here) and to play sounds.

There are a number of text files on your Workbench disk which you can display and, by using a simple AmigaDOS command, it will be possible to create a graphics screen for you to look at using MultiView as well. First, using either the Execute Command option or better still, by typing directly into an AmigaShell window, make a copy of one of the Amiga's text files by entering the following command:

```
COPY s:startup-sequence RAM:
```

This will make a copy of the file called startup-sequence and place it in the Ram Disk.

To view this file open MultiView by double-clicking on its icon which can be found in the Utilities drawer on the Workbench disk. This will launch a large file requester window which should be reasonably familiar to you by now. Click on the Volumes button at the bottom of the window and when the new listing is displayed, click on Ram Disk. This will display a list of the files and directories in the Ram Disk and the first one of these should be startup-sequence. Click on this twice and, within a flash or two, a large window will be opened and it will contain some curious looking text. In fact this is not text in the strictest sense but an AmigaDOS program! In fact it is the list of commands that your Amiga executes every time it is switched on!

Note that this window is like any other Workbench window and you can use the scroll bars to scroll up and down the text. You can exit from the display by press the Q key or by clicking in the Close window gadget in the normal fashion. If you have a large amount of text you can also scroll through this a page at a time by pressing the spacebar.

There are a few menus associated with this MultiView screen and the Edit menu also allows you to Print out from it if you have a printer attached.

The process is exactly the same for displaying any other type of file that can be read by MultiView. Simply run MultiView and then locate the file you want to see and MultiView will do the rest!

There is another string gadget based in the file requester window and this is called Pattern. By default this has the following text within it:

#?

This effectively means list all files and is called a *wildcard*.

If the text file you wish to display has an icon associated with it you can direct MultiView to load it directly from the Workbench. Select MultiView, hold down and keep held down the Shift key, then double-click on the text icon. You could try this out for yourself by opening the Ram Disk window and then selecting the Show All Files option from the Windows menu. Then click on the MultiView icon once, press and keep pressed the Shift key and then double click on the startup-sequence icon.

It is also possible to run MultiView from the AmigaShell. To do it simply type:

MultiView

at the prompt. You can load a file in much the same way, simply by specifying its full name (and path) after the command thus:

MultiView RAM:startup-sequence

SetMap

We have already touched on the subject of KeyMaps in Chapter 2. If you are using Workbench 2.1 or later it is a simple matter to install keymaps – you just ensure that the correct keymap icons are placed in the Keymaps drawer in the Devs directory on the Workbench disk. Then you open the Input Preferences Editor – located in the Prefs drawer to select the required keyboard type from the scrolling list.

However, things are not so straightforward if you are using release 2.04 or 2.05 of Workbench. This section explains what to do if you are using either of these versions of Workbench.

First of all the correct keymap file must be copied to the Keymaps drawer located in the Devs drawer of the Workbench disk. To do this proceed as follows:

1. Open the Workbench window and select Show All Files from the Window menu.

2. Scroll through the window and locate the Devs drawer. Open this and close the Workbench window.

3. Open the Keymaps window and close the Devs window.

4. Insert the Extras disk and select Show All Files from the Window menu.

5. Open the Devs drawer and close the Extras disk window.

6. Open the Keymaps window and close the Devs window.

You will now have two Keymaps windows displayed on the screen, one from the Workbench disk (which may contain the gb icon if you installed this earlier) and one from the Extras disk which contains the various keymaps.

7. Locate the keymap of your choice and drag this across into the Workbench keymaps window.

As this stage you may have to do a bit of disk swapping if you have a single drive. If you have a dual drive system then you should have the Workbench disk in one drive and the Extras disk in the other. Once this is done you can close the windows.

With the keymap in place it is now necessary to set the correct Tool Type. Open the System drawer and select the Setmap icon by clicking on it once. Then, from the Icons menu, select the Information option to display the Information window. Locate the New button in the bottom lefthand corner of the window and select this. The text gadget to the right will cease to be greyed out. Now type the following:

KEYMAP=gb

where gb is the keymap you copied across – gb in this case being Great Britain. Press Return and the newly typed information will appear in the Tool Types window. Select the Save button and the process is completed.

If you ever wish to change the keymap again, proceed as already outlined and then simply edit the Tool Type setting by clicking on the KEYMAP option at which point it will be copied into the text gadget and be accessible for editing.

Appendix A: Glossary

If you use a computer then you will inevitably encounter plenty of jargon. It's built into the Amiga in the form of the Workbench and its various features and into AmigaDOS with its commands. After all this is new technology so the designers of your Amiga are inventing it as they go along. And we try to keep up. We've tried to explain any new areas as we've reached them in the main text but there are other areas of using the Amiga to which you will now progress. So this glossary of terms is designed to recap on what you have bumped into so far but also to take you a few steps beyond the scope of this beginner's guide.

active screen

This is the screen currently displaying the active window.

active window

The window currently receiving input from a user. On the Amiga only one window can be active at any one time.

address

A number which identifies a storage location or the start of a particular object in the memory of the Amiga.

alert

A special red/black Amiga display used for emergency messages. These needn't mean you have experienced an irrecoverable problem.

algorithm

A series of rules (or a diagrammatic equivalent) that, when followed, results in a predetermined or predictable outcome. It is applied to the design of a computer program.

alias

An alternative name for a command. Useful for shortening long command sequences.

Alt keys

Two special command keys situated on the bottom left and bottom right of the Amiga's main keyboard. They are used in conjunction with other keys to get special characters.

Amiga keys

Two special keys situated either side of the spacebar. Used in conjunction with other keys to give shortcuts to menu choices.

angle brackets

These characters, < and >, are frequently used to identify command line parameters. For example: dir <filename> implies that filename is a parameter which you, the user, should supply.

ANSI C

An official standard for the C language that by early 1990 had been adopted by almost all major C compiler writers.

anti-aliasing

The dithering of coloured pixels to give the impression of smooth curves on screen.

applications gadget

A custom Amiga gadget used within an applications program.

ARexx

The Amiga version of Mike Cowlishaw's REXX programming language. ARexx is now distributed on the Amiga master disks which come with Workbench 2 and 3.

arguments

The values supplied when a command or function is used. These values are also often called parameters.

array

A data structure that allows an information set to be indexed by a subscripted variable. Used in database style programs.

ASCII

The American Standard Code for Information Interchange consists of a set of 96 displayable and 32 non displayable characters. The displayed alphanumeric characters make up the plain text we see on screen..

backup

To make a duplicate of a program or data disk. Back-up copies are usually made for either safety or security purposes. Important data should be backed up regularly

backdrop window

An Amiga Intuition window which always stays at the back of the screen display and cannot be depth rearranged.

background program

A program, task, or process, which is running somewhere in memory but not interacting directly via a terminal.

baseline

A desktop publishing term. The invisible line upon which the bases of most characters rest.

baud rate

A measurement of the rate of data transmission through a serial port. The baud rate divided by ten is a rough measure of the number of characters being transmitted per second.

binary

A number system using base 2 for its operations. It uses only 1 and 0, the equivalent of on and off, set and clear.

bit

An abbreviation of binary digit.

bitmap

An array of bits which form a system's display memory. Modifying the data in the bitmap alters the picture on the display. The Amiga uses a bitmap display consisting of a number of two dimensional bitplanes.

Blitter

Custom chip inside your Amiga for moving graphics around.

blocks

Selected areas, usually of text.

bold

Text shown in a thick, darker form. Font families can contain different levels of bold.

boot

To start up a computer system.

borders

The unprinted area around a document. Print borders can be set in the printer driver.

browsing

Scrolling through a text or text/graphics document, eg a directory listing.

buffer

An area of memory used to hold data temporarily whilst being collected or transmitted.

bug

A fault within a program that has not yet been found. Also see Debug.

bullets

Characters which can be typed in like text characters but which represent small pictures such as blobs, telephones etc. Used for lists on screen.

bus

The electronics which carries data between different components of the system.

C

One of the best high-level programming languages for creating programs on the Amiga.

caret

Vertical cursor at which text is typed.

character string

A sequence of printable characters.

checkmark

A small image, usually a tick, which indicates that a menu item has been selected by a user.

CLI

Command line interface.

click

A rapid press and release of a mouse button.

clipboard

A temporary memory store where deleted items are placed.

close gadget

A gadget in the top left corner of an Amiga window which allows you to remove the window from the display.

Co-processor

Powerful Amiga chip which handles much of the display work. This chip has its own instruction set which allows it to modify display characteristics without requiring 68000 processor intervention.

colour palette

A range of colours available for the screen at any one time, not necessarily all the colours that the Amiga can produce.

column

Words wrap within a narrow margin rather than at the page edge and at the bottom of the page, the cursor moves into the next column width.

Comma Separated Values (CSV)

ASCII data with each new item being separated by a comma. A way of transferring data between programs, eg from a wordprocessor into a database.

command file

An ordinary (usually ASCII) text file containing executable system commands.

comment

A remark written within a program.

composite video

A video signal which includes both picture and sync information. It can be transmitted using single co-ax cable.

control character

A character that signifies the start or finish of some process.

Copper

An abbreviation for the Amiga's co-processor chip.

CPU

Central Processing Unit. The 68000 series of chips at the heart of your Amiga.

crash

A term used when a computer program terminates unexpectedly or when the system hardware or software malfunctions. Usually reserved for serious problems that have no way of escape other than restarting the system.

CRT

Cathode Ray Tube.

current device/directory

The device or directory to which AmigaDOS's attention is currently drawn. All file access is done with reference to this status.

cut and paste

The action of removing an item from one place on the page/document and putting it back in another.

data set

A collection of data items.

debug

To eliminate errors within a program.

debugger

A program designed to help programmers find errors (bugs) in their programs.

default value

A value which will be supplied automatically if no other is given. Default values are used in Preferences unless you edit them.

depth arrangement gadget

An Amiga system gadget which allows a user to depth arrange (bring to front or send to back) a window in relation to other windows currently displayed.

device name

The name of a device which is incorporated into the Amiga system, eg the parallel port has the name PAR:.

destination file

A file being written to.

dictionary

A list of correct spellings against which the text in a document is checked.

digital-to-analogue converter

A hardware device which will convert a binary number into an analogue (continuously variable) level signal.

direct memory access

A method of data transfer whereby intelligent hardware devices can read and write to memory without the main microprocessor being involved.

directory

A collection of files grouped together under one heading.

disable

To prevent something from being used.

display memory

The RAM area that contains data used to produce the screen image.

display mode

A particular type of screen display: low resolution, high resolution, non-interlaced etc.

DMA

Direct Memory Access

double-click

Pressing and releasing a mouse button twice in quick succession.

drag

Shifting the position of a screen object by selecting it and, whilst holding the mouse button down, moving (dragging) it to another location.

enable

To make something available for use.

encrypt

To convert a file (or other information set) into a form which cannot easily be understood. Data is usually encrypted for security purposes.

extended selection

A method of selecting more than one option from a menu.

file

A set of data items held on diskette, tape or other medium.

filename

A name given to a file for identification purposes.

fill

To colour or draw a pattern into an enclosed area.

flag

A single bit within a microprocessor register or memory location which has been chosen to represent some TRUE/FALSE, YES/NO, type situation.

font

A collection of characters designed in a particular style. The Amiga supports fonts suitable for display on screen and for desktop publishing.

footer

A space at the bottom of a page reserved for page references and numbers (folio).

formatting

Preparing a blank disk for use. Also, a wordprocessing term for the way that text appears across the width of a document.

gadget

An Amiga icon type object. Amiga gadgets can represent on/off switches, one and two dimensional proportional sliders, can collect text string and number messages.

genlock

Hardware addon which combines a video signal with the computer graphics of the Amiga.

ghosting

Overlaying an image with a layer of dots making it slightly indistinct. Ghosting of gadgets and menu items is used to tell a user that certain options are not available.

glitch

A transient, usually unreproduceable, problem usually associated with some hardware malfunction.

global

Actions take place on specified elements without confirmation. Used, for instance, in searching and replacing text in a wordprocessor.

guttering

An extra margin on the inside of a facing page, providing space for folding. A DTP term.

hanging indent

The first line of a paragraph has a different left margin from the rest. DTP and wordprocessing term.

hard space

A space within text which is preserved after formatting.

hard copy

A printed listing or graphic dump of some computer output as opposed to the output displayed on a VDU screen.

header

Space at the top of a page reserved for repeating information about the document.

hexadecimal

A base 16 numbering system using the digits 0 - 9 and the letters A - F. Often the prefered system for programming.

highlight

Adding a print style, eg italic, to a block of text. Or, merely highlighting an area of text on the screen (also marking and selecting) before carrying out an operation on it, eg deleting.

Hold And Modify (HAM)

An Amiga screen mode capable of displaying all available colours.

hue

One of the ways of describing colour in a screen display.

hyphenation

When a word needs to be broken to retain text formatting which is pleasing to the eye, there are rules about which words can be split and how. These rules are held in a list which is checked against. A DTP/wp term.

I/O

Input/output.

icon

A picture representation.

import

The loading of external data types into a document.

indent

The space from a margin to the text.

inserting

When typing a new character it moves any existing character along the line to the right.

interactive

A program or system which reacts to input from you, the user.

interface

To connect up two different pieces of computer equipment and also the name for the electronics which provides this connection.

interlace

A way of producing double the number of display lines, from top to bottom, on screen.

Intuition

The Amiga's high level graphics interface, ie the overall Workbench orientated WIMP arrangement. Programmers take a much lower level view, regarding Intuition as a mass of system routines and object definitions which can be used to simplify their programming tasks. The Intuition approach allows programmers to easily create programs which use windows, gadgets, menus etc.

italic

Slanted text used for *highlighting.*

justification

The way that text is formatted between two margins.

kerning

A term from the world of desktop publishing. Moving text characters nearer to or further from each other to eliminate unwanted spaces between different shaped characters. A DTP term.

keymap

A translation table which describes the conversion of Amiga keyboard key presses into specific numerical codes.

leading

The space between lines of text.

linefeed

A new line of text is controlled by carriage return and linefeed codes. To avoid overprinting or double spacing the printer and computer need to match their use of codes.

local

An action which applies only to the current word or block. Opposite of global.

low-level language

A computer language whose primitive operations are closely related to the processor on which the language runs. Assembly languages are low-level.

macro

sequence of actions or instructions, eg selecting and moving text, grouped onto a single key press with a label. Shorthand.

matching

Finding a specified word in a document (wp) or a filename in AmigaDOS.

memory map

A diagram showing the allocation of the various parts of memory chosen for a particular system or program.

menu bar

A strip in an Amiga screen title bar which, when the right mouse button is depressed, displays the menu list categories.

menu button

The Amiga's righthand mouse button.

merging

Loading one file into another and then saving as a whole.

monospacing

Characters all take up the same space. The opposite of proportional.

multitasking

The means by which the Amiga runs more than one program at a time.

NTSC

The National Television Standards Committee standard for composite video. Used mainly in North America.

octal

A base 8 numbering system.

operating system

A collection of routines that performs the I/O and other hardware dependent chores that are needed for a computer to function.

Overscan

Most screen modes don't use the whole screen but have a border around them. An overscan mode fills the whole screen area. Used for video work.

overtyping

Typing a character deletes the one below. Opposite of inserting.

page break

Where one page ends and a new one is started. This will happen automatically when the defined page size is exceeded but can also be forced by the user.

page layout

Arrangement of blocks of text and graphics on a page.

PAL

Phase Alternate Lines. A composite video standard used widely in the UK and western Europe.

paragraph

A block of text with a press of Return at the end. The paragraph file format is common to a number of wordprocessors.

parallel port

Hardware device which, on the Amiga, is used for transmitting data eight bits at a time. Used mainly for printer connection.

parameter

Any value which must be explicitly passed to a subroutine, function, procedure or program in order for it to be properly executed.

peripheral

Any external or remote device connected to a computer system, eg a printer.

pixel

The smallest addressable part of a screen display.

playfield

Another name for a screen background.

point

A unit of measurement for type and design.

pointer

The arrow icon which appears on the Workbench and is controlled by the mouse in order to pull down menus and make selections.

Preferences

An Amiga system program which allows a user to set a large number of user-definable I/O characteristics.

primitives

Another name for Amiga library functions and system routines.

proportional

Individual characters take up an appropriate amount of space.

ragged

Describes unjustified edge of line of text.

RAM

Random Access Memory.

refresh

To redraw part (or all) of a graphics display.

render

Draw an image into a display area.

requester

An Intuition window which appears asking a user to provide some information.

resolution

The number of lines (pixels) which can be displayed on screen.

ribbon cable

A cable which connects an add-on with an Amiga port or edge connector.

ROM

Read Only Memory.

root directory

The top of the directory tree in AmigaDOS.

rubout box

A rectangular coloured box forming a background for text. A desktop video term.

ruler

Scale with units of measurement and tabulation marked on it.

Sans serif

Fonts without serifs.

script

A desktop video term. The text and graphics which go into the editing screen, not to be confused with an AmigaDOS script.

script

A term commonly used for AmigaDOS (and ARexx) programs. Usually, but not always, reserved for smallish programs.

scroll

To make a graphics display move upwards/downwards (vertical scrolling) or sideways (horizontal scrolling).

select box

The area of a gadget or menu within which Intuition can recognise a left-click select operation.

select button

The Amiga's lefthand mouse button.

sequence

Operations following each other in time.

Shell

An improved CLI interface which offers a number of useful new facilities including line editing and re-use of previously typed commands.

simulation

A program which tries to reproduce the real world.

sizing gadget

An Amiga system gadget which allows a user to drag-alter the size of an Intuition window.

software

Any program or routine for a computer.

sprite

A small graphical image. The term was originally applied to images whose movements were controlled directly by hardware. The Amiga supports both simple hardware sprites, virtual sprites, and a number of more sophisticated animation objects.

source file

A file from which data is being read.

submenu

A secondary menu which appears once a user has selected a specific menu item.

syntax

The formal grammatical structure of a language.

text editor

A program that enables text to be written, manipulated, stored etc. Wordprocessor programs are sophisticated text editors.

title bar

An optional strip at the top of a window or screen which may contain either a name, some system gadgets, or both.

tool

An Amiga Workbench name for an application program.

user-friendly

Designed to be easy to use.

user-definable

Part of a program which can be modified to suit.

VDU

Visual display unit. Your monitor or television.

wild card symbols

Symbols which may be used to represent any character in a pattern.

Workbench

The Amiga's inbuilt high-level interface applications program which allows users to interact with AmigaDOS, run applications programs etc, without getting involved with CLI/Shell commands.

Book Order Form

Full details of current books can be found in our Amiga Books appendix. Please rush me the following *Bruce Smith Books* books:

Amiga Gamer's Guide @ £14.95   £..........·......

Mastering AmigaDOS Vol. One Revised Edition @ £21.95   £..........·......

Mastering AmigaDOS Vol. Two Revised Edition @ £19.95   £..........·......

Mastering Amiga Workbench 2 @ £19.95   £..........·......

Mastering Amiga AMOS @ £19.95   £..........·......

Mastering Amiga Printers @ £19.95 with PD Disk   £..........·......

Mastering Amiga C @ £19.95 with Scripts & PD NorthC Disk   £..........·......

Mastering Amiga System @ £29.95 with Programs Disk   £..........·......

Mastering Amiga Assembler @ £24.95 with Programs Disk   £..........·......

Mastering Amiga ARexx @ £21.95 with Programs Disk   £..........·......

A600 Insider Guide @ £14.95   £..........·......

A1200 Insider Guide @ £14.95   £..........·......

Postage (International Orders Only): £..........·......

Total: £..........·......

I enclose a Cheque/Postal Order* for £   .   p.

I wish to pay by Access/Visa/Mastercard*

Card number ☐☐☐☐☐☐☐☐☐☐☐☐☐☐☐☐

Expiry Date: ..../......./..........

Name. ....

Address. ....

....

.... Post Code..............................

Contact phone number. ....

Signed ....

*Delete as appropriate. Cheques payable to Bruce Smith Books Ltd. E&OE

Send your order to:

Bruce Smith Books Ltd, FREEPOST 242, PO Box 382, St. Albans, Herts, AL2 3BR.

B:
Contacts

Owning a computer is a statement of intent: to get to grips with this new technology that can govern, but also liberate. And you are not alone. Computer owners tend to club together to share information and experience. The Amiga has so much potential that applications and approaches for its use are appearing daily. Sharing information is a way of not reinventing the wheel and of helping beginners get up to speed faster than through struggling in isolation.

You'll find that there are hundreds, nay thousands, of enthusiasts with Amiga experience who are willing to share their expertise and admit to where they went wrong in order to make your life a bit easier.

There are two types of club: local and by mail. Local groups tend to meet every month and to have a theme for each get-together. They put on demonstrations and invite companies to come and show their new creations. Secondhand auctions at Christmas and training sessions are also among the common activities of a local computer club. Check the magazines and the diary of events in your local press to find your nearest club.

By mail groups tend to be based upon a common interest in a particular hobby, eg music on the Amiga, or in a particular product, for instance programming in AMOS. Some are involved in producing newsletters or disk magazines, some provide a PD service too. You may find that the club runs on a swap basis or that there's a modest subscription.

So, get together with your fellow beginners to take your Amiga computing to its next stage, and tell them Bruce sent you!

Action Replay User's Club, 66 Muirside Avenue, Kirkinilloch, Glasgow, G66 3PR. Contact: Gordon Hagan.

Allbit Computer Club, 170 Claughton Avenue, Crewe, Cheshire CW2 6ET.

AMI-INFO, Homeside, Higher Warberry Road, Torquay, Devon, TQ1 1SF. Contact: Paul Caparn.

Amiga 500+ Club, 3 Islay Court, Irvine, Ayrshire, KA11 4JQ.

.**Amiga Addicts**, Clonkelly, Binn, Co. Ojffaly, Ireland. Contact: A Minnock.

Amiga Artists Club, 34 Roundhay Mount, Leeds, LS8 4DW. Telephone: (0532) 493942.

Amiga Athens Club, 9 Derfeld Road, Patisia, 11144, Athens, Greece, 01 2027973. Contact: Stephanos Papamichael.

Amiga BASIC Club, 15 Weybridge Road, Thornton Heath, Surrey, CR7 7LN. Telephone: 081-689 9102.

Amiga Beginners Club, 110 Whitehill Park, Limavidy, Co. Londonderry, BT49 0QG.

Amiga Boatowners, Lock, Branston Fen, Lincolnshire, LN3 5UN. Contact: D. Beet.

Amiga C Club, Tulevagen 22, 181 41 Lidingo, Sweden. Contact: Anders Bjerin.

Amiga Club, 190 Falloden Way, Hampstead Garden Suburb, London, NW11 6SE. Telephone: 081-455 1626.

Amiga Graphic Club, 16 Drumbawn, Enniskillen, Fermangh, BT74 6NF. Contact: Jonathan McBrien.

Amiga Helpline, 21 Skirsa Place, Glasgow, G23 5EE.

Amiga Mania, 88 Blackbull Road, Folkestone, Kent, CT19 5QX.
Contact: Dave Cryer.

Amiga Maniacs Help, 8 Tan-y-Grais, Caernafon Road, Bangor,
LL57 4SD.

Amiga Musicians Club, Guthrie Street, Carnoustie, Angus.
Contact: Gavin Wylie.

Amiga Navigation, 4a Allister Street, Neath, West Glamorgan.

Amiga Network International, 434 Denby Dale Road East,
Wakefield, West Yorks, WF4 3AE.

Amiga Special, Honeysuckle Cottage, 71 Green Lane, Studley,
Warwickshire, B80 7EY. Contact: Andrew Stanford.

Amiga Users Group, 25 Glen Eldon Road, Lytham St. Annes, Lancs,
FY8 2AX.

Amiga Users Klub, 1 Windsor House, 19 Castle Street, Bodmin,
Cornwall, PL31 2DX.

Amiga Users, Luton. Telephone: (0582) 502806.
Contact: Dave J. Noble.

Amiga Utd, 14 Linden Close, Hutton Rudby, Yarm, Cleveland,
TS15 0HX. Contact: David Collingwood.

Amiga Video Producers' Group, 8 Rochford Close, Grange Park,
Swindon, Wilts, SN5 6AB. Telephone: (0793) 87667.

Amiga Witham Users' Group, 85 Highfield Road, Witham, Essex,
CM8 1LW.

Amigaholics, 29 Wolfe Crescent, Charlton, London, SE7 8TS.
Contact: Kevin Bryan.

AmigaSoc, 17 St. Winifrid's Avenue, Manor Park, London, E12 6HQ.
Contact: Neil Cartwright.

AMOS Programmers Club, 6 Brassey Avenue, Broadstairs, Thanet,
Kent, C10 2DS.

AMOS Programming, 132 rue Jean Follain, 50000 Saint-Lo, France,
315220 02. Contact: F Moreau.

Amos Programmers Group, 62 Lonsdale Street, Workington, Cumbria, CA14 2YD. Contact: John Mullen.

Angus Amiga CDTV Club, 22a High Stret, Brechin, Angus, DD9 6ER. Telephone: (0356) 623072. Contact: J. Robertson.

Artman, 40 Northwell Gate, Otley, West Yorks, LS21 2ND. Telephone: (0943) 466476.

Asia Amiga Association, Room 11c, Fortune Court, 4-6 Tak Hing Street, Kowloon, Hong Kong, 7245196. Contact: Pete Alex.

AUGFL vzw, Meesberg 13, 3220 Holsbeek, Belgium. Contact: Lieven Lema.

Avon Micro Computer Serious Club, 16-18 King Square, Bristol. BS2 8JL. Fax: (0272) 311642.

BASIC Programmers Group, 68 Queen Elizabeth Drive, Normanton, West Yorks, WF6 1JF.

Beaconsfield and District CC, 27 Russell Court, Chesham, Bucks. Contact: Phillip Lishma.

Bloomfield Video and Computing, Nashville, 50 Glynderi, Carmarthen, Dyfed, SA31 2EX. Telephone: (0267) 237522. Contact: Mrs Beryl Hughes.

Bournemouth Amiga Club, 36 Homeoaks, 30 Wimborne Road, Bournemouth, Dorset BH2 6QA. Telephone: (0202) 296714. Contact: P. Chamberlain

BR and CJ Computer Club, 23 Fairway Road, Shepshed, Loughborough, Leicestershire, LE12 9DS. Telephone: (03922) 841296. Contact: B. Robinson

Camberley User Group, Telephone: (0252) 871545. Contact: F Wellbelove.

CDTV Users Club, 113 Fouracres Road, Newall Green, Manchester, M23 8ES. Contact: Julian Lavanini.

Chester-le-Street 16 Bit Computer Club, Newcastle Road, Chester-le-Street. Telephone: 091-385 2939.

Chic Computer Club, PO Box 121, Gerrards Gross, Bucks. Telephone: (0735) 884473. Contact: Steve Winter.

Chud, 103 Neward Road, Bulford, Salisbury, Wilts, SP4 9AH. Telephone: (0980) 33154. Contact: Mr M. Sellars.

City Centre Amiga Club, Loughton Lower, Newcastle, Co. Dublin, Republic of Ireland. Contact: Sean Corrigan.

Club 68000, 59 Walton Park, Pannal, Harrogate, North Yorkshire, HG3 1EJ. Telephone: (0753) 884473. Contact: Chris Hughes.

Club Amiga, 5 Bowes Lea, Shiney Row, Houghton-Le-Spring, Tyne and Wear. Telephone: 091-385 2627. Contact: Chris Longley.

Comp-U-Pal, 116 Macarthur Street, Sale, Victoria 3850, Australia.

Darlington Commodore Users Club, 1 Ruby Street, Darlington, County Durham, DL3 0EN. Contact: S. Wheatley.

East Midlands Amiga Users Group, 70 Felstead Road, Apsley, Nottingham, NG8 3HF. Contact: Richard Haythorn.

Edinburgh Amiga Group, 37 Kingsknowe Road North, Edinburgh, EH14 2D. Contact: Neil McRea.

Enfield Amiga Club, 32a Hoe Lane, Enfield, Middx. Telephone: 081-804 2867. Contact: Sean Clifton.

Exeter 16 Bit User Group, 25a Gloucestershire Road, Exwick, Exeter, EX4 2EF. Telephone: (0392) 72889. Contact: Andrew Deeley.

FST Amiga Club, 17 Grasmere Close, Penistone, Sheffield, Yorks, S30 6HP.

Fylde Computer Club, 90 The Esplanade, Fleetwood, Lancs FY7 7BQ. Telephone: (0253) 772502. Contact: Colin Biss.

GFA Basic Forum, 52 Church Road, Braunston, Nr. Daventry, Northants, NN11 7HQ. Contact: J Findlay.

Gibraltar Amiga Users Club, 7 Lime Tree Lodge, Montagu Gardens, Gibraltar, 010 350 79918. Contact: Paul Jennings.

Hereford Amiga Group, Alma Cottage, Allensmore, Hereford, HR2 9AT. Telephone: (0981) 21414. Contact: John MacDonald.

Hermit Computer Club, Hermit Centre, Shenfield Road, Brentwood, Essex CM15 8AG. Telephone: (0277) 218897. Contact: John Mynard.

Hynburn Amiga Users Club, 7 Brecon Avenue, Oswaldtwistle, Lancashire BB5 4QS. Telephone: (0254) 395289. Contact: Nigel Rigby.

In Touch Amiga, PO Box 21, Lingfield, Surrey, RH7 6YJ. Telephone: (0342) 835530. Contact: Pete Allen.

Independent Commodore Products Users' Group (ICPUG), PO Box 1309, London N3 2UT. Telephone: 081-346 0050. Contact: Bob Rigby.

Kent Youth Computer Group, The North Youth Centre, Essellar Road, Ashford, Kent. Telephone: (0233) 629804. Contact: Jim Fanning.

Lothian Amiga Users Group, 52 Biniegill Avenue, Bathgate, West Lothian, EH48 2RR. Telephone: (0506) 630509. Contact: Andrew Mackie.

Macclesfield Computer Group, 36 Stapleton Road, Macclesfield, Cheshire, SK10 3NP. Telephone: (0625) 429667.

Maritime Amiga Club, GN Ships Refit Office, 51 Rue de la Bretonniere, 50105 Cherbourg, France. Contact: Cdr K. Osei.

Megamigamaniacs, PO Box 37216, Chempet 7442, Cape Town, Republic of South Africa. Contact: Nick Oliver.

N. Ireland Amiga Users, 98 Crebilly Road, Ballymena, Co Antrim, BT42 4DS. Contact: Stephen Hamer.

Newhall Amiga Users Club, 115 Stanley Street, Accrington, Lancashire. Telephone: (0254) 385365. Contact: Bill Grundy.

Pascal Programmers Group, 93 Manchester Road, Wilmslow, Cheshire, SK9 2JQ. Contact: Colin Yarmall.

Pennine Amiga Club, 26 Spencer Street, Keighley, West Yorkshire, BD21 2BU. Contact: Neville Armstrong.

Perth and District Amateur Computer Society, 137 Glasgow Road, Perth. Contact: Alastair Macpherson.

Redbourn Computer Users Group, Telephone: (0294) 313624. Contact: Ruby Anderson.

Robotronix Amiga Club, 36 Century Road, Cobholm,
Great Yarmouth, Norfolk, NR31 0BX. Contact: P Symonds.

Rye Amiga Group, 71 The Mint, Rye, East Sussex, TN31 7EW.
Contact: Oliver Campion.

Shropshire Amiga Link, 2 Dodmoor Grange, Randlay, Telford,
Shropshire, TF3 2AW. Telephone: (0952) 591376.
Contact: N. Cockayne.

Sittingbourne Co-op Computer Club, Unit 11, The Mall, 121-127
East Street, Sittingbourne, Kent, ME10 4AQ. Contact: Andy.

Slim Agnus, 115 Brocks Drive, North Cheam, Sutton, Surrey,
SM3 9UW. Contact: Phillip Worrel.

South Wales Computer Club, 53 West Avenue, Trecenydd,
Caerphilly, CF8 2SF. Contact: D. Allen.

The Amiga Club, 31 Pine Lea, Brandon, Durham, DH7 8SR.
Contact: G. Starling.

Wrexham District Computer Club, 3 Ffordd Elfed, Rhosnesi,
Wrexham, Clwyd, LL12 7LU. Contact: Paul Evans.

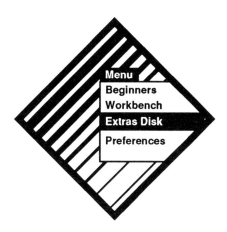

Mastering Amiga Guides

Bruce Smith Books are dedicated to producing quality Amiga publications which are both comprehensive and easy to read. Our Amiga titles are being written by some of the best known names in the marvellous world of Amiga computing. Below you will find details of all our currently available books for the Amiga owner.

Titles Currently Available

- Mastering Amiga Workbench2
- Mastering AmigaDOS Vol. 1
- Mastering AmigaDOS Vol. 2
- Amiga Gamer's Guide
- Mastering Amiga AMOS
- Mastering Amiga C
- Mastering Amiga Printers
- Mastering Amiga System
- Mastering Amiga Assembler
- Mastering Amiga ARexx
- Amiga A600 Insider Guide
- Amiga A1200 Insider Guide

Brief details of these guides along with review segments are given below. If you would like a free copy of our catalogue *Mastering Amiga News* and to be placed on our mailing list then phone or write to the address below.

Our mailing list is used exclusively to inform readers of forthcoming Bruce Smith

Books publications along with special introductory offers which normally take the form of a free software disk when ordering the publication direct from us.

Bruce Smith Books,
PO Box 382,
St. Albans, Herts, AL2 3JD
Telephone: (0923) 894355
Fax: (0923) 894366

Note that we offer a 24-hour telephone answer system so that you can place your order direct by 'phone at a time to suit yourself. When ordering by 'phone please:

- Speak clearly and slowly

- Leave your full name and full address

- Leave a day-time contact phone number

- Give your credit card number and expiry date

- Spell out any unusual names

Note that we do not charge for P&P in the UK and endeavour to dispatch all books within 24-hours.

Buying at your Bookshop

All our books can be obtained via your local bookshops – this includes WH Smiths which will be keeping a stock of some of our titles, just enquire at their counter. If you wish to order via your local High Street bookshop you will need to supply the book name, author, publisher, price and ISBN number.

Overseas Orders

Please add £3 per book (Europe) or £6 per book (outside Europe) to cover postage and packing. Pay by sterling cheque or by Access, Visa or Mastercard. Post, Fax or Phone your order to us.

Dealer Enquiries

Our distributor is Computer Bookshops Ltd who keep a good stock of all our titles. Call their Customer Services Department for best terms on 021-706-1188.

Compatibility

We endeavour to ensure that all *Mastering Amiga* books are fully compatible with all Amiga models and all releases of AmigaDOS and Workbench.

NEW! Great value! 368 pages for £14.95.

Amiga Gamer's Guide by Dan Slingsby

Everyone loves games and Amiga games are growing in sophistication, always setting new playing challenges while introducing ever more gasp-producing graphics and sound effects. Even the techies at Bruce Smith Books are not immune to the games phenomenon. This latest book for the discerning Amiga owner, is a highly illustrated guide to your favourite Amiga games, including classics like Shadow of the Beast and recent top ten hits like Putty, Formula One Grand Prix, Streetfighter 2 and Indiana Jones.

From sports sims to arcade adventures, Amiga Gamer's Guide gives you the hints and tips, hidden screens and puzzle solutions which you are looking for. Completed by a massive A to Z of tips and tricks for over 300 games, Amiga Gamer's Guide is the most masterful of games guides yet published.

Written by CU Amiga editor Dan Slingsby, Amiga Gamer's Guide contains a wealth of background information to the most popular Amiga games. The graphically appealing layout with hundreds of pictures used to illustrate the games and their story lines, makes this one of the most attactive Amiga books to be found on the bookshelves.

The games featured, with full scenarios, hints and tips and solutions are:

Another World; Chaos Strikes Back; Dungeon Master; Elvira 2; Epic; Formula One Grand Prix; Gobliiins; Indiana Jones & the Fate of Atlantis; Ishar; John Madden American Football; Kickoff 2; Lure of the Temptress; Monkey Island 2; Populous 2; Project X; Putty; Robocod; Sensible Soccer; Shadow of the Beast 1, 2 and 3; Speedball 2; Streetfighter 2; Striker; Supremacy; Zak McKracken.

Amiga Gamer's Guide
by Dan Slingsby

ISBN: 1-873308-16-7, price £14.95, 368 pages.

Mastering AmigaDOS 2

Our 700-page plus dual volume set covers all versions of AmigaDOS from 1.2, including 1.2, 1.3, 1.3.2 and 2.x. Volume One is a complete tutorial for AmigaDOS users, both beginners and experts alike. Volume Two is a detailed and comprehensive reference to all AmigaDOS commands.

Here's what the press said:

"If you're a complete beginner or unsure of a few areas, this book is an amazingly informative read." Amiga Format on Volume One

"As a reference book it's very useful. So far as I know there isn't any similar book...If you need to know how every AmigaDOS command works get this book...it is a definitive reference" Amiga Format on Volume Two.

"The Reference book that Commodore forgot to commission" Keith Pomfret of New Computer Express on Volume Two.

"The book can be strongly recommended....and even more strongly to those having difficulty getting to grips with its various commands. You won't find a better guide to, or a more useful book on, the Amiga than this" Micronet AmigaBASE.

"No other authors have investigated AmigaDOS with the thoroughness of Smith and Smiddy and every page provides useful information. Put off getting that new game, and buy this instead. You won't regret it." Micronet AmigaBASE.

And if you don't know if you need either or both books here is what Amiga Format suggested: *"If Volume 1 is so good what is the point of having Volume 2? Volume 1 is a tutorial, it teaches you how to use AmigaDOS. Volume 2 is more of a manual."*

Mastering AmigaDOS 2 Volume One – Revised Edition
by Bruce Smith and Mark Smiddy

ISBN: 1-873308-10-8, price £21.95, 416 pages.

FREE Utilities disk when ordered direct – £1.50 to cover p&p otherwise.

Mastering AmigaDOS 2 Volume Two – Revised Edition
by Bruce Smith and Mark Smiddy

Foreword by Barry Thurston, Technical Director, Commodore Business Machines (UK) Ltd.

ISBN: 1-873308-09-4, price £19.95, 368 pages.

Mastering Amiga C

C is without doubt one of the most powerful programming languages ever created, and it has a very special relationship with the Commodore Amiga. Much of the Amiga's operating system software was written using C and almost all of the Amiga technical reference books assume some proficiency in the language.

Paul Overaa has been writing about C and the Amiga for as long as the machine has been in existence. He knows the Amiga-specific pitfalls that can plague the beginner, knows how to avoid them, and above all he knows about C. Best of all he's prepared to share that experience. The result is a book which is guaranteed to get the Amiga owner programming in C as quickly and as painlessly as possible.

This introductory text assumes no prior knowledge of C and covers all the major compilers, including Lattice/SAS and Aztec. What is more it also covers NorthC – the Charityware compiler – so that anyone who is interested in learning C can do so for just a few pounds. This book assumes no prior knowledge of C and features:

- Easy to follow tutorials
- All major C compilers
- Explanations of special Amiga C features
- Amiga problem areas
- Debugging and testing

Here's what CU Amiga thought of Mastering Amiga C: *"This book has been written with the absolute novice in mind. It doesn't baffle with jargon and slang"*.

Writing in Amiga User International, Mike Nelson called Mastering Amiga C: *"Very thorough, Paul Overaa has gone to considerable lengths to keep up to date with developments the in real world of C and the ANSI Standards......this book will go a long way to help you master C on your Amiga"*.

Mastering Amiga C
by Paul Overaa

ISBN: 1-873308-04-6, price £19.95, 320 pages.

FREE Programs Disk and NorthC Public Domain compiler when ordered direct from Bruce Smith Books.

Mastering Amiga Printers

Next to the Amiga itself, your printer is the largest and most important purchase you're likely to make. It's surprising then, that so little help is available for those about to take this step, whether it be for the first time, or for the purpose of upgrading from an old, trusted but limited model to one of today's much more versatile and complex machines. The problem of course is that you can't take one home on trial to find out what it does.

Today's printers are extremely sophisticated and complex devices, with a wide range of capabilities, so it's all too easy to make a mistake at the stage of buying if you don't know what to look for, the right questions to ask and the sort of comparisons to make between similarly priced models from different manufacturers. Since a printer is such a large investment, quite possibly more expensive than the micro itself, choosing the right type and model for your needs is doubly important, because you'll have to live with your decision for a long time.

Unfortunately for the user, neither computer nor printer manufacturers see it as their responsibility to offer guidance or assistance to users in this important purchase.

Mastering Amiga Printers fills this gap perfectly. Making no assumptions about previous printer experience, the explanations begin with the basic principles of how printers work, including a run-down of the different types most commonly used with home and business micros.

After a comprehensive grounding in the abilities and methods of the different types of printer hardware you'll then learn how to install them in the Amiga. Preference selections and printer drivers are thoroughly explained for both Workbench one and two, so you'll know not only which choices to make, but what they mean. There's also a thorough grounding in the direct use of printers from the command line, which you'll need if you want to write your own programs.

Additional chapters take a logical approach to trouble-shooting and routine maintenance, vital to the newcomer. These chapters include the sort of information and knowledge which is normally only available after long experience, the very thing the new user lacks. *Mastering Amiga Printers* is a must for every user who wants to the best out of their Amiga and its printer.

Mastering Amiga Printers

by Robin Burton

ISBN: 1-873308-05-1, price £19.95, 336 pages.

FREE utilities and printer drivers disk when ordered direct from Bruce Smith Books.

Mastering Amiga Workbench 2

The Workbench is one of the most important aspects of the Amiga, yet so few users really understand how to use it to its full potential. From it you can access virtually all of the Amiga's functions and determine how your computer will operate from the moment it is switched on. With the advent of Workbench 2, running under the much enhanced AmigaDOS 2, the options open to the Workbench users are greater than ever before.

In this book Bruce Smith explains everything you will want to know about the Workbench version 2.x, using screen illustrations throughout for ease of reference. The book is geared towards all types of users, whether you have a single floppy disk or a hard disk to operate from.

Starting from first steps the book explains the philosophy of the Workbench and how it ties in with your Amiga. It then moves on to describe the best way to perform basic housekeeping tasks such as disk copying, file transfer and how to customise your own Workbench disks for different occasions and requirements.

The author works his way through each of the menu options with full descriptions of their use, providing many hints, tips and tricks *en-route*. By this stage you will already be an accomplished Workbench user, but as the books enters its final stages you will make the transition to expert status as areas such as Preferences, Tools and Commodities are fully explained.

In effect *Mastering Amiga Workbench 2* provides you with a complete guide to your Workbench and Extras disks in an easy to read style guaranteed to upgrade you to full proficiency on your Amiga.

Mastering Amiga Workbench

by Bruce Smith
ISBN: 1-873308-08-6, price £19.95, 320 pages.

Mastering Amiga System

A complete tutorial to Amiga System programming with copious examples. A basic knowledge of C is required but the book begins with short examples which only later build into full-scale programs. Serious Amiga programmers need to use the Amiga's operating system to write legal, portable and efficient programs. But it's not easy! Paul Overaa shares his experience in this introduction to system programming in the C language, the natural language for getting the best out of the Amiga. And there's a free programs disk included in the price with lots of examples and utilities.

Readers will learn how to communicate with the system, how to handle tasks and processes and work with libraries and how to incorporate IFF graphics into their own applications. They will also find out how to harness the power of Intuition, the routines behind the Amiga's classic graphical interface. At no time is the reader left to produce code from general explanations. The author keeps it specific and presents skeleton programs which are fully documented so that they can be followed by the newcomer to Amiga programming. The larger programs are fully-fledged examples which can serve as templates for the reader's own ideas as confidence is gained.

Paul Overaa spells it out in a step by step fashion as he proceeds to explain devices and the custom chips which make the Amiga the all-time great graphical microcomputer. In dealing with a difficult subject, Paul Overaa has avoided merely duplicating standard documentation. Instead he has entered on a journey through the different aspects of the Amiga's system, finding the safest and most effective routes to practical programs. Mastering Amiga System is an invaluable purchase for the Amiga programmer who wants to master the system software.

The free disk which accompanies this book contains both source code and runable versions for all of the programs discussed within the text. In addition to this, a number of document files have been provided which deal with compilers and compiling, ANSI C and K&R C (including notes on ANSI C <-> K&R C program conversion), header files and guru numbers. As well as the tutorial style examples, the disk also contains a number of utility programs including a MIDI message analyser, a generalised minterm expression evaluator, and a recursive search disk routine that could be used as the basis of a number of disk catalogue programs. Source code files for each of these utilities have been provided.

Mastering Amiga System
by Paul Overaa
ISBN: 1-873308-06-X, price £29.95, 398 pages.
FREE progams disk when ordered direct from Bruce Smith Books.

Mastering Amiga Assembler

Although the 68000 processor series is well-documented, the use of assembly language to write efficient code within the unique environment of the Amiga is only now explained in this hands-on tutorial. It teaches how to generate machine code from the popular Amiga assemblers, all of which are supported by the many program examples in this book. These programs also appear as source code and runable programs on the free support disk.

The Amiga is a powerful machine but the sheer complexity of its operating system has provided a major obstacle to many programmers wishing to enter the world of Amiga assembly language programming. Mastering Amiga Assembler holds the reader's hand, introducing topics through short examples, with diagrammatic explanation where necessary. Longer programs of a practical nature come only later, as the required techniques are practised and mastered.

Topics covered include:

- Fundamental assembly language concepts.

- The 68000 processor and its important instructions.

- The 68000 addressing modes.

- Use of system header files and the official Amiga documentation.

- Working with the Amiga libraries.

- CLI/Shell and Workbench programming.

- Low-level Intuition and graphics programming.

- Introductions to some advanced topics including Exec interrupts and mixed code programming.

- Details of popular assembler environments including HiSoft's Devpac and the PD 68K assembler.

Mastering Amiga Assembler
by Paul Overaa
ISBN: 1-873308-11-6, price £24.95, 416 pages.

FREE disk with programs from the book and extra utilities when ordered direct from Bruce Smith Books.

Mastering Amiga AMOS

AMOS has very quickly developed into one of the most exciting and most accessible programming language environments on the Amiga. Its easy to use interface and familiar BASIC structure are augmented by powerful libraries for games and graphics programming.

Phil South provides a fascinating introduction, tries out all the main features and provides lots of example code for the reader to experiment with. He also brings you right up to date on 3D, graphics, demo programming and developments such as Easy AMOS, AMOS Professional and third party support.

If you are a novice programmer, or are looking for the next step after BASIC then AMOS is for you and you'll enjoy learning AMOS in the company of this step by step tutorial. Like any programming language AMOS has many shortcuts and clever ways of doing things, most of which are presented with examples in this book.

AMOS has also gathered around it a number of powerful utilities which can be used to augment the language in particular ways and provide materials such as windows, text and menus, screens, sprites and bobs, icons and screen blocks, sound and music, object movement, SpriteX, CText and TOME, AMOS compilers, 3D and advanced AMAL. These are covered in detail with information about how to get hold of them and how to join up with AMOS clubs and program libraries.

Anyone following the various series on AMOS which are appearing in the Amiga magazines will find Mastering Amiga AMOS a handy reference and source of programming ideas. The example programs listed have been selected to demonstrate a wide variety of programming techniques.

Whether you have a specific program that you wish to write or you intend to do some programming as a hobby, AMOS opens the door; this book takes you by the hand and leads you through it. Sit yourself down at the keyboard with Phil South's many examples and you'll soon find impressive results can be obtained easily.

Mastering Amiga AMOS
by Phil South
ISBN: 1-873308-12-4, price £19.95, 320 pages.

Mastering Amiga ARexx

ARexx is the Amiga version of the REXX programming language Commodore have adopted as part of Workbench 2/3. With this sort of official endorsement ARexx is set for a very bright future and Amiga users are now asking the questions: Is ARexx a replacement for AmigaBASIC? Can ARexx replace AmigaDOS? Can real programs be written with ARexx? How does ARexx allow programs to talk to each other? In short, people want to know what ARexx is and how it can be used. It is exactly these types of question for which this book provides the answers!

ARexx is in many ways an unusual programming language. For a start it is easy to learn and even those new to the Amiga soon find that simple ARexx script programs give added weight to an already powerful operating system.

The creator of ARexx is Bill Hawes and the general consensus is that his initial interpretation of the REXX language and the subsequent programming has been nigh-on faultless. This has resulted in ARexx being one of those relatively rare third party products officially endorsed by Commodore. ARexx is of course now provided as part of Workbench 2 and 3 but it has been happily running on the Amiga through both 1.2 and 1.3 versions of the operating system. Even nowadays you do not need to be a Workbench 2 user to benefit from ARexx because ARexx is still available as a separate package

This latest guide to ARexx is from programming expert Paul Overaa and is guaranteed to get the Amiga owner into the world of ARexx programming quickly, productively and enjoyably.

Topics covered include: how to install ARexx on any Amiga, introductions to the ARexx language and comparisons with languages like BASIC, in depth discussions of the ARexx language's main features, explanations of how ARexx is used to control other programs, details of ARexx's built-in functions and support libraries, methods for creating well structured ARexx programs, introductions to many advanced ARexx programming topics plus tips and tricks, programming and debugging guidelines, tutorials, and much more.

When ordered direct from Bruce Smith Books, Mastering Amiga ARexx also comes with a free support disk containing the many example programs from the book.

Mastering Amiga ARexx
by Paul Overaa

ISBN: 1-873308-13-2, price £21.95, 336 pages.

FREE disk with program examples and utilities when ordered direct from Bruce Smith Books.

Amiga A600 Insider Guide

A perfect companion for all A600 and A600HD users. This book provides you with a unique insight into the use of Workbench and AmigaDOS on all versions of the Amiga A600.

Assuming no prior knowledge it shows you how to get the very best from your machine in a friendly manner and using its unique Insider Guide steps (see A1200 description below).

Amiga A600 Insider Guide
by Bruce Smith
ISBN: 1-873308-14-0, price £14.95, 256 pages.

Amiga A1200 Insider Guide

Assuming no prior knowledge, it shows you how to get the very best from your A1200 in a friendly manner and using its unique Insider Guide steps. Configuring your system for printer, keyboard, Workbench colours, use of Commodities and much much more has made this the best-selling book for the A1200.

As well as easy to read explanations of how to get to grips with the Amiga, the book features 55 of the unique Insider Guides, each of which displays graphically a set of step by step instructions. Each Insider Guide concentrates on a especially important or common task which the user has to carry out on the Amiga. By following an Insider Guide the user learns how to control the Amiga by example. Beginners to the A1200 will particularly appreciate this approach to a complex computer.

The disks which come with the A1200 contain a wealth of utilities and resources which allow you to configure the computer for your own way of working. The step by step tutorials take you through using these point by point, anticipating any problems as they go. There are also fully fledged programs such as MultiView and ED which can seem impenetrable for the new user but which become clear when observed in use over the shoulder of author Bruce Smith.

Great new features such as the colour wheel, Intellifonts, using MSDOS disks with CrossDos and configuring sound are dealt with in detail. A useful appendix acts as a file locater so that any of the many files on the Amiga disks can be quickly found.

Amiga A1200 Insider Guide
by Bruce Smith
ISBN: 1-873308-15-9, price £14.95, 256 pages.

Contents Lists

These pages list the chapter headings for some of our published books. This should give you a better indication as to their full content.

Mastering AmigaDOS 2 Volume One Revised Edition

Introduction, AmigaDOS and Workbench, About Directories, AmigaDOS Command, Formatting and Copying, The Shell, The RAM Disk, Wildcards and Pattern Matching, File Protection and Assigning, ED – The Screen Editor, Multi-tasking Amiga, Environmental Variables, Command Bits and Pieces, The Bootable RAM Disk, Devices, More About LIST, Introduction to Scripts, Structured AmigaDOS, Evaluating and Manipulating, Startup-sequences, AmigaDOS 1.2 Startup-sequence, AmigaDOS 1.3 Startup-sequence, AmigaDOS 2.04 Startup-sequences, Customising Disks, Practical Scripts, Scripts That Write Scripts!, Recursive Scripts, Commodities Exchange, Fountain, MEMACS, Backing Up with BRU, Multi-User Machine, Pipes, Original AmigaDOS2 Startup-sequence.

Mastering AmigaDOS 2 Volume Two

AmigaDOS Command Reference Section, ADDBUFFERS, ADDMONITOR, ALIAS, ASK, ASSIGN, AUTOPOINT, AVAIL, BINDDRIVERS, BINDMONITOR, BLANKER, BREAK, BRU, CD, CHANGETASKPRI, CLICKTOFRONT, CLOCK, CMD, COLORS, CONCLIP, COPY, CPU, DATE , DELETE, DIR, DISKCHANGE, DISKCOPY, DISKDOCTOR, DISPLAY, DPAT, ECHO, ED, EDIT, ELSE, ENDCLI, ENDSHELL, ENDIF, ENDSKIP, EVAL, EXCHANGE, EXECUTE, FAILAT, FASTMEMFIRST, FAULT, FF, FILENOTE, FIXFONTS, FKEY, FONT, FORMAT, GET, GETENV,. GRAPHICDUMP, ICONTROL, ICONX, IF, IHELP, INFO, INITPRINTER, INPUT, INSTALL, JOIN, LAB, LIST, LOADWB, LOCK, MAGTAPE, MAKEDIR, MAKELINK , MEMACS, MERGEMEM , MORE, MOUNT, NEWCLI, NEWSHELL, NOCAPSLOCK, NOFASTMEM, OVERSCAN, PALETTE, PARK, PATH, PCD, POINTER, PREFERENCES, PRINTER, PRINTERGFX, PRINTFILES, PROMPT, PROTECT, QUIT, RELABEL,REMRAD, RENAME, RESIDENT, REXXMAST, RUN, SAY, SCREENMODE, SEARCH, SERIAL, SET, SETCLOCK , SETDATE, SETENV, SETFONT, SETMAP, SETPATCH, SKIP, SORT , SPAT, STACK, STATUS, TIME, TYPE, UNALIAS, UNSET, UNSETENV, VERSION , WAIT, WBPATTERN, WHICH, WHY, Wildcards, ;,? ,<, >, >> ,*,"",*,',CTRL+\ ,ALT+' , AmigaDOS Error Codes, The Virus Menace, The Interchange File Format, The Mountlist, Telling FIBs.

Mastering Amiga C

Introduction, Making a Start, Types, Operators and Expressions, Functions, Program Documentation and Portability, Flow Control, The C Preprocessor, Arrays and Pointers, Input and Output,

Structures and Bitfields, Character Strings, Storage Classes, Data Types Revisited, Files, Special C Features, The Real Problem, Some Amiga Specifics, Resource Allocation, Intuition and the Graphics Library, Making the Most of C's Modularity, Debugging and Testing, Last Words, Glossary, Bibliography, The Lattice/SAS C Compiler, The Manx Aztec C Compiler, The NorthC Compiler, Bits and Bytes, ANSI C Summary, ASCII Character Set, Useful Programming Tools.

Mastering Amiga Printers

Consider the Printer!, Types of Printer, Connected Matters,   Initial Setting-up, Controlling Printers, Printer Commands, Graphics Commands, Printer Peculiarities, Elements of a System, Printer Installation, Printer Preferences, Printer Driver Facilities, Taking Control, Command Line Control, BASIC Control, Graphicus Horizontalis, Graphicus Verticalis, Graphics Preferences, Graphics Options, Screen Dumping, Deluxe Paint, Problems, Problems... Printer Driver Commands, Decimal-hexadecimal-binary-ASCII Conversions, Glossary.

Mastering Amiga Workbench 2

Take Off, The Workbench, Drawers and Directories, Disks and Drawers, Copying Files, The Menus, The Ram Disk, The Utilities Drawer, The Tools Drawer, The Shell, The System Drawer, Commodities Exchange, The Preferences Editors, The Recoverable Ram Disk, Icons and IconEdit, Information and Tool Types, Printer Installation, Graphics Printing, Fonts, Useful AmigaDOS, ED – The Text Editor, Customising Workbench Disks, MEmacs, Tool Types Revisited, The Virus Factor, Hard Disks, Goings On, Creating a Text File, Tool Type Summaries, File Location Guide

Mastering Amiga System

An Overview, Preliminary Style and Programming Notes, Exec Memory Management, Tasks and Processes, Lists and Nodes, Libraries, Libraries and More Libraries, Intuition's Screens and Windows, Resource Allocation, Talking to Intuition, Exec Messages and Ports, Intuition's Text, Line Drawing and Image Facilities, Intuition's Gadgets, Intuition's Menu System, Devices: An Introduction, The Amiga's Serial Device, Interrupts: Making a Start, The Amiga's Co-Processor, Blitter First Steps, Troubleshooting Software Problems, Last Words.

Mastering Amiga Assembler

Contents, Fundamental Concepts, The 68000 Chip and its Assembly Language, Solving Simple Problems, Subroutines and Parameter Passing, Program Design Issues, Program Documentation, An Introduction to the Amiga Environment, The Amiga System Include Files, Macro Programming and its Benefits, Libraries and the Amiga,

An Overview Of Some Important Rules, Some Introductory Shell/CLI Programs, Exec Messages and Ports, Making a Start With Intuition, A Complete Intuition Example, Where To Go From Here, The 68000 Instruction Set, The C Language, Library Function Tables, The 68K Assembler, Bibliography

Mastering Amiga ARexx

Contents, The ARexx Language, The ARexx Environment, Making A Start, Simple Variables, Operators & Expressions, Functions, Flow Control, Program Documentation & Coding Conventions, Putting Some Pieces Together, Compound Variables, Program Design – Some Guidelines, Parsing, Files and Other I/O Issues, More Coding Practice, Interrupt Signalling, Tracing & Debugging, ARexx Communications, Interprogram Communications1 – The User Angle, Interprogram Communications 2 –The Inside Story, Where To Go From Here, The Complete ARexx Package, The Commodore Connection, Public Domain Offerings, Glossary, Bibliography

New publications and their contents are subject to change without notice.

E&OE.

Index

Symbols

3D graphics 144

A

A500 Plus..........................20, 23

A600 ....20, 24

A600HD 20, 24

A1200 ....21, 235

AmigaDOS........................51, 192

AMOS 199, 203-209

animation 144, 149

archive.................................160

ARexx...................................192

assembly language 194

backdrop 72

B

backing up.............................41

BASIC 193, 198

baud.....................................158

bitmap 149

booting 24

bulletin board...............158, 160

C

CAD...............................142, 144

Calculator 61

camcorder..............................151

Cancel 39

CDTV 152, 228, 238, 253-254

change directory.....................89

Clock.....................................57

close 31

Colors 63

colour cycling 149

commands 52

Commodity 258, 261

comms 157

compression 162

Continue 40

copy 42, 45-47

copy command 83, 85-87

Copy_of_ 43

corrupted 43

CrossDOS 258

cursor 43

D

daisywheel 110

data....................................185

database..............................182

Deluxe Paint........139, 144, 148

desktop................................25

desktop publishing.....112, 188

desktop video 145, 152

destination...........................41

devices 51

DF0: 38

digitiser 225

Dir..54, 89

directory 54, 79

Disk Copy 42

disk formatting.....................38

disk magazine.....................247

disk swapping......................45

diskspace 44

dot matrix.....................11, 117

double-click 29

drawer 79-82, 88

E

ED 91

editing keys 73

electronic mail....................158

Epson 109

execute command.................52

External drive 85

Extras 61, 261

F

fax......................................228

field 183

filing system........................80

Fish disks............................248

floppy disk 37, 43, 45

floppy drive 19, 219

Format 83

fractal 147

freespace 32

front/back......................31, 32

G

gadget 30

games...........................163, 233

genlock 152, 154, 227

graphic printing..................112

graphics 139

graphics objects 142

H

hacker 157

hard disk 19, 41, 219-222

hardware......................18, 217

hierarchical...........................80

high level 212

hot key.................................36

hot spot 70

hypermedia.......................185

I

icon ....
.......25, 26, 29, 34, 79, 102-107

IconEdit.............................103

image processing...............140

inbetweening 145

information provider..........157

inkjet 110

integrated software 187

international 27

K

keymap 24, 27

KeyShow 64

kickstart................................24

L

laser 111

low level 212

M

machine code.....................194

magazine disk....................247

mandelbrot 147

marqueeing...........................48

master disks 22, 41, 42

menu.......................25, 26, 35

MIDI 153, 171, 175, 226

modem...................158, 229

monitor 223

mouse 27, 224

MSDOS...........................259

multimedia 151

music 171

N

network............................227

NTSC 152

O

object oriented 195

outline fonts 112

P

PAL....................................152

parallel port.......................117

path name..........................82

PCs ....
.....163, 164, 230-232, 257-260

PhotoCD 255

pointer...........................25, 26

PostScript..........................111

Preferences 59, 65-72

Presets 68, 71

printer buffer.....................113

printer driver......109, 118, 119

printer ink 115

printer installation 117-123

printer paper 113, 121

procedure 201

program 18

program loop.....................201

projects...........................34, 101
public domain 241-246

Q

Quick Format 40

R

RAM......................46, 218, 230
Ram Disk.........................34, 46
ray tracing 146
record 182
relational 184
rename.................................42
Return key 24

S

sampling sound 172
scanner 226
screen 35, 224
scroll.............................31, 33
serial port 117, 229
SetMap 269
shareware 241, 248
Shell...........................53, 73-77
size 31
software.......................18, 233
sound.................................171
source 41
spreadsheet 186
string 200
structured drawing.............142
subdirectory 81
System 26
system request 39

T

telecommunications 157
terminal 158
text editor............................91
Time....................................60
title 31, 32
tools...........................34, 101
trackerball 225
trashcan........................34, 49

U

unformatted.........................38
upgrade..............................217
user-definable.......................65
utilities 57

V

Verify 40
versions 19, 22
video...........................151-155
virus 211-216
volume 40

W

wild card 183
WIMP 25
window 25, 26, 29, 31
wordprocessor.............177-181
Work 26
Workbench.............................
.........18, 24, 29-36, 66-69, 137

Z

zoom............................31, 33